101 Best Resumes
for Grads

OTHER BEST-SELLING CAREER BOOKS BY JAY A. BLOCK AND MICHAEL BETRUS:

101 Best Resumes

101 More Best Resumes

101 Best Cover Letters

101 Best Tech Resumes

2,500 Key Words to Get You Hired

101 Best Resumes
for Grads

JAY A. BLOCK, CPRW

MICHAEL BETRUS, CPRW

McGraw-Hill

New York   Chicago   San Francisco   Washington, D.C.   Auckland   Bogotá
Caracas   Lisbon   London   Madrid   Mexico City   Milan
Montreal   New Delhi   San Juan   Singapore
Sydney   Tokyo   Toronto

McGraw-Hill

A Division of The **McGraw·Hill** *Companies*

1 2 3 4 5 6 7 8 9 0   QPD/QPD   0 9 8 7 6 5 4 3 2

ISBN 0-07-139506-7

McGraw-Hill books are available at special quantity discounts to use as premiums and sales promotions, or for use in corporate training sessions. For more information, please write to the Director of Special Sales, Professional Publishing, McGraw-Hill, Two Penn Plaza, New York, NY 10121-2298. Or contact your local bookstore.

 This book is printed on recycled, acid-free paper containing a minimum of 50% recycled, de-inked fiber.

I would like to dedicate this book to little Michael,
who has brought more to my life than I ever thought a little boy could.
—Michael G. Betrus

I also want to thank and dedicate this book to my two sons,
Ian and Ryco.
—Jay A. Block

Contents

Alphabetical Listing of Resumes/Cover Letters

Alphabetical Listing of Resumes/Cover Letters

Contributors

Liz Benuscak, CPRW, IJCTC
Bi-Coastal Resumes, Inc.
32 Old Schoolhouse Road
New City, NY 10956
www.bi-coastalresumes.com
bi-coastal@prodigy.net

Dr. Jerry Bills, IJCTC, CPRW
The Resume Center, Inc.
theresumecenter@aol.com

Camille Carboneau, CPRW, CEIP
CC Computer Services & Training
459 Gullane Circle
Idaho Falls, ID 83401
www.cccomputer.com
camille@cccomputer.com

Jean Cummings, M.A.T., CPRW, CEIP
A Resume For Today
123 Minot Road Concord, MA 01742
www.AResumeForToday.com
careers@AResumeForToday.com

Marie Ditta, CEIP
First Impression Career Services
328 Flatbush Avenue, Suite 216
Brooklyn, NY 11238
www.firstimpressioncareerservices.com
amditta@firstimpressioncareerservices.com

Dayna Feist, CPRW, CEIP
Gatehouse Business Service
265 Charlotte Street Asheville, NC 28801
www.bestjobever.com
gatehouse@aol.com

Anne Follis, B.A., CPRW
CareerPro Resume Service
6738 N. Frostwood Parkway
Peoria, IL 61615
www.aaaprofessionalresumes.com
aaaprofessionalresumes@yahoo.com

Nancy Karvonen, CPRW, CEIP, CCM, IJCTC
A Better Word and Resume
4490 CountyRoad HH
Orland, CA 95963
www.aresumecoach.com
careers@aresumecoach.com

87, 121-122,
131, 144, 151, 164-165, 195

Roland L. LaPointe, CPC, CIPC, CPRW, IJCTC, CCM
RO-LAN Associates, Inc.
725 Sabattus Street
Lewsiton, ME 04240
rlapointe@aol.com

109-110, 128-129,
130, 134, 191-193, 223

Tracy M. Parish, CPRW
CareerPlan, Inc.
PO Box 325
Kewanee, IL 61443
www.careerplan.org
resume@careerplan.org

88-90, 106-107, 157, 190, 202-204,
208-209, 215

Barbara Poole, CPRW
Hire Imaging
1812 Red Fox Road
St. Cloud, MN 56301
eink@astound.net

93-94, 118, 132-133, 139, 161-162,
176-177, 189, 228-229

Janice Worthington, CPRW, JCTC, CEIP
Worthington Career Services
6636 Bellshire Street
Columbus, OH 43229
www.worthingtoncareers.com
janice@worthingtoncareers.com

80, 81, 108, 126, 147,
152-153, 173-174, 205

Vivian Van Lier, CPRW, JCTC, CEIP
Advantage Resume and Career Services
6701 Murietta Avenue
Los Angeles, CA 91405
www.cuttingedgeresumes.com
vvan@aol.com

82, 104-105, 124-125, 140, 146,
172, 226

Acknowledgments

We would like to thank all the members of the Professional Association of Resume Writers (PARW) who collectively have raised the bar of excellence in the area or resume writing and job coaching. Their contributions have made it possible for more people around the globe to find passion and purpose in their work.

We would like to thank Philip Ruppel and and Michelle Howry for sponsoring and editing the *101 Best* ... series, and enabling our message to reach career designers everywhere.

101 Best Resumes
for Grads

1

How to Use This Guide

Welcome to the fifth installment in the *101 Best* . . . series of career books. Because it is so important for new graduates and students to secure good jobs and learn good career-management skills early, developing a resource guide like this is both important and rewarding. The past resume books in this series have been focused on traditional occupations, such as general management, sales, finance, etc. However, there was little emphasis on the needs of students and recent graduates.

This guide offers a variety of tools for you. Like previous installments, we review the different sections and components of a resume. We review different resume formats, and which to use for various occasions. The largest portion of the book is dedicated to showcasing the best resumes that members of the Professional Association of Resume Writers have created for their clients. Every resume has been produced by a Certified Professional Resume Writer and was actually used by a client.

We have done enough research on this subject to know that most people buy a book like this for the sampling it provides, and the instruction that accompanies it may or may not be read. So, if you choose not to read the guidelines we have set forth, please consider the following tips in using the book:

- Even if a particular sample resume is not in your area of expertise or from your major, look it over anyway. It may include an appealing format or approach you like. For example, many different headlines and title styles are sampled.

- Notice the relaxed writing style in the cover letters. Try not to write in too stiff or formal a manner.

- Review the "Tips to Get You Hired" starting on page 61. They will provide you with savvy tips you won't find anywhere else.

Again, look at the many sample resumes provided by the Certified Professional Resume Writers. Whatever your major or academic emphasis, you should still look at the formats of *all* the resumes for ideas on layouts, different ways of writing, and the impact of including graphics and clip art in your resume. The resumes also exemplify a variety of different ways that people have utilized the "5 Ps" you will learn about in Chapter 6.

2

Finding Job Openings

For students and recent graduates, there are several primary sources of job leads:

- On-campus recruiting
- Networking
- Online services
- Career fairs
- Direct contact with companies
- Classified advertisements
- Executive recruiters and employment agencies

There are several unique elements to job searching if you are fresh from school compared to if you have several years of work experience. There are differences in the tactical approaches to the job search, and we provide some suggestions and guidelines for you to help get that resume in front of the right people.

ON-CAMPUS RECRUITING

You will find that different companies will recruit at different universities—trying to be geographically diverse, focusing on the top schools only, or focusing on those schools that have brought them the best recruiting success in the past. Resumes from these targeted schools will often be reviewed with a little more attention than resumes sent through the mail or by fax. If the company you are targeting doesn't recruit at your school, you still have good options—we discuss some of them later in this chapter.

If your targeted company is visiting your campus to recruit. you should register with the school's career center to obtain an interview. When that is scheduled, do some preliminary research on that company. Most on-campus recruiting companies are large enough to have a detailed Web site and be "in the news." Visit their site so you can see their direction, and conduct some media searches to learn more. Then, drop this information in the interview when appropriate. You will learn more and make a stronger impression on the interviewer.

Now suppose your targeted company is visiting your campus but you cannot secure an interview due to your major or grades. Don't give up; employ some creative tactics.

- Try having a favorite professor "sponsor" your effort, and try either to work with the campus career center or the recruiter to grant you an interview.
- Make a special effort with the dean of your department or the director in charge of the career center to convince him or her you are worthy and should not be overlooked. If your grades are poor, it may help to have some justification, such as working 20 hours a week. If you have a different major, point out that over two-thirds of all professionals work in fields that are different than their emphasis in college.
- Suppose the company is large, like Verizon. Go to a Verizon store and network with the store manager to see if someone internal can get you any additional pull to secure an interview.

There are many ways to get in the door, and you should not give up at the first push back. If the company is recruiting, perhaps you can get an interview—even if you do not get one on campus. If you know that a company like Verizon is recruiting, go directly to them and apply for a position.

If you have secured your interview on campus, perform some research on the company so you are prepared to discuss how you can fit into their organization. In addition to anticipating some questions that the recruiter might ask you, your research should stimulate good questions for you to ask the recruiter. Here are some sample questions to consider asking a recruiter.

- What brought you to this company, and how does it differ there from other places?
- How would you rate the overall leadership and direction at this organization, and how is morale overall?
- How would you describe the management culture in your company?

Finding Job Openings

- What is one characteristic that demonstrates leadership skills in your organization?

- What do you feel is your biggest competitive threat in the next several years? How would you describe the culture of your company?

- Could you describe a typical day in the life of a [whatever discipline you're interviewing for] person?

- What are some of the challenges you face on a day-to-day basis?

- What is the average length of time that entry-level recruits remain with the company?

- Did your company face significant layoffs in the most recent recession, and if so, how were those laid off selected?

- What types of continuing education programs do you offer your employees?

- What support mechanisms are currently in place that foster your company's innovative culture?

NETWORKING

The buzzword of job searching is networking—connecting with people. And it's your best strategy today. Networking *is* people-connecting, and when you connect with people, you begin to assemble your network. Once your network is in place, you will continue to make new contacts and communicate with established members. People in your network will provide advice, information, and support in helping you to achieve your career goals and aspirations.

Networking accounts for up to 70 percent of the new job opportunities uncovered. So what is networking? Many people assume that they should call all the people they know, personally and professionally, and ask if they know of any companies that are hiring. A successful networker's approach is more targeted and refined.

Leverage Alumni and Faculty

College grads and seniors should use their colleges' alumni for networking sources. Generally speaking, most people are pretty willing to help you network if you ask them to do something specific, rather than simply ask for general advice or ask for a job. The trick is getting in the door to those connected professionals. Here are some tips on networking with alumni.

- If you hear of alumni presenting at your college in your area of interest, attend and make sure you make contact with the presenters. If appropriate, ask for their cards for future reference.

- Ask professors in your discipline if they know of any graduates who work in the area you are interested in, or for companies you are targeting.

- Suppose you are interested in obtaining an accounting job with Ford Motor Company. Go to professors in other departments, such as the engineering department or the marketing department, who may be connected with alumni or managers within Ford. Large companies employ countless disciplines, and you need to leverage any "in" you can uncover.

- Find out which faculty members work in the consulting arena in the private sector and seek their advice and contacts.

- Focus on recent graduates. They were more recently in your shoes, and may be better sources of tips and leads than more established alumni.

- Go to alumni gatherings. For example, in Dallas, the Michigan State University alumni association has more than 100 members. Alumni, especially from major universities, are *everywhere*. Visit them in the cities where you wish to live and work. Become friendly with the chapter president.

Make sure you treat alumni as respected networking sources and utilize the principles outlined later in this section. Don't send them your resume, and don't ask them for a job. Be well organized, and think through what you want to ask them so they can give you very targeted advice. If your networking is not focused, your alumni contacts will not be able to help and may find the whole exercise frustrating.

A successful networker starts by listing as many names as possible on a sheet of paper. These can include family, relatives, friends, coworkers, managers (past and present), other industry contacts, and anyone else you know.

The next step is to formulate a networking presentation. Keep in mind that it does not need to address potential openings. In networking, the aim is to call your contacts asking for career or industry advice. The point is, you're now positioning yourself not as a desperate job hunter, but as a *researcher*.

It is unrealistic that you will go far asking people for advice like this:

> *John, thanks for taking some time to talk with me. My company is likely to lay people off next month, and I was wondering if your company had any openings or if you know of any.*

This person hasn't told John what he does, has experience in, or wants to do. John is likely to respond with a, "No, but I'll keep you in mind should I hear of anything." What do you think the odds are that John will contact this person again?

A better approach is to ask for personal or industry advice and work on developing the networking Web:

> *John, Amanda Mancini at BMI suggested I give you a call. She and I have worked together for some time, and she mentioned that you work in finance and are the controller of Allied Sensors. I work in cost accounting and feel you'd probably be able to offer some good career advice. I'd really appreciate some time. Could we get together for lunch some time in the next week or so?*

You have now asked for advice, not a job. People will be much more willing to help someone who has made them feel good about themselves or who appears genuinely to appreciate their help. This strategy can be approached in many ways. You can ask for job-search advice (including resume or cover-letter advice); overall career advice (as shown above); industry advice; key contacts they may know; information about various companies, people, and industries; or details about other people they may know.

It is important that the person you network through likes you. When someone gives you a reference, it is a reflection of that person. They will not put themselves at personal or professional risk if they aren't confident that you will be a good reflection on them. Finally, send each person you speak with a thank-you letter. That courtesy will be remembered for future contacts.

In addition to traditional networking for opportunities, there is another very effective way to leverage networking in today's economy. Suppose you go to an online resume board and uncover a great opportunity with Cisco Systems, Bristol-Myers Squibb, or some new e-commerce company. Before blindly sending in your resume and a brief cover letter to that company (or recruiter), immediately ask around and try to find a reference you can leverage to get to them. Following the rules of "six degrees of separation," there is a good chance you can ask around and get a personal introduction to that hiring manager.

When you do, you have engineered a reference and networked your way to the back door. Another terrific strategy to help you in this quest is to proactively have your best references send in letters of recommendation to that hiring manager during the interview process. The determination you demonstrate by developing these references from your network will be perceived as the kind of determination you will demonstrate on the job. Companies desperately need good employees. Sell yourself as one of these, and most companies will find a place for you.

A client of ours, Mark, was looking to find a position with Voicestream, a wireless telecommunications company. Their Web site had a posting for an open position in Atlanta. But how could he avoid being lost in the plethora of resumes these companies receive for each posting?

We worked with Mark to see if he knew *anyone* at Voicestream. After a few days of asking around, it turned out that Mark's girlfriend's friend (in Chicago) used to work there. So, we called her and got the name of her vice president. Mark called him in Seattle and the VP actually picked up the phone himself, in part because Mark called before hours, when things were slow. Mark gave him a quick "elevator pitch" of his background and what his goals were, and the VP referred him to that region's VP. Mark then reached the Atlanta VP—and by now had a few names to drop, positioning himself as a referred candidate.

The new VP had Mark get in touch with an HR recruiter in Kansas City, and weeks later, Mark had secured an interview *and* a position. That whole networking exercise took just two days, but enabled Mark to scoop thousands of other candidates. You too should think of creative ways to network internally.

ONLINE SERVICES

When searching for job opportunities, online sites will be a huge resource for you. Many resources exist today that specialize in guiding you through the maze of job searching online. Though a comprehensive direction is beyond the scope of this publication, you should recognize that after networking, online searches will probably be a good resource for uncovering a high number of quality job opportunities.

The top sites that house these opportunities include:

- Monster.com (*www.monster.com*)
- Headhunter.net (*www.headhunter.net*)
- Jobs.com (*www.jobs.com*)
- America's Job Bank (*www.jobsearch.org*)
- HotJobs (*www.hotjobs.com*)
- JobOptions (*www.joboptions. com*)
- CareerBuilder (*www.careerbuilder.com*)

Though there are many great resources to help you in your online search, here are a few tips to keep in mind:

1. Have a good idea of what types of jobs you are seeking. That will make the search on these online sites narrower in scope and productive. Have geography and keywords prepared in advance. These two objectives should be complete anyway as part of developing your resume.

2. Have two resumes ready at hand: a "finished" Microsoft Word document to send as an attachment, and a nonformatted, text-only resume to copy and paste in an email. The content should be the same, but the latter should be stripped of formatting that will not be preserved through the email exchange.

3. Plan to post your resume at these sites as well as send them directly to recruiters and employers.

4. Take the time to read and understand how the sites work before jumping in headfirst.

5. Print out copies of everything you see that is of interest on a site. It will help you for future reference. Also, catalog who you send emails and resumes to, so you won't send redundant applications.

6. Provide a personal email address, not the one you use at your current job. Check your email daily, as that is commonly the first reply you will receive.

7. We will cover this later in more detail in Chapter 6, but make sure your resume is very tight and focused. The hiring managers reading these resumes are doing so online and will not lend a lot of time to each, so make it easy for them to get to your qualifications and objectives quickly and effortlessly.

Career fairs are often-overlooked chances to uncover good career opportunities. In 1997, Grace Matherly, 26, was looking for a new marketing job in Dallas. She networked with some former colleagues, checked the classifieds, and contacted some executive recruiters. Still, she had not yet uncovered the position that was a good fit. Then she heard of a career fair for engineers and technical managers. Though she was not looking for that type of position, she went anyway to network.

There she met some recruiters from Sprint, and they informed her that Sprint had a big marketing presence in Dallas and that they were hiring. They put her in touch with them, and within 60 days she secured exactly the position for which she was looking. She uncovered an opportunity that had not been advertised and had no executive recruiter supporting it.

Even if the career fair is for a different specialty than your own, it still provides an excellent networking opportunity to uncover new leads. Generally, career fairs are advertised in local papers and held at hotels or convention centers, and from 5 to 15 companies may be participating, even more in large fairs in major markets.

Career fairs can sometimes be crowded, with long lines of candidates waiting to interview. You can maximize your productive time with good preparation. Try to register electronically at the organizer's Web site if possible. This eliminates standing in line at the entrance. Get there early, before the long lines, if you can. No matter what time you show up, go first to the companies that your research has indicated will be the best match—then hit the rest. Do take the time to visit as many companies as you can. Below are some tips to insure that you get noticed.

Tips

- Develop your "elevator pitch." This is a two-minute overview of your background and the type of position for which you are looking. It should include professional and academic information, not personal information. However, when delivering, you can interject some personal information to build rapport, demonstrate a high-energy personality, and distinguish yourself. Just don't overdo it.

- Bring at least one good copy of your resume for each company participating in the fair, as well as a few extras in case you network in other areas.

- Research the employers attending. Learn more about each company, its products, services, etc., and current challenges. You can find terrific information on a company's Web site and in media reviews. Try going to the company's trading symbol on financial Web sites and looking in the "news" sections. Or, just type in the name of the company in a good search engine and click on what comes up.

- Bring a folder to carry resumes and a notepad for notes.

- Dress professionally. Dress professionally. Dress professionally.

- Prepare for the interviews. Review the tips for interviewing section in this book, as well as Ron Fry's *101 Best Answers to Interview Questions*.
- Prepare questions you want employers to answer.
- Go alone. If you go with friends or family, walk the fair by yourself.
- Be aware of time demands on employers. Do not monopolize an employer's time. Ask specific questions and offer to follow up after the fair, as appropriate.
- Be direct. Introduce yourself. If you are job seeking, state the type of position in which you are interested. If you are gathering information, let employers know that you are only interested in materials and information.
- When greeting a recruiter, introduce yourself and look confident by initiating a handshake with a smile.
- Ask the company what the next step is and how to follow up.
- Get appropriate contact information and ask for a business card.
- After the career fair, send a thank-you card and reconfirm interest in the position and company. In the note, include exactly when *you* will follow up, and then do so. Put the burden of follow-up on yourself, because they may intend to contact you but be too busy and put it off or forget.

CONTACTING COMPANIES DIRECTLY

Aren't there one or two companies you've always been interested in working for? Ideally, you may know someone who will introduce you to key contacts there or inform you of future openings. The best way to get introduced to a targeted company is to have a current employee personally introduce you or make an introductory phone call for you. You could make the introduction and reference the employee you know. We get into this later, but if you don't know anyone at a targeted company, a recruiter may be a good source of contact for you, even if it involves no job order for them.

You could send an unsolicited resume, but the likelihood of this materializing is low. Most large-profile companies receive thousands of resumes a year, and few are acted on. Corporate recruiters Jackie Larson and Cheri Comstock, authors of *The New Rules of the Job Search Game*, don't regard mass-mailed resumes very seriously. Part of the problem is that too many resumes are written as past job descriptions and are not *customized* toward a targeted position.

Conrad Lee, a retained Boca Raton recruiter, believes, "information is the most important thing in contacting companies directly. Don't call just one person in the company and feel that is sufficient. That person may have their own job insecurities, or be on a performance improvement plan. You should contact 5 to 10 people and only then can you say you contacted that company directly." New job-search strategies all suggest targeting a select few smaller companies (under 750 employees) intensely rather than blanketing a thousand generically. Contacting the head of your functional specialty in that company is a good start.

Is it hard? Of course. You're facing rejection, probably feeling like you're bothering busy people, begging, or maybe even feeling inferior. But ask yourself this: Would you feel inferior if you were calling hotels and ticket agencies for Super Bowl information? Of course not. So what if some can't help you? You just get back on the phone and keep calling until you achieve your goal. These contacts should be approached the same way. You have a great product to sell—yourself. Position yourself as someone of value and as a product who can contribute to the target company.

The key is to position yourself for individual situations. This requires specialized letters, resumes, and strategies tailored for each situation.

When you do contact the company, you can do it directly through yourself, or through a reference or networking source. A third-party endorsement lends credibility to you, and will differentiate you from the other applicants. The networking section in this chapter is a good guideline on how to contact companies directly.

CLASSIFIED ADVERTISEMENTS

When you depend on classified advertisements to locate job openings, you limit yourself to only 7–10 percent, or less, of all available jobs—plus you are competing with thousands of job hunters who are reading the same ads. Keep in mind that the majority of these ads are for lower wage positions. Do not disregard the classifieds, but at the same time, don't limit your options by relying too heavily on them. Answering ads is more effective at lower levels than higher. An entry-level position or administrative-support position is more likely to be found using this method than a director's position. But it is easy to review advertisements. Check the local paper listings on Sunday, the paper of the largest metropolitan area near where you live, and even a few national papers, like the *Wall Street Journal* (or their advertisement summary, *The National Business Employment Weekly*) or the *New York Times*.

You may gain company insight by looking at the ads that don't necessarily match your background. You may see an ad that says, "Due to our expansion in the Northeast we are looking for . . ." You have just learned of an expanding company that may need you. Review papers that have good display ads, like the *Los Angeles Times, The Chicago Tribune*, or any other major Sunday edition.

EXECUTIVE RECRUITERS AND EMPLOYMENT AGENCIES

Employment agencies and executive recruiters work for the hiring companies, not for you. There are thousands of employment agencies and executive recruiters nationwide. Employment agencies generally place candidates in positions with a salary range under $40,000, which may bode well for many recent graduates. Executive recruiters place candidates from temporary service at the administrative or executive level to permanent senior-level management. Recruiters can be a great source of hidden jobs, even if they do not have a position suitable for you at a given time.

Recruiters and agencies will have a greater chance of successfully locating a position for you if your professional discipline is of a technical or specific nature, such as accounting, engineering, or sales.

All of the above methods are excellent and necessary in your career design.

3

What Skills Do You Possess?

Have you ever known a highly successful sales professional who didn't have a firm grasp and knowledge of his or her product? An award winning professor who did not know his or her material? Ask experienced salespeople what the secret to success is, and they'll say that it's knowing the product, knowing the customer, and matching the benefits of the product to the needs of the customer. This is a powerful success formula.

The job search is a sales and marketing endeavor. There is simply no way around this: You are the product, you are the salesperson, and you must define your customers and promote yourself to them. So, like the highly successful salesperson, the key to your success is knowing your product (you) inside and out, and matching the benefits of the product to the needs of your potential customers (prospective employers). In sales, we call this "selling features and benefits." You must know the features of the product (your marketable skills) and determine what specific benefits result from those features that would interest a prospective employer. In other words, the only reason for someone to hire you is for the benefit that you offer that person or company. If an interviewer were to ask you what your strengths are, what skills you bring to the table, or what contributions you feel you could make to the company, he or she is actually asking you to identify your features and the benefit that the company would realize by hiring you.

In order to effectively communicate the features and benefits of the product, namely you, you must first take an inventory of your skills. In the simplest of terms, there are three categories of skills:

- Job-related (or academic) skills
- Transferrable skills
- Self-management skills

JOB-RELATED SKILLS

There are four categories of job-related skills: 1) working with people, 2) working with data and information, 3) working with things, and 4) working with ideas. Though most of us work with all four categories at one time or another, we tend to be attracted to one or two areas in particular. Successful teachers, customer service representatives, and salespeople must be particularly skilled at working with people. Financial controllers, meteorologists, and statistical forecasters possess outstanding skills in working with data and information. Engineers, mechanics, and computer technicians enjoy using their skills to work with things, and inventors, writers, and advertising professionals must have solid creativity and idea skills.

Which category do you lean toward? *You need to determine which job-related skills you are strongest in and which you enjoy the most.* Then write a brief paragraph stating why you feel that you are skilled and qualified to work with the category you selected.

Since as a recent grad you may have limited job experience, it is your academic accomplishments and learnings that will comprise most of your job-related skills. You should be prepared to articulate in writing and orally what skills you possess that will be most valuable to a potential employer.

TRANSFERRABLE SKILLS

Transferrable skills are just that—transferrable from one environment to another. If you enjoy working with people, your specific transferrable skills might include leadership, training, entertainment, mentoring, mediation, persuasion, public speaking, conflict resolution, or problem-solving skills. If you enjoy working with data and information, your specific transferrable skills might include research, analysis, proofreading, editing, arranging, budgeting, assessing, measuring, evaluating, surveying, or pricing. If you enjoy working with things, your specific transferrable skills might include knowledge of equipment, repair, maintenance, installation, set-up, troubleshooting, or building. And finally, if you enjoy working with ideas, your specific transferrable skills might include creating, developing, reengineering, restructuring, painting, writing, problem solving, planning, or brainstorming.

So take 15 minutes, sit down with a pen and paper, and write down all the skills and abilities *you possess that have value to a company.*

Transferrable skills are marketable and tangible qualifications that will have value to many organizations. An accountant, human resources manager, or logistics manager at General Motors has tangible transferrable skills that are of value to many companies both in and out of the automotive industry.

SELF-MANAGEMENT SKILLS

Self-management skills are skills that are personality centered and value oriented. Self-management skills are those that describe your attitude and work ethic. They include creativity, energy, enthusiasm, logic, resourcefulness, productive competence, persistence, adaptability, and self-confidence. One cautionary note, however: *Try not to be too general in describing your self-management skills*. When you identify a specific skill, always be prepared to explain how that skill will benefit a prospective employer. For example, if you're analytical, how does that make you better prepared for a position you have designed for yourself?

When you identify and recognize your skills, you begin to know your product. If you know your product inside and out, you will never be caught off guard in an interview. In fact, you will be able to reinforce your value by emphasizing specific accomplishments you've achieved in the past using those specific skills.

In summary, writing a powerful resume requires that you identify your marketable skills because they represent the heart of the resume. Your ability to sell yourself confidently in an interview despite stiff competition depends on knowing your skills and communicating the benefits of those skills to the interviewer. Strategic resume preparation begins with identifying what you have to offer based on where you plan to market yourself. It is the foundation for developing a powerful resume, and will be the foundation of successful interviewing as well.

4

What Is a Resume?

The resume is the driving force behind career design. Ironically, it's not just the resume itself that is critical; it's the energy, planning, strategy, and commitment behind the resume. For a professional athlete or actor, it's the preparation that makes or breaks the performance. In career design, the effort that goes into the preparation of your resume will play a major role in the outcome of your campaign. If you invest quality time and energy in developing a comprehensive and focused resume, you'll get quality results! On the other hand, if you put your resume together without much thought or reason, simply writing down your life's story and distributing it to potential employers, chances are you'll experience less than impressive results. In fact, you'll probably end up in the unenviable position of joining the "80 Percent Club"—that 80 percent of people who are dissatisfied with their jobs.

The resume is the driving force of career design—if it is constructed in a strategic and methodical manner. With this in mind, let's define the word *resume*. Webster defines it as "a statement of a job applicant's previous employment experience, education, etc." This definition is hardly adequate, so let us offer you a clear and concise definition.

A resume is a formal written communication, used for employment purposes, noting a potential employer that you have the skills, aptitude, qualifications, and credentials to meet specific job requirements. A successful resume is a marketing tool that demonstrates to a prospective employer

that you can solve his problems or meet her specific needs, and thus war-
rant an employment interview in anticipation of being hired.

In order to demonstrate that you can meet the needs of employers, you must have specific goals and objectives. Too many job seekers have vague, ambiguous, or uncertain career goals. They say, "I want a good-paying job with a progressive organization," or, "I'm open to most anything." Forget that approach! You wouldn't say to a travel agent, "I'd like to go on a vacation somewhere interesting," or, "I'm open to most anything." The age-old question applies: "If we don't know where we're going, how will we ever get there, or know when we've arrived?" There is no doubt that the quality of your career—the quality of your life—is a matter of choice and not a matter of chance only if a choice is made.

How does all this tie into writing resumes? There are only two types of resumes that have proven to be effective in career design, and most people use neither type. If you took all the resumes in circulation today and put them end to end, they would circle the earth over 26 times. That amounts to about 650,000 miles of resumes. And here is a statistic that is truly astonishing: Approximately 98 percent of all resumes being circulated today don't do justice to the candidates they describe. In other words, most of the resumes are autobiographical in nature, describing just the background and experience of a candidate. The problem with autobiographical resumes is that they simply don't work.

Hiring managers and personnel professionals don't read resumes for education or entertainment. The bottom line is this: If you can identify an employer's needs or problems and *explicitly* demonstrate that you can fill those needs or effectively solve those problems, you'll be interviewed and eventually hired. It's logical and makes good common sense. In Chapter 5 we explain which resumes work, and why.

5

Successful Styles and Formats for Resumes

Here are the two types of resumes that are powerful and that work:

- The Targeted Resume
- The Inventory Resume

If you know the job classification and/or the industry or environment in which you want to work, you are a candidate for a *targeted resume*. In essence, you can identify (target) what you want to do either by job title, by industry, or both.

If you are a generalist, open to a number of options or unable to identify clearly what you want to do, but able to identify your marketable skills, you are a candidate for an *inventory resume*. An inventory resume promotes one's marketable skills to a diversified audience.

TARGETED RESUME

If you know your target audience, you must create a resume that emphasizes your skills, abilities, and qualifications—and that *matches* the needs of your target. Position the text on your resume to match the job requirements as closely as possible. For example, if you're seeking an entry-level marketing position but are not fussy about what industry you sell in, you would identify the key assets and value that you bring to the table. Five such assets might be:

1. Experience and familiarity with marketing research techniques and databases
2. Experience, perhaps through an internship, with advertising or brand guidelines at a large corporation
3. High grades earned in marketing-oriented case studies, or an academic award-winning project
4. Solid curriculum of marketing and related course work
5. Familiarity with target company products and the competitive landscape

The problem with most entry level resumes is that people simply list their career objectives and do not focus on even little accomplishments that may relate to the targeted industry, company, or position.

INVENTORY RESUME

If you cannot clearly identify your target, then your resume should highlight your accomplishments and skills in a more generic manner. What benefits will a prospective employer receive in return for employing you? What skills do you bring to the table that will enhance and contribute to the organization?

Let's take the example of an accounting graduate looking for her first job after graduation. She might have five specific skills that she can market to any number of industries, so she would develop an inventory resume with a portfolio of inventory assets that might include the following:

1. Internship with a major accounting firm at tax time
2. Concentration in auditing
3. Good writing skills (backed up by some academic recognition)
4. High grades in core classes
5. Some other accomplishment that demonstrates being a well-rounded individual, such as participation in intramural sports

After advertising these specific skills on the resume, the balance of the document would focus on specific achievements in these five areas.

Regardless of which resume type you choose, you must incorporate pertinent information that addresses the needs, concerns, and expectations of the prospective employer or industry. Samples of both resume types are included in this book.

COMMUNICATING CRUCIAL MESSAGES

A resume must communicate *crucial messages*. What are crucial messages? A resume is a 30-second advertisement. Understanding that, crucial messages are likened to "hot buttons," using marketing terminology. Crucial messages are messages that the reader of your resume needs to read. They ignite enthusiasm and eventual action—which is an interview.

Career design is an exercise in self-marketing, and it's okay to be creative and to get excited about your future. When it comes to marketing yourself, there is just one ironclad rule for resume writing, and here it is:

There can be no spelling or typographical errors, and the resume must be well organized and professionally presented, consistent with the industry you are pursuing.

That's it! Yes, brief is better—one page for most students or graduates, unless you have a unique situation. And today, many successful career designers are incorporating graphics into their resumes, packaging them in a vibrant, exciting, and professional manner. For the first time, career designers are getting enthusiastic and excited about their resumes. After all, if *you* can't get excited about your resume, how do you expect anyone else to get excited about it? Just be careful on the graphical creativity when it comes to email and scanning.

So to this end, there are two main objectives to a resume. The obvious one is that the resume is a hook and line, luring a prospective employer to take the bait and invite you to an interview. And the second objective of the resume is to get you pumped up, and prepare you for the interview and the process of securing a job.

RESUME FORMATS

Chronological Format

The chronological format is considered by many employment professionals and hiring authorities to be the resume format of choice because it demonstrates continuous and upward career growth. It does this by emphasizing employment history. A chronological format lists the positions held in a progressive sequence, beginning with the most recent and working back. The one feature that distinguishes the chronological format from the others is that under each job listing, you communicate your 1) responsibilities, 2) skills needed to do the job, and, most importantly, 3) specific achievements. *The focus is on time, job continuity, growth and advancement, and accomplishments.* Nearly all resumes of students and recent graduates follows the chronological format. This is because as a rule recent graduates have not yet developed enough experience and skills from which to focus a resume. There are many examples of the chronological format.

Functional Format

A functional format emphasizes skills, abilities, credentials, qualifications, or accomplishments at the beginning of the document, but does not correlate these characteristics to any specific employer. Titles, dates of employment, and employment track record are deemphasized in order to highlight qualifications. *The focus is squarely on what you did, not when or where you did it.*

The challenge of the functional format is that some hiring managers don't like it. The consensus seems to be that this format is used by problem career designers: job hoppers, older workers, career changers, people with employment gaps or academic skill-level deficiencies, or those with limited experience. Some employment professionals feel that if you can't list your employment history in a chronological fashion, there must be a reason, and that reason deserves close scrutiny. Few recent graduates have developed the marketable skills required to focus a resume on specific functions, and most of the resumes in this book are variations of the chronological format. However, some examples of a functional theme are illustrated on pages 117 and 192.

Combination Format

This format offers the best of all worlds—a quick synopsis of your market value (the functional style), followed by your employment chronology (the chronological format). This powerful presentation first addresses the criteria for a hire—promoting your assets, key credentials, and qualifications—supported by specific highlights of your career that match a potential industry or employer's needs. The employment section follows with precise information pertaining to each job. *The employment section directly supports the functional section.*

The combination format is very well received by hiring authorities. The combination format actually enhances the chronological format while reducing the potential stigma attached to functional formats. This happens when the information contained in the functional section is substantive, rich with relevant material that the reader wants to see, and is later supported by a strong employment section.

Curriculum Vitae (CV)

A curriculum vitae (CV) is a resume used mostly by those professions and vocations in which a mere *listing of credentials* describes the value of the candidate. A doctor, for instance, would be a perfect candidate for a CV. The CV is void of anything but a listing of credentials such as medical schools, residencies performed, internships, fellowships, hospitals worked in, public speaking engagements, and publications. In other words, the *credentials do the talking*.

The Resumap

The resumap is a new format that clearly breaks with tradition. The writing of the resume is a left-brain exercise in which thoughts occur in a rational, analytical, logical, and traditional manner. By engaging the right brain in this endeavor (the creative, imaginative, and stimulating side of the brain), the resume becomes a more dynamic document.

HOW TO SELECT THE CORRECT FORMAT

Considering the fact that you probably have limited work experience, either the chronological or functional format can work well. If your discipline is fairly technical in nature, such as engineering or accounting, a functional format may work well, leading off with your academic accomplishments. Contemplate using a combination format if you have few deficiencies in experience, education, or achievements.

In the end, exercise common sense and design a resume that best promotes *you*. There are no rules, only results. Select the format that will afford you the best chance of success.

6

The Five Ps of Resume Writing

Now it's time to review the five Ps of an explosive resume:

- Packaging
- Positioning (of information)
- Punch, or Power Information
- Personality
- Professionalism

PACKAGING

Packaging is a vital component to sales success. Most people wouldn't think of purchasing something from a store if the packaging was slightly broken. Paper stock, graphics, desktop publishing, font variations, and imaginative presentations and ideas are parts of the packaging process. Most resumes are prepared on white, ivory, or gray paper. Conforming may be a recipe for disaster, so make your resume professionally stand out from the crowd. You'll want to remain professional, and in some cases, on the conservative side. There are various paper styles and presentation folders that are professional (but unique) and provide a competitive edge. Office supply stores or your local printer will be a good source of different paper stocks.

POSITIONING OF INFORMATION

Positioning means organization. Organize the data on your resume so that it's easily accessible and the reader is able to grasp significant information quickly. You need to create a section of the resume (the introduction, as we discuss later) in which the key information will be displayed. In other words, by creating a highly visible section within the resume, you manipulate the reader's eyes to zero in on information that you deem essential to getting an interview. By doing this, you make the best use of the hiring authority's 10 to 20 seconds of review time.

You can have the best credentials in the world, backed by a powerful personality, complemented by the strongest references, but these career-making credentials are useless if your resume is sloppy, poorly organized, and difficult to read. No matter how superior you are to your competition, the prospective employer will almost never read a poorly presented document.

PUNCH, OR POWER INFORMATION

This "P" is by far the most important. When you deliver the punch, you deliver the information that the hiring manager wants to see. It means that you are supplying the reader with *power information*. Power information *matches a career designer's skills, abilities, and qualifications to a prospective employer's needs*. Quite simply, power information is delivering the knockout punch, indicating to a prospective employer that you meet the criteria for hire.

The employers' task is to locate candidates whose overall credentials and background meet their needs. Your task is to demonstrate, in your resume and later during interviews, that you have what they are looking for. So the starting point of all career-design resumes is projecting and anticipating hiring criteria. You need to be aware of the types of people who will be reviewing your resume. Furthermore, you must determine what kind of information they seek that will provide you with a clear competitive advantage and spark enough interest to warrant an interview.

The challenge for so many people writing resumes is to address directly the concerns of hiring authorities. The challenge is to get into the hiring people's heads. What are they thinking? What do they want? What can you show them that will make them react? In many instances, it's specific, quantifiable achievements.

This is a good time to emphasize the importance of noting specific accomplishments on your resume. The fact that you were responsible for doing something in a past job in no way assures anyone that you were successful! If your resume is full of generalities, responsibilities, and job descriptions, and lacks specific successes and achievements, how do you expect prospective employers to differentiate your resume from the other 650,000 miles of documents? The majority of attention should be placed on your accomplishments and achievements. Responsibilities don't sell. Benefits, results, and successes sell. What you were responsible for in the past has little impact on your future. *What you specifically accomplished highlights your past and determines your hireability.*

PERSONALITY

Hiring managers want to hire people with pleasing personalities. Your resume can have its own personality. Packaging can convey a unique personality, and so can words. We are suggesting that by the use of sumptuous vocabulary, you can turn a rather dull sentence into a more lavish and opulent one. Substitute the word "ignited" for "increased." Change the term "top student" to "academic leader." Instead of "majoring in...," show that you were "created special projects that resulted in...."

Remember, words are power. Make use of the more than 750,000 available to you in the English language. A resume does not have to be a lackluster instrument. Lighten up and let your resume dance a bit, sing a little, and entertain the reader. By displaying a personality, you display emotion. And more than any other single element, emotion sells!

PROFESSIONALISM

Countless hiring managers believe that how people present themselves professionally will determine how professionally they will represent their company. We purchase expensive clothing, practice good hygiene, and make sure we look our very best when going to an interview because we want to make a good, lasting, and professional first impression. The resume must do the same. Once again, you are the product, and you are the salesperson. Your resume is your brochure. Would you hire yourself, based on the professionalism of your resume?

What is professionalism? Well, would you ...

- Send your resume out without a cover letter, or would you enclose a personal cover letter, addressed specifically to a targeted individual, on matching stationery?
- Fold your resume into thirds and stuff it in a business envelope, or would you send the resume out in an attractive flat envelope without folding it at all?
- Send the resume by regular mail, or use overnight or two-day air mail to make a more powerful entry into the organization of destination?
- Expect the prospective employer to call you after receiving your resume (reactive responsibility), or would you make it clear that you will telephone him or her within a week to arrange an interview?

The Five Ps of Resume Writing

Think about these questions for just a moment. What would seem more professional to you? There is a tremendous shortage of professionalism out there. Embrace professionalism and you'll discover that you'll be invited to more and more interviews. That means more opportunities.

7

Anatomy of a Career-Design Resume

Regardless of the resume type you choose or the format you decide upon, there are six primary sections that make up a successful career-design resume, along with numerous subsections that can also be incorporated. The five primary sections are:

1. Heading
2. Introduction
3. Education
4. Employment
5. Miscellaneous

THE HEADING

The heading, also referred to as your *personal directory*, consists of your name, address (with full zip code), and phone number (with area code). If you carry a portable phone or pager or have a fax machine, you can include these phone numbers in your heading. We do not recommend that you include a work number. Many hiring managers do not look favorably upon furnishing a work number. They may conclude that if you use your present company's phone and resources to launch a job-search campaign on company time, you might do the same while working for them.

There are two basic methods for setting up your heading: the traditional method and the creative method. The traditional method is the centered heading. This is effective for any resume, including those that will be scanned by a computer. The creative style consists of any heading that is not centered. Look at some of the many different examples of headings in the sample resumes. For style and layout ideas, look at resumes even if they do not represent your profession.

Coletta Staggers

517-555-2491

328 WESTERN MILL
OKEMOS, MICHIGAN 48821

THE INTRODUCTION

An effective, power-packed introduction consists of *two or three sections*. The introduction sets the tone of the resume and swiftly connects your area(s) of expertise with the prospective employer's needs. It must answer the initial query, "What do you want to do?" or, "What value can you provide for my company?"

The first section of the introduction identifies who you are and what you have to offer. It is delivered in one of the following three forms:

- Title
- Objective
- Summary

For functional resumes (the choice of most students), you should consider leading with your education and associated academic skills as the opening summary. The purpose of the this introduction is to convey the scope of your experience and background and to indicate to the reader your key strengths and areas of expertise. *The first section of the introduction must ignite initial interest and make the reader want to continue.*

Here is an example of a student's introduction, focusing on educational experience:

SUMMARY OF QUALIFICATIONS

Education	**Master of Business Administration**, (expected 2003) *Central Michigan University*, Midland, Michigan GPA 3.0/4.0
	Bachelor of Arts in Communications, 2000 *Central Michigan University*, Midland, Michigan GPA 3.4/4.0
Honors/Awards	◆ High school valedictorian ◆ Won citywide essay competition senior year in high school

- Won "Best Essay" contest out of 800 students at Armstrong State College
- Invited to statewide Academic Recognition Ceremony at state capitol
- Awarded distinguished *Silver A* award from Armstrong State College

Skills/Strengths

- Strong understanding of financial markets and market development
- Proficient with all Microsoft Windows-based programs
- Extensive background with performing strategic analysis of corporations
- Developed multiple presentations outlining strategic recommendations
- Proven tact and diplomacy in handling interpersonal relationships

THE EDUCATION SECTION

The education section, as any other section, should position your credentials in the very best light without being misleading. List your highest degree first and work back. If you have attended six different colleges but have no degree, you might think that these efforts indicate that you are a lifelong learner. But it could also be interpreted as *project incompletion*, and work against you. Think carefully, strategize, and do what's right for you.

Generally, the education section appears at the beginning of your resume if you have limited work experience. A recent high school, technical school, or college graduate will, in most cases, fall into this category. As your portfolio of experience and achievements gains momentum, the education section will drop toward the end of the resume, while newly formed experiences, skills, and accomplishments will begin to outweigh educational experience in the eyes of a prospective employer. Finally, if your educational credentials are seen as crucial, or are superior to those of competing candidates, you'll want to introduce this section early in the resume.

If you have a post-high-school degree, you need not list high school credentials on the resume. A job seeker with no post-high-school degree should include high school graduation on the resume. Particular details you might want to address under the heading of education include:

- Grade point average (GPA), if 3.0 or higher
- Class ranking
- Honors and awards
- Scholarships
- Intramural or varsity sports
- Clubs and special classes
- Relevant course work, if directly related to your target profession (mostly for recent graduates)

- Special theses or dissertations
- Internships
- Research projects
- Extracurricular activities (tutoring, volunteer work, student activities or politics, school newspaper)
- Career-related jobs and activities while attending school

The following is an example of what the education section might look like. It is the same one illustrated in the introduction section, because they often are the same on student resumes with little professional experience.

Here is an example of a student's introduction, focusing on educational experience:

EDUCATION	**Master of Business Administration**, (expected 2003)
	Central Michigan University, Midland, Michigan
	GPA 3.0/4.0
	Bachelor of Arts in Communications, 2000
	Central Michigan University, Midland, Michigan
	GPA 3.4/4.0

HONORS/AWARDS	◆ High school valedictorian
	◆ Won citywide essay competition senior year in high school
	◆ Won "Best Essay" contest out of 800 students at Armstrong State College
	◆ Invited to statewide Academic Recognition Ceremony at state capitol
	◆ Awarded distinguished *Silver A* award from Armstrong State College

THE EMPLOYMENT SECTION

The employment section is a very important part of the resume for an experienced professional. However, for a student, the emphasis is more academic; a robust professional background is not expected. If you do have good work experience relevant to the position for which you are applying, list it here.

This section highlights your professional career and emphasizes experience, qualifications, and achievements. The employment module normally begins with your most recent position and works back. (Allocate the most space to the most recent positions and less space as you go back in time.) If you have a sensible and strategic reason to deviate from this guideline, and it enhances your document, go for it. Otherwise reference the following information for each employer:

1. Name of company or organization
2. City or town, and state where you worked
3. Dates of employment
4. Titles or positions held

Experience is not limited to paying jobs. If applicable and advantageous, include volunteer work that enhances your candidacy. Do not include salary, reasons for leaving, or supervisor's name unless you have a very specific reason for doing so. Salary history and requirements, if requested, should be addressed in the cover letter.

HOW THE EMPLOYMENT SECTION SHOULD LOOK

When using a chronological or combination format, provide specific information for each employer you worked for and for each job you performed. Include three pieces of information for each employer and job:

1. Basic *accomplishments* and industry- or company-specific information
2. Special skills required to perform those responsibilities
3. General responsibilities

The listing of your job accomplishments and responsibilities should read like a condensed job description, describing how you made a difference. Bring out only the highlights, not the obvious. Finally, use positive and energy-oriented words. The words you choose should reflect your energy level, motivation, charisma, education level, and professionalism. Emotion and action sell; use action and power words.

Briefly describe any special skills you used in carrying out past responsibilities. These skills might include computers that you operated, special equipment used, and bilingual capabilities. Other examples of skills that you might have employed include problem solving, communications, organization, and technical mastery. Review your daily tasks and you'll be surprised at the skills you use every day but take entirely for granted.

The major focus of the employment and experience section should be on your specific accomplishments, achievements, and contributions. What you did in terms of day-to-day functions has little impact. *What you accomplished through those functions determines hireability.* Achievements vary from profession to profession. You need to consider:

- Revenue increases
- Reengineering successes
- Awards and recognitions
- New technology introduction
- Mergers and acquisitions
- Problems identified and resolved
- Profit improvement
- Productivity improvements
- New policies and procedures
- Start-ups and turnarounds
- Inventory reductions
- Contributions made
- Expense savings
- Systems enhancements
- Quality improvements
- Reducing employee turnover
- Adding value to the company

When using a functional format, simply list the information—company name, city and state, dates of employment, and titles—and leave it at that.

Here is an example of what this section might look like:

VOLUNTEER ACTIVITIES AND PREVIOUS WORK EXPERIENCE

■ **Merrill Lynch,** Lansing, Michigan
Intern (Summer 2000, 1999)
Performed financial analysis of prospective investment opportunities and worked directly with clients to support account manager. Helped develop new process flow that reduced temporary-help expenses by over 22%.

■ **Sigma Alpha Mu Fraternity,** Central Michigan University, MI
Kitchen Steward (Academic Season 1999, 2000, 2001)
Established kitchen procedures, many still in use, for newly chartered chapter of this fraternity. Responsible for budgeting food, purchasing food and supplies, interviewing and hiring kitchen personnel, supervising kitchen and dining room operations, and preparing food. Also held positions of Scholarship Chairman and Fundraising Chairman.

OVERCOMING OBSTACLES

This is a good place to talk about hiding information. There are some very imaginative methods of trying to hide weaknesses, and without exception, they all fail. But that doesn't mean you should accentuate any flaws in brilliant colors for all to see. The best way to overcome a weakness is to identify a corresponding strength that will more than make up for the weakness. If you have an associate's degree in business when a bachelor's degree is required, what can you do? Pinpoint areas of experience in which you've proven yourself, especially where practical experience and a proven track record stand out. Demonstrate high energy and enthusiasm, and stress your commitment to give 200 percent. Also, enroll in a community school and begin earning your bachelor's degree, and state this in your resume and/or cover letter.

You need to address your weakness honestly by demonstrating powerful strengths and assets. Even if you are successful in initially fooling a hiring authority, you can be sure that the interview will be quite uncomfortable. If questions are asked that you can't answer satisfactorily, you're in for an embarrassing, defensive, and unproductive meeting. You will come across as conniving and unethical.

MISCELLANEOUS SECTIONS

Military

If you served your country and received an honorable discharge, it is fine to mention this briefly in your resume. Unless your experience in the military is directly related to the profession you are pursuing (e.g., U.S. Navy aircraft mechanic applying for a job as a mechanic with an airline), keep it very short, one to two lines at most. The more your military background supports your future career goals, the more emphasis you should give it. Underscore key skills and achievements.

Finally, and this is very important, translate military jargon into English. Many civilian employers were not in the military and can't relate to or understand military vernacular. If you are not sure of the proper equivalent civilian terminology when translating military verbiage to business terminology, seek out assistance. After going through the painstaking effort of getting hiring or personnel managers to read your resume, you want to be absolutely certain they can easily understand the messages you are sending.

Interests

Interests are inserted to add a human element to the resume; after all, companies hire people, not robots. This is a section that should be kept brief, tasteful, and provocative, insofar as the interviewer can use this information as an "ice breaker," and to set the tone of the interview. It helps to build rapport.

Obviously, you will want to use an interest section when your interests match job requirements, skills, or related activities that enhance your chances of getting an interview, and a job offer. A country club manager may want to include tennis, golf, and swimming as hobbies. A computer teacher may want to list reading, attending motivational workshops, and surfing the Internet as hobbies. A salesperson may want to include a competitive sport as a hobby, because many sales managers view strong competitive skills as a valuable asset in the highly competitive sales arena.

Provide one line (no more unless you have a compelling reason to do so) of information to show the reader your diversification of interests. You might try two or three athletic interests, two or three hobbies, and/or two or three cultural interests. This gives the prospective employer a good profile of who you are outside of work.

Community Service, Special Projects, and Volunteer Work

Many organizations place a high degree of importance on community service. They value fundraising efforts, volunteering time to charities, and contributing to community improvement. In many cases, it is good P.R. and enhances a company's image in the eyes of the public. Organizations that value these activities believe in the adage that "what we get back is in direct proportion to what we give." If you feel that supporting community activities, the arts, and other such causes will enhance your overall credentials, then by all means, include them on your resume.

Professional and Board Affiliations

Memberships and active participation in professional and trade associations demonstrate to a prospective employer that you 1) are a contributing member of your profession, 2) desire to advance your own knowledge and improve your skills, and 3) are committed to the future of your vocation. Pertinent affiliations should appear in your resume.

If you sit on boards of directors, this also indicates that you are well respected in your community and that you give your time to other organizations, be they profit or nonprofit entities. These distinguishing credits should be included in your resume.

Awards, Honors, and Recognitions

Clearly, these are crucial to your resume because they represent your achievements in a powerful and convincing manner. It's one thing to boast about your accomplishments—and that's good. But flaunt your accomplishments *supported by specific awards and recognitions*, and that will often be the one thing that separates you from your competition.

You can illustrate your honors and recognitions:

1. In the introduction section of your resume
2. Under professional experience
3. As a separate section

Technical Expertise and Computer Skills

Incorporating a section describing your specific technical and computer skills may be an effective way to introduce your skills quickly to the reader. In a high-tech, ever-changing business environment, employers are looking for people with specific skills and, even more importantly, for people who have the ability to learn, adapt, and embrace new technologies.

In this section, consider using short bullets so the information is easily accessible. Information and data tend to get lost and confused when lumped together in long sentences and paragraphs.

Teaching Assignments

If you have conducted, facilitated, or taught any courses, seminars, workshops, or classes, include this on your resume, whether you were paid for it or not. Teaching, training, and educating are *in-demand* skills. They exhibit confidence, leadership, and the ability to communicate. If you have experience in this area, consider stating it on your resume.

Licenses, Accreditation, and Certifications

You may choose to include a section exclusively for listing licenses, accreditation, and certifications. Consider using bullets as an effective way to communicate your significant qualifications quickly and effectively.

Languages

We live and work in a global economy, in which fluency in multiple languages is an asset in great demand. Be sure to list your language skills at the beginning of the resume if you determine that these skills are crucial to being considered for the position. Otherwise, clearly note them toward the end.

Personal Data

Personal data consists of information such as date of birth, marital status, social security number, height, weight, gender (if your name is not gender specific), health, number of dependents, citizenship, travel and relocation preferences, and employment availability.

Employers, by law, cannot discriminate by reason of age, race, religion, creed, gender, or color of your skin. For this reason, many job seekers leave personal information off the resume. Unless you have a specific reason to include it, it's probably a good idea to limit or eliminate most personal information. For example, if you are applying for a civil service position, a social security number might be appropriate to include on the resume. Or, if you are applying for a position as a preschool teacher and have raised six children of your own, you may want to include this information on the resume.

Here's a good test for determining whether or not to include personal information on a resume. Ask yourself, "Will this information dramatically improve my chances for getting an interview?" If the answer is "yes," include it. If the answer is "no," or "I don't know," omit it.

8

An E-Guide to the Electronic Resume

We have been primarily discussing how to develop a resume through traditional means. Nearly everyone is used to writing a resume using a word processing document, finding nice stationery, printing it up, and sending it out in the mail with a stamp.

Today, the Internet environment brings a new way of distributing your resume. Mail with a stamp is still useful, to be sure, but email and Web site postings are, too. In fact, for those of you in the Internet-related industries, email and Web site communications are so prevalent that you should consider those communications vehicles your first priority.

First, let's assume that there are two kinds of e-resumes. One is the resume as an email attachment. The other is as text copy inserted into a Web site input field or directly pasted into an email.

E-RESUMES AS ATTACHMENTS

This is the easiest method and has the fewest complications. What this means is that you take the file of your resume that you created in a word processing software program, like Microsoft Word, and "attach" it in the email. We will assume that you know how to do this. If you do not know how to do this, you probably shouldn't be applying for a position in Internet-related businesses.

We would always recommend that you attach your resume in email and posting communications, where possible. The hiring managers and recruiters will invariably print the email with your resume on it. If you have a good version attached, that will be easier to read than a text-only file that might be graphically displeasing or difficult to sort through. If you attach your email, all the guidelines previously discussed still hold true.

E-RESUMES AS TEXT FILES

Another way you can offer your resume is as a text file. This means that you are providing the bare content of your resume in text, but without the graphical enhancements. This can mean that you no longer get to use tabs, bullets, certain spacing, boxes, shading, bold print, etc. This can make the creation of the resume both easier and more difficult.

It can be easier to create a resume in text-only format because you are in fact eliminating the graphical enhancements and formatting. You're simply writing in straight text. However, making an effective presentation without that ability to format actually makes it a more difficult task. This is very important! You need to make your resume appealing given the limitations just described.

E-RESUMES AS TEXT FILES—WRITING MODIFICATIONS

For the next few sections, please refer back to Chapter 7, "Anatomy of a Career-Design resume." We take each section that defines how to write up the resume, and offer up tips on modifying it for the text-only version.

The Heading

Keep the heading free of any bullets, changes in fonts, and underlines. Use commas instead. Your new text-only heading might look something like this:

Kathy Morris, 3628 Eastmore Street, San Francisco, CA 94123, 415-555-1257, kmorris@winklink.com

The Introduction

Since this is going to be reviewed online, you need to get to the point as concisely as possible. A good introduction is very important here. Try to boil your accomplishments down to 3 or 4, preferably quantifiable ones, and make them as terse as possible. Whatever a reader's attention span is on paper, it is even shorter reading plain text on a monitor.

* 5 years' experience in telecommunications
* Accomplished background in telecommunications engineering and product development
* Sales and product-management background in wide area network (WAN) design, ATM, Frame Relay, and Internet services

The Employment Section

Keep this section free of any bullets, change in fonts, and underlines. Use commas instead. Your new text-only employment section might look something like this (only listed one for demonstrative purposes):

SPRINT CORPORATION, San Francisco, CA, 1996 to Present
Advanced Sales-Support Manager/Field Product Manager
- Provided technical and product-related support for Sales-Support divisions on leading-edge technologies for approximately 200 engineering and sales-management employees.
- Led sales support for data services for highest-performing region in Sprint, which in 2000 was 213% of plan.
- Developed analyses of competitors' product offerings and evaluated customer demand for new product-feature offerings through market surveys. Provided recommendations to Marketing and Business Development on needed enhancements to product portfolio.

The Education Section

Keep this section free of any bullets, changes in fonts, and underlines. Use commas instead. Your new text-only education section might look something like this:

EDUCATION
COLLEGE OF WILLIAM AND MARY, Williamsburg, VA,
Bachelor of Science, May 1996

The Finished Product

Here is an example of what a finished product might look like. This is a good example of how the completed resume would be formatted:

Kathy Lucy Morris, 3628 Eastmore Street, San Francisco, CA 94123, 415-555-1257, kmorris@winklink.com

PROFESSIONAL PROFILE
- 5 years of experience in telecommunications
- Accomplished background in telecommunications engineering and product development
- Sales and product-management background in wide area network (WAN) design, ATM, Frame Relay, and Internet services

SPRINT CORPORATION, San Francisco, CA, 1996 to Present
Advanced Sales-Support Manager/Field Product Manager
- Provided technical and product-related support for Sales-Support divisions on leading-edge technologies for approximately 200 engineering and sales-management employees.
- Led sales support for data services for highest performing region in Sprint, which in 2000 was 213% of plan.
- Developed analyses of competitors' product offerings and evaluated customer demand for new product-feature offerings through market surveys. Provided recommendations to Marketing and Business Development on needed enhancements to product portfolio.

EDUCATION
COLLEGE OF WILLIAM AND MARY, Williamsburg, VA,
Bachelor of Science, May 1996

Following are two more examples of e-resumes written in plain ASCII format, that is, stripped of all formatting. Note, these are not specific to students, but taken from our previous guides to professionals.

Robert Atkinson
4548 Sierra Lane
Jupiter, FL 33445
(561) 555-5934
robert.atkinson@aol.com
ACCOUNTING MANAGER

PROFILE:

Passed CPA exam in state of Florida

Well versed in all relevant computer software programs, including Peachtree, DacEasy, Lotus 1-2-3, AccountPro, Excel, and most other Windows-based applications

Experience in cost accounting in manufacturing environments and public auditing

Develop plan; conduct audits and variance analyses; process payroll, payroll tax reports, and filings; and maintain and update accurate inventories

KEY ACHIEVEMENTS:

Instrumental in the negotiation and acquisition of $3-million home care and retail pharmacy stores; negotiated a $14-million contract for pharmaceuticals, resulting in a savings of 1.5%–3% on cost of goods for each retail store
- Saved $87k in annual corporate-management salaries through comprehensive management of the financial programs and credit administration of the group
- Managed accounting department consisting of controller, billing auditor, and accounting staff

EMPLOYMENT:

Wellington Regional Medical Center, West Palm Beach, FL
1994–Present
Accounting Manager

- Manage accounting staff reporting to CFO
- Design, implement, and manage all centralized accounting, management information systems, and internal control policies and procedures
- Manage accounting department consisting of A/P, A/R, cost management, and general ledger maintenance
- Prepare all federal and state tax requirements, including corporate, partnership, payroll, and property tax returns.

Diversified Centers, Inc., Palm Beach, FL
1988–1994
Staff Accountant

- Acted as staff accountant for real estate development firm
- Coordinated all financing and external reporting with financial institutions for the group
- Held full general ledger management responsibility
- Managed accounts payable for two years
- Managed accounts receivable for 18 months
- Prepared and administered operating and cash budgets for each retail profit center.

EDUCATION: Florida Atlantic University, Boca Raton, FL
                Bachelor of Arts: Accounting, 1987

Renee Christian
2724 Cameron Street
Washington, DC 20008
W (703) 555-1212, H (202) 555-1212
renee.christian@mail.argi.net

EXPERIENCE

A.T. Kearney—EDS Management Consulting Services
Washington, DC
Principal, 1996–present
Senior Manager, 1994–1996

Specialized in the development of business plans for emerging wireline and wireless telecommunications companies. Responsible for client relationship management and sales into preexisting client base. Responsible for managing large work teams (up to 30 people). Provided advice to senior management on a broad variety of strategic and operational subjects, including:

– Business strategy and planning
– Financial modeling
– Competitive assessment
– Market segmentation
– Operations design and optimization
– Mergers and acquisitions
– Implementation assistance
– Churn management

Deloitte & Touche Management Consulting
Washington, DC
Manager, 1993–1994
Senior Consultant, 1991–1993

Primarily focused on developing market-entry strategies for telecommunications clients. Developed very strong financial-modeling skills. Responsible for managing smaller projects and developing client deliverables.

EDUCATION

B.S. in Physics, Montana State University, 1989
MBA in Finance, Carnegie Mellon University, 1991

PUBLICATIONS AND SPEECHES

"An Ice Age Is Coming to the Wireless World: A Perspective on the Future of Mobile Telephony in the United States," 1995

Thought Leadership Series, EDS Management Consulting

"Analysis of the FCC's Order Regarding Ameritech's Application to Provide InterLATA Toll Services Within the State of Michigan," A.T. Kearney White Paper, 1997

Presented at over two dozen industry conferences, workshops, and panels

9

Cover Letters and Email

You must include a cover/email letter when sending your resume to anyone. Resumes are impersonal documents that contain information about your skills, abilities, and qualifications, backed by supporting documentation. In most cases, you'll send the same resume to a host of potential employers. A resume is a rather rigid instrument, and unless you customize each document for a specific audience, the resume is, for the most part, inflexible.

Phoebe Taylor, in her 1974 publication, *How to Succeed in the Business of Finding a Job*, provides advice on cover letters that, after 30 years, still holds true:

> *If you stop to think about it for a moment, all resumes have basic similarities. Librarians' resumes are look-alikes; accountants' resumes have much in common; and so on. To get the employer to single out the "paper you," you'll have to demonstrate some ingenuity to separate yourself from the crowd.*

> *The cover letter provides additional pertinent information and reemphasizes your qualifications consistent with the employer's needs. As your "personal messenger," it shows your uniqueness and your ability to express yourself on paper and gives a glimpse of your personality. Addressed to a real person, "Dear Mr. Johnson" or "Dear Ms. Winters," it becomes a personal communiqué. It proves to the reader that you made the effort and used your resourcefulness to find out his or her name and title.*

A cover letter allows you to get more personal with the reader. It is the closest you can get to building rapport without meeting in person. It is a critical component in getting an interview and, eventually, the job.

Cover letters should be brief, energetic, and interesting. A polished cover letter answers the following questions concisely and instantaneously:

1. Why are you writing to me and why should I consider your candidacy?
2. What qualifications or value do you have from which I could benefit?
3. What are you prepared to do to further sell yourself?

Cover letters work best when they are addressed to an individual by name and title. They should be written using industry-specific language and terminology. And finally, you must initiate some future action. Specifically, you want to let the reader know that you will be contacting him or her for the purpose of arranging an interview, or whatever the next step will be. Be proactive! Don't expect the employer to call you; when possible, you should launch the next step, and do so with confidence and an optimistic expectation.

MEET THE NEEDS OF THE EMPLOYER

Marketing principles revolve around the 4 Ps: product, place, promotion, and price. Your self-marketing principles should revolve around the same principles. Given that, it makes sense to draw the parallels even further.

Marketers attempt to create and position a product to meet the needs of their target sales segment. You too should position yourself in a manner that meets the needs of your targeted employers. Once marketing does their thing, it is up to sales to complete the process. This is the place, or distribution element of the marketing mix. Your sales element is in full force when you are in the interviewing stage, but even prior to that you need to set up the stage for a strong sell.

In some industries, a sale is nothing more than *transactional*—the sales department is selling a commodity, simply taking and filling orders. A company that provides long-distance service to businesses is a good example of a transactional seller. They are selling a simple product that has many alternate vendors, and the product may have few features that differentiate it, other than price. The salespeople don't have to sell a concept or stress the relationship between the customer needs and their product, other than the ability to make calls for less.

However, what if the salespeople worked for IBM's consultative branch touting Real Solutions? Then they would sell an integrated solution that may include long distance along with managed network services, Internet access, data-transport products, and WAN service. In order to make that sale, the salespeople would absolutely have to understand the needs of the customer.

Enter *consultative* sales. Consultative sales calls for you to really understand the needs of the customers (or your prospective employers) and sell them a product (you) to meet those needs. So, in order to rise above the pack in the job-search process, you need to demonstrate to the prospective employers that you clearly understand their needs and that you can fill the gap they have in their organization to meet those needs.

Here are a few examples of things to look for in an organization. These are things that you should understand and research prior to the process of beginning the cover letter and sending your resume, so you can address those items in your communications.

- existing products
- new products
- geographic presence
- climate of their industry
- competitive products and companies
- emerging trends in both the industry and within the organization
- profile of current staff
- profile of desired staff skill set
- key business or market drivers

You need to try hard to learn about what is important to your prospective employers. Then you can better position yourself as someone who can help them achieve their goals, rather than someone who needs a job. The research should take place prior to sending the cover letter and resume, so you can then customize them to meet the needs you uncovered.

You can learn about these things several ways. The Web is a great place to start to learn about the industry or the organization. You can order a company's annual report or call various employees and ask them about the organization.

When you have uncovered that information, you can use it in two ways. In your resume you should position, spin, or highlight your accomplishments consistent with their overall goals. Your cover letter is the vehicle to formally address what you have learned and how you can help them meet their goals.

Take a look at the letters at the end of this chapter and look for the ways that each letter opens with a level set of where the company is and where it is going. Then look for the way the writers are connecting the company needs with their skills. If you can master this concept you will be not just very successful in your job search, but in your overall career.

For more suggestions on developing your cover letter or email, review our book, *101 Best Cover Letters* (McGraw-Hill, 2000).

ANATOMY OF A COVER LETTER

What follows is the skeletal structure for a successful cover letter:

1. Your heading and the date
2. Recipient's name and title
3. Company
4. Address
5. Salutation
6. First paragraph: Power opening—talk about the organization, not you
7. Second paragraph: Purpose of this correspondence and brief background
8. Third paragraph: Punch the "hot button(s)"—what precisely can *you* do for *them*?
9. Fourth paragraph: Closing and call to action (initiate your next move)
10. Sign-off

Consider the following quotation:

> *I would be lying if I told you that I read every resume that crossed my desk. But I have almost never not looked at a resume that was accompanied by a solid, well-written cover letter. The lesson here is that you must learn how to write a strong letter. A cover letter should do more than serve as wrapping paper for your resume. It should set you apart from other candidates.*

This quote comes from Max Messmer, CEO of Robert Half International, Inc., one of the world's largest staffing firms. Messmer suggests that most cover letters emphasize what candidates are looking for and not enough about the contributions that a candidate can make to an organization. Therefore, when you are composing your letters, avoid overusing the pronoun "I," and focus instead on the contributions that you will make to the company. Don't rehash what you deliver in the resume. Whenever possible, mention information that reflects your knowledge of the organization to which you are writing or the industry as a whole. Bring current news or events into the letter that will show the reader you are up-to-date and current with industry trends.

THE BROADCAST LETTER

Though the broadcast letter is not necessarily the best tool for those with limited experience, like a recent graduate, it is a great tool for those who do have some experience under their belts, such as internship or a job in their chosen field. It's also a good tool for future reference, if you get a job and decide that you're ready to make a change.

There are times when a career designer is gainfully employed, content with the job, but restless enough to want to explore alternatives. Maybe you're bored, not earning what you feel you deserve, foresee trouble ahead, or just want a career change to try something different. *The challenge in this situation is that you don't want to take the chance of your current employer's finding out that you're looking for other work.* That could cause really big trouble. The day you send out your first resume, you risk exposure. You can never be 100 percent sure about where your resume will end up. Consequently, the moment you broadcast to anyone that you are exploring employment opportunities, you run the risk of exposing this to your present employer. The broadcast letter is a means to protect you to a certain degree, though even the broadcast letter is not foolproof.

The broadcast letter can also be used by those who have had multiple jobs in a short amount of time, who take time off from work on occasion, or who are returning to the workplace following an extended absence.

The broadcast letter becomes half cover letter, half resume. Though you'll need a resume sometime down the road, a broadcast letter is a technique used to attract initial attention without providing extensive detail or exposing information that you'd rather not divulge at this time. Some career designers use this letter format because they feel that people are more apt to read it than a resume. Secretaries, for instance, who screen incoming mail may not screen out broadcast letters as quickly as they do resumes.

Broadcast letters provide an effective means for discreetly communicating your employment intentions to executive recruiters or employment agencies, or for informing key people in your network of your goals and objectives. The broadcast letter, by definition, *broadcasts your strengths and abilities in more depth than a cover letter but in less detail than a resume*. There are many advantages to sending out a broadcast letter. With it, you can:

- Avoid chronology of employment
- Provide a partial listing of former employers
- Communicate that you are presently employed and are, therefore, uncomfortable in advertising the identity of your present employer until there is interest in you as a viable candidate
- Speak about your strong employment record and accompanying assets without mentioning educational credentials that may be viewed by others as weak
- Overcome a challenging past, including alcohol or substance abuse difficulties, time spent in jail, physical or emotional encounters, or other similar obstacles

A broadcast letter can be an effective way to introduce yourself and spark interest in your candidacy. You must be prepared, however, to address any challenges in subsequent communications with employers who show an interest in you after having reviewed the broadcast letter.

Throughout the book you will see select cover letters joined to resumes to give you examples and ideas. Look at each one and notice how many are written less formally than you might expect—this allows the writer more creativity than a traditional resume might. Try not to write the cover letter in too formal a style. Many entry-level candidates tend to write very stiff, "professional" letters that prevent the reader from getting to know them.

YOUR COVER LETTER AS AN EMAIL

If you are sending an electronic or emailed resume, your email should open with a note. This is your new cover letter. The dynamics of a cover letter sent online are probably more different than the change with your resume. Emailed cover letters should be considered short introductions—not nearly as long as what you might write out and put in the mail.

Your cover letter might also be used as a source of key words for computer searches, so, like with your resume, make it rich with at least a few key words (nouns) that will give the reader an overview.

The same general purposes of a cover letter hold true for an emailed one. However, it is crucial to keep it short and maintain the same formatting guidelines assumed for the electronic resume.

EMAIL COVER LETTER

To: advertisingjobs.net;jobsearch.net
Date: May 14, 1998
Subject: Seeking advertising account executive position

I am interested in finding a position with a Big 6 advertising firm in the capacity of advertising account executive. I have worked in advertising for 3 years, and past accounts include Procter and Gamble, Dave and Busters, Cisco, and Ethan Allen.

I am the lead account manager for Dave and Busters and Cisco. Duties include contract negotiation, liaison between client and company, and overseeing creative development.

Please see attached resume if you are interested. If you know of any relevant contacts, please forward leads to me, or feel free to forward this email and the attached resume. I really appreciate it!

Sincerely,

Mary Beth Rouse
mbrouse@sprintmail.com   Attachment: [resume.doc]

Dear Ms. Pappas:

My experience in business management and marketing is an excellent fit for your new telecommunications start-up in Houston. I have watched with much envy as you launched your PCS network in other markets, and wanted to take this opportunity to introduce myself.

Though I did not see a market development opening on your Web site, I am confident that I am a good fit and would like to be available for consideration should a good fit come along.

Though I am currently employed, I am very interested in Sprint, and would like the opportunity to discuss your future market developments.

Sincerely,

RG Matherly
rgmatherly@hotmail.com
3255 Phillips Street
Irving, TX 77299
(214) 555-5687

Personal Calling Cards

It may not be practical to carry your resume everywhere you go or to every meeting or event you attend. But everywhere you go and at every meeting or event you do attend you should be networking. If you connect with an individual who might be of some assistance to your career design efforts, you must be prepared to leave a calling card. We highly recommend that you have 500 to 1000 personal calling cards printed (they are not expensive), and make it a point to hand out 100 to 150 a week for starters! Include just the basic information such as name, address, phone number, and the career objective or short summary of qualifications.

Thank-You Notes

You should send thank-you notes to every person who makes even the most infinitesimal impact on your career design. Stock up on some stylish, classy notecards, because even a small item like a thank-you note can make a huge difference in the outcome of your labors.

Following are two cover letter examples that demonstrate how you should write in a way that validates that fact that you understand the needs of the employer and meet those needs.

MISTI DeORNELLAS
45227 Michigan Avenue, Chicago, IL 24197 (312) 555-3125

March 9, 1999

Ms. Maria Lane, Executive Vice President
Hyde and Smithson Public Relations, Inc.
1800 Scenic View, VT 19877

Dear Ms. Lane:

Over the last few months I've noticed your firm moving into consulting with several health-care firms. After speaking with Tom Aimee, I am aware that you are bidding on the upcoming opening of two new Columbia hospitals. You will no doubt need significant health-care industry expertise to drive this account. Health-care can really get complicated when trying to balance aggressive marketing and sales techniques along with a more public entity image.

The two new locations in Portsmouth and Springfield will be delicate openings, given the amount of bad press Columbia has received in the last year or two. Columbia has been in trouble with both the IRS and FBI for tampering with federal aid and overbilling to Medicare. They will undoubtedly need good advice on how to position their openings to get off on the right foot.

I have been working in marketing and public relations for 9 years, most recently with Humana in Florida. We successfully opened 11 new hospitals over the last 6 years, and even experienced a storm when we opened the one in Orlando. That one opened in the midst of a major citywide controversy regarding the for-profit nature of Humana versus the for-the good-of-the-people persona hospitals have maintained. Under my direction Humana successfully overcame that encounter and now that hospital is one of the most successful in the region.

My skills are very much in line with the needs of both your firm and your clients:

- 15 years in public relations
- 15 years in the health-care industry
- Expertise in new launches and crisis management
- Key contacts within the industry

Please expect my telephone call in the next week so that we might be able to set a time to meet and discuss employment possibilities that would serve our mutual interests.

Sincerely,

Misti DeOrnellas

URSULA N. MORRIS
2524 Santa Monica Blvd.
Los Angeles, CA 90021
(222) 555-0996

October 19, 1999

Joel Pels, Program Director
Greater Los Angeles Jewish Community Center
1818 Wilson Road
Los Angeles, CA 90022

Dear Mr. Pels:

Joanne Green provided me with your name and thought it might be beneficial if we got together and discussed your Cultural Arts programs.

I set up the Cultural Arts program at the JCC in Marblehead, MA and today, 10 years after its inception, the program is considered one of the best in the country. I would like to make your Cultural Arts program the benchmark for all others to emulate. Below are a few career highlights:

Achievements
Leadership role in successful start-up of Marblehead JCC Cultural Arts program
Recipient of Irving Cohen Award for Outstanding Achievement in Program Development
Awarded JCC Program Director of the Year
First full-time Cultural Director for School of the Arts, Salem, MA

Education

Master of Education	Boston University
Bachelor of Arts in Education	Northeastern University
Certificate of Achievement, Jewish Studies	University of Tel Aviv

Past Employment

Program Developed/Director	JCC Marblehead, MA
Director—Cultural Arts	School of the Arts
Fund-raiser/Volunteer Supervisor	American Cancer Institute

If you believe, as I do, that my qualifications and credentials merit further review on how I can best serve your community center's cultural needs, I would appreciate the opportunity of meeting with you. Please expect my telephone call in the coming week to arrange such a meeting. Thank you for your consideration.

Sincerely,

Ursula N. Morris

10
Keywords

Keywords are those descriptive words, usually nouns, that are associated with specific disciplines or industries. Keywords are important because they are considered standardized for specific industries. For example, if you were an accountant, keywords might be: *cost accounting, budget analysis, auditing, tax,* etc. Keywords can be crucial in the world of job searching. Employers and recruiters may take your resume and cover letter (especially if sent electronically) and scan a search for whatever the keywords are that they are looking for. For example, a finance director for Microsoft might have a scan or search of resumes and cover letters completed for the words listed above, and if they aren't on your materials, you could miss the first cut.

That said, it is our belief that scanning and electronic searching of resumes and cover letters is more hype than a real part of most corporations. OCR software still isn't that accurate, and based on our research with many hiring managers and recruiters, it doesn't happen that often in practice. Keywords probably play a larger role in the real world in the scenario described below.

Keywords can be very important outside the computer-search arena. In many cases, the initial scan of resumes is completed by either a human resources person or an assistant to the hiring manager. Even the most competent people doing this function can only do a high-level job of resume scanning if they are not intimately aware of the position or are not hiring for themselves. That is why it is important to keep a certain amount of "boilerplate" in your resume.

A client of ours named David Robinson comes to mind. He worked for PrimeCo Personal Communications and was curious about an advertisement he saw for a position with Ericcson. We updated his resume in the style that looks like that on pages 56–57 from our first book, *101 Best Resumes*. The key to that resume style is the use of the left column for a listing of accounts—that really becomes the core of the resume if you work in an account-driven environment like sales. The hiring manager called David for an interview, and told him, "We've had so many resumes that I told my assistant not to bring me any more unless they look like a perfect fit. The way that you listed your accounts on the first page of the resume was a great way to show us who your contacts are." So, the initial screening was conducted by his assistant, who was only scanning resumes for key items (words, even things like industry-specific terms, product names, etc.), and his resume effectively illustrated his sales accounts. Don't make the readers work to learn what you're all about; the competition for good jobs is too stiff.

As you can see, keywords are not limited to just descriptive nouns, but can be anything that in a terse manner tells the reader about you and your skills. Below is a broad list of keywords that are discipline oriented, but by no means a complete listing. There are many, many more. At the very least, you will get a sense of what we're talking about by reviewing this list. Not included in this list but just as important can be the names of other companies or products, as illustrated in the above example.

Accounts Payable	Cash Management
Accounts Receivable	Catering
Administration	Cellular
Administrative Assistant	Chemical Engineering
Administrative Support	Chemical Scientist
Advertising	Chief Executive Officer
Architecture	Chief Financial Officer
Artificial Intelligence	Chief Information Officer
Asset Management	Chief Technology Officer
Asynchronous Transfer Mode (ATM)	Clinical Studies/Services
Auditing	Commercial Banking
Backbone	Commercial Credit
Bookkeeping	Competitive Intelligence
Brand Image	Contract Administrator
Budgeting	Contracts
Business Development	Copy Editing
Call Center	Copy Writing
Case Management	Corporate Communications
	Corporate Development

Corporate Image

Cost Accounting

Cost Center

Cost Reduction

Credit

Credit and Collections

Customer Loyalty Programs

Customer Retention

Customer Service

Data Communications

Design Engineer

Director of Finance

Director of Information Services

Director of Information Technology

Director of Marketing

Director of Public Affairs

Distribution Channel

E-Commerce

Electrical Engineering

Email

Emerging Technologies

Employee Relations

Environmental Engineer

Equal Employment Opportunity (EEO)

Event Management

Executive Presentations

Executive Secretary

Financial Planning

Financial Restructuring

Focus Groups

Food and Beverage Management

Food Cost Control

Foreign Exchange

Frame Relay

Fraud

Full Time Equivalent (FTE)

Fund-raising

Government Affairs

Graphic Design

Group Manager

Health Care Administrator

Home Health Care

Hospitality Management

Human Resources

Insurance

Investment Analysis

Investment Banking

Investor Relations

Labor Relations

LAN

Law (with all derivatives)

Leasing

Legal Affairs

Litigation

Loan Processing

Managed Care

Manufacturing Engineer

Market Development

Marketing Communications

Marketing Management

Media Buys

Media Relations

Meeting Planner

Merchandising

Mergers/Acquisitions

MIS

Multihospital Network

National Accounts

Not-for-Profit

Nuclear Engineer

Nursing

Occupational Health

Office Management

Order Processing

Personal Communication Services (PCS)

Plant Manager

President

Press

Primary Care

Product Development

Product Manager
Product Marketing
Product Support
Profit/Loss Statement
Project Manager
Public Relations
Public Speaking
Purchasing
Quality Control
Quality Training
Radio Frequency Engineering
Recruiting
Reengineering
Regulatory Manager
Research
Research Specialist
Return on Assets (ROA)
Return on Equity (ROE)
Return on Investment (ROI)
Risk Management
Sales Administration
Sales Management
SEC

Service Mark
Software Engineer
Staffing
Strategic Planning
Systems Engineering
Systems Leader
Team Leader
Telecommunications
Telemarketing
Telesales
Trade Shows
Trademark
Training
Transportation
Turnaround Specialist
Underwriting
Vice President
Video
Voice
Volunteer
WAN
Web Design

11

Tips to Get You Hired

25 UNCONVENTIONAL TECHNIQUES FOR UNCOVERING AND SECURING NEW OPPORTUNITIES

1. If you see a classified ad that sounds really good for you, but it only lists a fax number and no company name, try to figure out the company by trying similar numbers. For example, if the fax number is 555-4589, try 555-4500 or 555-4000. If this works, get the full company name and the correct contact person so you can send a more personalized letter and resume.

2. Send your resume in a Priority Mail envelope to serious job prospects. It only costs $3, but it will stand out and get you noticed.

3. Check the targeted company's Web site; they may have postings there that aren't listed elsewhere.

4. If you see a classified ad at a good company but for a different position, contact them anyway. If they are new in town (or even if they're not), they may have other nonadvertised openings.

5. Always have a personalized card with you in the event that you meet a good networking or employment prospect.

6. Always have a quick personal briefing rehearsed to speak to someone.

7. Network in nonwork environments, such as a happy-hour bar (a great potential location) or an airport.

8. Network with your college alumni office. Many college graduates list their current employers with that office, and they may be a good source of leads, even out of state.

9. Most newspapers list all the new companies that have applied for business licenses. Check that section and contact the ones that appear appealing to you.

10. Call your attorney and accountant and ask them if they can refer you to any companies or business contacts; perhaps they have a good business relationship that may be good for you to leverage.

11. Contact the Chamber of Commerce for information on new companies moving into the local area.

12. Don't give up if you've had just one rejection from a company that you are targeting. You shouldn't feel like you have truly contacted that company until you have contacted at least three different people there.

13. Join networking clubs and associations that will expose you to new business contacts.

14. Ask your stockbroker for tips on which companies they identify as fast growing and good companies to grow with.

15. Make a list of everyone you know, and use them as a network source.

16. Put an endorsement portfolio together (see *101 Best Cover Letters* [McGraw-Hill], Chapter 16), and mail it out with targeted resumes.

17. Employ the hiring-proposal strategy (see *101 Best Cover Letters* [McGraw-Hill], Chapter 17).

18. Post your resume on the Internet, selecting news groups and bulletin boards that will readily accept it and match your industry and discipline.

19. Don't forget to demonstrate passion and enthusiasm when you are meeting with people, interviewing with them, and networking through them.

20. Look in your industry's trade journals. Nearly all industries and disciplines have many such publications, and most have an advertising section in the back that lists potential openings with companies and recruiters.

21. Visit a job fair. Most don't recruit for managerial positions, but you may discover a hot lead. If a company is recruiting, you should contact them directly for a possible fit.

22. Don't overlook employment agencies. They may seem like a weak possibility, but they may uncover a hidden opportunity or serve as a source through which to network.

23. Look for companies that are promoting their products using a lot of advertising. Sales are probably going well, and they may be good hiring targets for you.

24. Call a prospective company and simply ask them who their recruiting firm is. If they have one, they'll tell you, and then you can contact that firm to get in the door.

25. Contact all the recruiters in town. Befriend them, and use them as a networking source if possible. Always thank them, to the point of sending them a small gift for helping you out. This will pay off in dividends in the future. Recruiters are always good contacts.

25 TIPS FOR USING THE INTERNET IN YOUR JOB SEARCH

1. When typing your resume out with the intent of emailing, make sure it is in an ASCII format (see pages 43–44).

2. Use keywords heavily in the introduction of the resume, not at the end.

3. Keywords are almost always nouns, related to skills such as financial analysis, marketing, accounting, or Web design.

4. When sending your resume via email in an ASCII format, attach (if you can) a nicely formatted one in case it does go through and the reader would like to see your creativity and preferred layout. If you do attach it, use a common program like MS Word.

5. Don't focus on an objective in the introduction of the resume. Concentrate on your accomplishments, using keywords to describe them.

6. Don't post your resume to your own Web site unless it is a very slick page. A poorly executed Web page is more damaging than none at all.

7. Before you email your resume, experiment by sending it to yourself and to a friend as a test drive.

8. Look up the Web site of the company that you are targeting to get recent news information about new products, etc., and look for their job postings for new information.

9. Before your interview or verbal contact, research the company's Web site.

10. Use a font size between 10 and 14 point, make it all the same for an ASCII-format resume, and don't create your email resume with lines exceeding 65 characters.

11. If you think that your resume may be scanned, use white paper with no borders and no creative fonts.

12. Include your email address on your resume and cover letter.

13. Don't email from your current employer's IP network.

14. Don't circulate your work email address for job search purposes.

15. In the "subject" of your email (just below the "address to" part), put something more creative than "Resume Enclosed." Try, "Resume showing eight years in telecommunications industry," for example.

16. For additional sources of online job searching, do a search on the Web for job searching, your company, and your specific discipline, for additional information.

17. Be careful of your spelling on the Internet. You will notice more spelling errors on email exchanges than you will ever see in mailed letter exchanges.

18. Try to make sure that your resume is scannable. This means that it is in a simple font, has no borders, no boldface, no underlining, no italics, and limited if any use of columns. Though the practice of scanning is overestimated, it should still be a consideration.

19. Purchase or check out of a library an Internet directory listing the many links to job opportunities out there. There are thousands.

20. If you are using the email as your cover letter, keep it brief. If the readers are reading on screen, their tolerance for reading long information is reduced dramatically.

21. Always back up everything you can on a disk.

22. If you post your resume to a newsgroup, make sure that is acceptable to avoid any problems with other participants.

23. Remember that tabs and spaces are the only formatting that you can do in ASCII.

24. Make sure that you check your email every day. If you are communicating via the Internet, people may expect a prompt return.

25. Don't send multiple emails to ensure that one gets through. Try to send it with a confirmation of receipt, or keep a look out for a notice from your ISP that the message didn't go through.

25 TIPS FOR JOB SEARCHING WHILE STILL EMPLOYED

1. Do not let your current employer find out about your intent to look around. This means no loose resumes left on the copy machine, no mailing from the office, no signal that could jeopardize your current position.

2. Get organized and commit to the process. Without the immediate pressures of unemployment to motivate you to look for a job, you may run the risk of being sporadic in your job search efforts. You must schedule time for the search and stick to it.

3. Don't feel guilty about looking around while employed. You owe it to yourself to make the most of your career, especially in today's environment. Companies are looking out for their own financial health; you should, too.

4. Get a voice mail pager or a cellular phone to enable yourself to return calls quickly, or invest in a reliable answering machine or voice mail system at home.

5. Do not circulate your work number for new employment purposes.

6. Do not send your resume or any other correspondence on your current employer's stationery.

7. Take advantage of different time zones to make calls, if this applies to you. This enables you to make calls early in the morning or after work.

8. Use a nearby fax (if you don't have one at home) for correspondence (but not the one at work).

9. Do not use any resources of your current employer's.

10. Commit to 10–12 hours per week, and schedule your activities for the week on the weekend.

11. Utilize executive recruiters and employment agencies. In some cases, they will be able to cut down on your legwork significantly.

12. Target direct mail efforts on the weekends.

13. Make use of lunchtime during the week to schedule phone calls and interviews.

14. Network through your family and friends.

15. Use electronic means to speed up your search, including surfing the Internet for job listings and company information.

16. Try to schedule interviews and other meetings before the workday (e.g., breakfast meetings) and after 5 p.m. You'll be shocked by how many potential employers will try to accommodate this, and they'll appreciate your work ethic.

17. Though the hit rate may not be great, you may consider identifying a direct mail company to help you directly contact many companies. They could even direct fax for you, and the rates aren't usually too high.

18. Network off-hours and through a few professional contacts, using caution and good judgment as to whom should be contacted.

19. If you are concerned about your current employer finding out about your search, leave your employer off your resume, and note this in your cover letter.

20. Consider using a broadcast letter in lieu of resume (see page 55).

21. In confidence, utilize vendors, customers, and other people associated with your current position, especially if you want to remain in your current industry.

22. Contact your stockbroker for ideas about which companies are growing.

23. Create a business or calling card with your name and personal contact information. Hand them out in sync with your one-to-two-minute prepared pitch about yourself.

24. Do not be critical of your current employer.

25. Read your newspaper cover to cover to determine which companies are growing, not who's advertising for jobs.

25 RESUME-WRITING TIPS

1. Absolutely no spelling, grammar, punctuation, or typographical errors.

2. Know your audience before you begin to prepare the document. Then write the resume for your defined audience.

3. The resume must match your skills and abilities to a potential employer's needs.

4. A resume must address your *market value* and, in twenty seconds or less, answer the question, "Why should I hire you?"

5. Key in on accomplishments, credentials, or qualifications.

6. Sell your features and benefits. What skills do you possess, and how will they contribute to the organization's goals and objectives?

7. Avoid fluff. Ambiguities and generalities represent fluff; they render a resume inept.

8. Be different, courageous, and exciting. Boring resumes lead to boring jobs.

9. Package the resume in an exciting way.

10. Be sure that the resume is well organized.

11. The resume must be professionally presented, consistent with the industry you are pursuing.

12. Your resume can have a distinct personality to it. Choose your language carefully; it can make a world of difference.

13. A *chronological resume format* emphasizes employment in reverse chronological order. Begin with your most recent job and work back, keying in on responsibilities and specific achievements. Use this format when you have a strong employment history.

14. A *functional resume format* hones in on specific accomplishments and highlights of qualifications at the beginning of the resume, but does not correlate these attributes to any specific employer. Use this format when you are changing careers, have employment gaps, or have challenges in employing the chronological format.

15. A *combination resume format* is part functional and part chronological—a powerful presentation format. At the beginning of the resume you'll address your value, credentials, and qualifications (functional aspect), followed by supporting documentation in your employment section (chronological component).

16. A *curriculum vitae* is a resume format used mostly by professions and vocations in which a mere listing of credentials describes the value of a candidate. Examples include actors, singers or musicians, physicians, and possibly attorneys or CPAs.

17. The five major sections of a resume are: 1) Heading, 2) Introduction, 3) Employment, 4) Education, and 5) Miscellaneous sections.

18. Miscellaneous sections can include Military Experience, Publications, Speaking Engagements, Memberships in Associations, Awards and Recognition, Computer Skills, Patents, Languages, Licenses and Certification, or Interests.

19. Write the resume in the third person, and avoid using the pronoun "I."

20. Salary history or compensation requirements should not appear in the resume. The cover letter is made for this purpose, if it needs to be addressed at all.

21. Always include a cover letter with your resume.

22. If you are a graduating student or have been out of the workforce for a while, you must make a special effort to display high emotion, potential, motivation, and energy. Stress qualitative factors and leadership roles in the community, on campus, or elsewhere. By employing a degree of creativity and innovation in your career-design campaign, you are

communicating to a hiring authority that you can be resourceful, innovative, and a contributing team member.

23. Employment gaps, job-hopping, and educational deficiencies can be effectively handled by using the combination format (or the functional format).

24. The resume should be a positive document. It must tell the truth, but not necessarily the whole truth. Don't lie, but you need not tell all, either. Keep negative thoughts and concepts out of your resume.

25. The shorter the better—one to two pages in most cases.

25 TIPS FOR WRITING COVER LETTERS

1. Use customized stationery with your name, address, and phone number on top. Match your stationery to that of your resume—it shows class and professionalism.

2. Customize the cover letter. Address it to a specific individual. Be sure that you have the proper spelling of the person's name, his or her title, and the company name.

3. If you don't wish to customize each letter and prefer to use a form letter, use the salutation, "Dear Hiring Manager." (Do not use "Dear Sir." The hiring manager may be a woman.)

4. The cover letter is more informal than the resume and must begin to build rapport. Be enthusiastic, energetic, and motivating.

5. The cover letter must introduce you and your value to a potential employer.

6. Be sure to date the cover letter.

7. An effective cover letter should be easy to read, have larger typeface than the resume (12-point type is a good size), and be short—four to five short paragraphs will usually do the job.

8. Keep the cover letter to one page. If you are compelled to use two pages, be sure that your name appears on the second page.

9. The first paragraph should ignite interest in your candidacy and spark enthusiasm from the reader. Why is the reader reading this letter? What can you do for him or her?

10. The second paragraph must promote your value. What are your skills, abilities, qualifications, and credentials that would meet the reader's needs and job requirements?

11. The third paragraph notes specific accomplishments, achievements, and educational experience that would expressly support the second paragraph. Quantify these accomplishments if possible.

12. The fourth paragraph must generate future action. Ask for an interview or tell the reader that you will be calling in a week or so to follow up.

13. The fifth paragraph should be a short one, closing the letter and showing appreciation.

14. Demonstrate specific problem-solving skills in the letter, supported by specific examples.

15. Unless asked to do so, don't discuss salary in a cover letter.

16. If salary history or requirements are asked for, provide a modest window, and mention that it is negotiable (if it is).

17. Be sure that the letter has a professional appearance.

18. Be sure that there are no spelling, typographical, or grammatical errors.

19. Be sure to keep the letter short and to the point. Don't ramble.

20. Do not lie or exaggerate. Everything you say in a cover letter and resume must be supported in the eventual interview.

21. Be careful not to use the pronoun "I" excessively. Tie together what the target company is doing and what their needs might be. To come full circle, explain how you fit into their strategy and can close potential gaps in meeting their objectives.

22. Avoid negative and controversial subject matter. The purpose of a cover letter and resume is to put your best foot forward. This material (job-hopping, prior termination, etc.) can be tactfully addressed in the interview.

23. If you are faxing the cover letter and resume, you do not need to send a fax transmittal form as long as your fax number is included in the heading along with your telephone number.

24. To close the letter, use Sincerely, Sincerely yours, Respectfully, or Very truly yours.

25. Be sure to sign the letter.

25 NETWORKING TIPS

1. Two-thirds of all jobs are secured via the networking process. Networking is a systematic approach to cultivating formal and informal contacts for the purpose of gaining information, enhancing visibility in the market, and obtaining referrals.
2. Effective networking requires self-confidence, poise, and personal conviction.
3. You must first know the companies and organizations for which you wish to work. That will determine the type of network you will develop and nurture.
4. Focus on meeting the "right people." This takes planning and preparation.
5. Target close friends, family members, neighbors, social acquaintances, social and religious group members, business contacts, teachers, and community leaders.
6. Include employment professionals as an important part of your network. This includes headhunters and personnel-agency executives. They have a wealth of knowledge about job and market conditions.
7. Remember, networking is a numbers game. Once you have a network of people in place, prioritize the listing so you have separated top-priority contacts from lower-priority ones.
8. Sometimes you may have to pay for advice and information. Paying consultants or professionals or investing in Internet services is part of the job search process today, as long as it's legal and ethical.
9. Know what you want from your contacts. If you don't know what you want, neither will your network of people. Specific questions will get specific answers.
10. Ask for advice, not for a job. You cannot contact people asking if they know of any job openings. The answer will invariably be "no," especially at higher levels. You need to ask for things like industry advice, advice on geographic areas, etc. The job insights will follow but will be almost incidental. This positioning will build value for you and make the contact people more comfortable about helping you.
11. Watch your attitude and demeanor at all times. Everyone you come in contact with is a potential member of your network. Demonstrate enthusiasm and professionalism at all times.
12. Keep a file on each member of your network and maintain good records at all times. A well-organized network-filing system or database will yield superior results.
13. Get comfortable on the telephone. Good telephone communication skills are crucial.
14. Travel the "information highway." Networking is more effective if you have email, fax, and computer capabilities.
15. Be well prepared for your conversation, whether in person or over the phone. You should have a script in your mind of how to answer questions, what to ask, and what you're trying to accomplish.
16. Do not fear rejection. If a contact cannot help you, move on to the next contact. Do not take rejection personally—it's just part of the process.
17. Flatter the people in your network. It's been said that the only two types of people who can be flattered are men and women. Use tact and courtesy.
18. If a person in your network cannot personally help, advise, or direct you, ask for referrals.
19. Keep in touch with the major contacts in your network on a monthly basis. Remember, out of sight, out of mind.
20. Don't abuse the process. Networking is a two-way street. Be honest and brief, and offer your contacts something in return for their time, advice, and information. This can be as simple as buying a lunch or offering your professional services in return for their cooperation.

21. Show an interest in your contacts. Cavette Robert, one of the founders of the National Speakers Association, said, "People don't care how much you know, until they know how much you care." Show how much you care. It will get you anywhere.
22. Send thank-you notes following each networking contact.
23. Seek out key networking contacts in professional and trade associations.
24. Carry calling cards with you at all times to hand out to anyone and everyone you come in contact with. Include your name, address, phone number, areas of expertise, and/or specific skill areas.
25. Socialize and get out more than ever before. Networking requires dedication and massive amounts of energy. Consistently work on expanding your network.

25 "WHAT DO I DO NOW THAT I HAVE MY RESUME?" TIPS

1. Develop a team of people who will be your board of directors, advisors, and mentors. The quality of the people you surround yourself with will determine the quality of your results.

2. Plan a marketing strategy. Determine how many hours a week you will work, how you'll divide your time, and how you'll measure your progress. Job searching is a business in itself—and your marketing strategy is your business plan.

3. Identify 25 (50 would be better) companies or organizations that you would like to work for.

4. Contact the companies, or do some research to identify hiring authorities.

5. Define your network (see "25 Networking Tips" on pages 72–73). Make a list of everyone you know, including relatives, friends, acquaintances, family doctors, attorneys, and CPAs, the cleaning person, and the mail carrier. Virtually everyone is a possible networking contact.

6. Prioritize your list of contacts into three categories: 1) strong, approachable contacts; 2) good contacts, or those who must be approached more formally; and 3) those who you'd like to contact but can't without an introduction by another party.

7. Set up a filing system or database to organize and manage your contacts.

8. Develop a script or letter for the purpose of contacting the key people in your network, asking for advice, information, and assistance. Then start contacting them.

9. Attempt to find a person, or persons, in your network who can make an introduction into one of the 25 or 50 companies that you've noted in number 3.

10. Spend 65 to 70 percent of your time, energy, and resources networking, because 65 to 70 percent of all jobs are secured by this method.

11. Consider contacting executive recruiters or employment agencies to assist in your job search.

12. If you are a recent college graduate, seek out assistance from the campus career center.

13. Scout the classified advertisements every Sunday. Respond to ads that interest you, and look at other ads as well. A company may be advertising for a position that does not fit your background, but they may say in the ad that they are "expanding in the area," etc. You have just identified a growing company.

14. Seek out advertisements and job opportunities in specific trade journals and magazines.

15. Attend as many social and professional functions as you can. The more people you meet, the better your chances are of securing a position quickly.

16. Send out resumes with customized cover letters to targeted companies or organizations. Address the cover letter to a specific person. Then follow up.

17. Target small to medium-sized companies. Most of the opportunities are coming from these organizations, not large corporations.

18. Consider contacting temporary agencies. Almost 40 percent of all temporary personnel are offered permanent positions. Today, a greater percentage of middle and upper management, as well as professionals, are working in temporary positions.

19. Use online services. America Online, Prodigy, and CompuServe have career services, employment databases, bulletin boards, and online discussion and support groups, as well as access to the Internet.

20. If you are working from home, be sure the room in which you are working is inspiring. organized, and private. This is your space, and it must motivate you!

21. If your plan is not working, meet with members of your support team and change the plan. You must remain flexible and adaptable to change.

22. Read and observe. Read magazines and newspapers and listen to CNBC, CNN, and so on. Notice which companies and organizations are on the move, and contact them.

23. Set small, attainable, weekly goals. Keep a weekly progress report on all of your activities. Try to do a little more each week than the week before.

24. Stay active. Exercise and practice good nutrition. A job search requires energy. You must remain in superior physical and mental condition.

25. Volunteer. Help those less fortunate than you. What goes around comes around.

25 EMAIL TIPS

1. Proofread everything, and make sure that your email is set up to check spelling before sending all emails. *No typos*.

2. Maintain two versions of every resume; one formatted in MS Word and one in plain text, stripped of all formatting (see example on page 43).

3. To ensure that you are eliminating all formatting, make sure that you are removing all bullets and underlining, and check to be sure that all the text is the same, with no indentations.

4. Include the position title and your name in the subject line of the email. This makes it easier for the recipient to keep organized.

5. Include your email address in your resume heading, possibly an email link.

6. When you attach your resume as a Word document, name the file "your name.Resume," such as *John Smith.Resume*.

7. Keep your email cover letter short, perhaps shorter than a mailed cover letter.

8. Do not send multiple emails, but do call to verify that it was received, if possible.

9. If you do send a cover letter formatted in Word as an attachment, place the plain text of it and the resume in the body of the email just in case the attachment ends up corrupted.

10. In the body of the email, make sure that the cover letter is easily separated from the resume by a line of asterisks, dashes, etc.

11. Save all of your emails, by either blind copying yourself or dragging the sent email to a storage folder.

12. Make sure that you never send a file larger than 1 MB without prior permission, as it can really clog up someone's dial-up connection, and many corporate employees dial up from remote locations.

13. Having trouble finding a prospective employer's email address? Go to the company's Web site and find their domain name. Generally, a person's email address is one of the following configurations, working with the name John G. Smith and the company domain of Author.com: jsmith@author.com; john.smith@author.com; john.g.smith@author.com; or jgsmith@author.com. Just try them one at a time so it looks professional. The incorrect ones will be returned.

14. Use a reference as soon as possible in the email to grab the attention of the reader.

15. Signature lines are very important when posting messages on discussion groups. If the recipients are interested in your posting and want to get in touch with you directly, the information contained in a signature line might make them pick up the phone or look at your Web site.

16. DO NOT TYPE IN ALL CAPS. This is very difficult to read and it generally gives a negative impression to the reader.

17. Be careful what you write because the email is likely to get forwarded around if the recipient is interested in what you wrote.

18. Don't use email jargon or acronyms, such as "LOL," BTW," "FYI," etc.

19. Don't abbreviate words.

20. Try to maintain consistency with your email address—don't change it frequently. The more established your email address becomes, the better for future contacts.

21. Try to set up your email program so that you can be identified when the recipient has received the email.

22. Make sure that your return email address is professional and relates to your name.

23. Don't establish your own Web site unless it's really good, relevant, and professional. A mediocre Web site will do more harm than good.

24. If you enter into an email exchange, and you are commenting on something in your response, restate what you are responding to from the initial email so the reader does not have to go back and read the chain of emails to see to what you are referring.

25. No typos!

Sample Resumes

GRETCHEN KONNEY

286 Tallowood St.
Bexley, OH 43209

Residence: (614) 555-1212
Email: email@email.com

GENERAL ACCOUNTING

Highly skilled, **entry-level accounting professional** with proven record of effectively managing multiple tasks without compromise to quality. Employs innovation, creativity, and enthusiasm when approaching projects while being recognized for strong work ethic, integrity, and commitment to success.

✓ Analytical individual with demonstrated competencies in general accounting environments with progressive learning and responsibilities in diversified basic tax preparation and general account support.

✓ Key role participating in reconciling financial records, astute at recognizing areas needing balancing, with the ability to implement necessary changes.

✓ Thorough research abilities utilizing innovative methods, including Internet, accounting software, and educational facilities, to fulfill much needed information-retrieval tasks.

"As an intern she displayed the ability to tackle jobs and learn new methods with ease...I am confident in how valuable Gretchen will be in the dawn of her career." Ronald C. Wendell, Accounting Manager, PLOMO, VISCHEY & GARFINKLE CONSULTING SERVICES.

EDUCATION, HONORS, & ORGANIZATIONS

The Ohio State University ... Columbus, OH

BS—Accounting—2001

Relevant Coursework: Accounting Principles, Advanced GAAP, Advanced Tax Preparation, Tax Laws & Regulations, Accounting Software

PC Skills: Microsoft Windows, Microsoft Office, QuickBooks, Lotus Notes

Beta Theta Phi Fraternity—Member, Officer

Dean's List—1998, 1999, 2000, 2001

Big Ten Scholar Athlete Award—1998, 1999

Varsity Soccer Team Captain, Cocaptain—1998, 1999

Ohio Society of Accountants—Member

Accountants Club of America—Member

Active Fundraiser for March of Dimes—1999, 2000, 2001

Neighborhood Block Watch Program—1999, 2000

Walk-For-Food Homeless Fundraiser—2000, 2001

CAREER SURVEY

Plomo, Vischey & Garfinkle Consulting Services

Accounting Clerk (1999–2001)

Shadowed Beta Theta Pi staff accountant; responsible for collecting annual dues, maintaining financial accounts, and addressing expense-control concerns. Developed monthly member meetings to present financial reviews related to current financial standing and upcoming obligations.

ACCOUNTING

LEIGH J. REYNOLDS, C.P.A.

3197 Monarch Avenue • Boston, Massachusetts 02108 • (717) 555-1212 • email@email.com

TAX ACCOUNTING • FINANCIAL SERVICES • AUDITING

Educated to strengthen internal controls through solid financial reporting, strategic planning, and analysis...

Resourceful and proactive MBA graduate with hands-on experience supporting financial and accounting applications for leading companies. Substantial familiarity with business processes while exceeding expectations within retail, customer service, and territory sales.

Applicable Knowledge Includes

Corporate/Business Taxation • Tax Strategies • Auditing and Assurance Service • Finance • Financial Management
Managerial & Cost Accounting • Auditing for E-Business • Option & Futures • Information Technical Management

ACADEMIC HIGHLIGHTS

EDUCATION

Kenan-Flager Business School—Chapel Hill, NC, 2001

MBA—Finance and Accounting
Bachelor of Science—Accounting
Certified Public Accountant, 2001

INTERNSHIPS

Corporate Finance Associates

Supported managing director with ongoing accounting functions of local office middle-market merger and acquisition consulting firm. Afforded opportunity to seek out and interface with potential clients, as well as consult with attorneys and accountants regarding structuring and negotiating of transactions.

Maxwell Banker Commercial Corporation

Assisted in the firm accounting responsibilities during set-up of business-brokerage division within commercial real estate.

CAREER CHRONICLE

ONECLICK DIRECTORIES—SALES ASSOCIATE   October 1998 to March 2000
Columbus, OH/Irvin, TX

Recruited to market print advertisements for monthly publication listing latest and most popular e-commerce Web sites, features, and links. Credited with strategic contributions for establishing more efficient ways of administering accounting processes. Successfully completed Management Problem-Solving and Decision-Making seminar.

CONNECTION CELLULAR—ASSISTANT SALES MANAGER   April 1996 to September 1998
Columbus, OH

Oversaw all aspects of store operations, including inventory, accounts payable/receivable, and personnel procedures. Assisted manager in addressing root causes of decreased productivity by implementing necessary strategies to achieve sales and marketing goals. Successfully motivated, monitored, and trained four employees in proven sales techniques, quality customer service, product, and competitor pricing information.

DON PABLOS—SERVER   March 1994 to November 1996
Bedford, TX

Encouraged a hospitable, safe, and clean eating environment while assisting customers with menu selections.

EXCELLENT REFERENCES FURNISHED UPON REQUEST

LIZ WARNER

6701 Morning Glory Road
Los Angeles, California 90022

(310) 555-1234
email@email.com

TARGET: POSITION IN ACCOUNTS RECEIVABLE/PAYABLE

✔ Solid academic training in all aspects of accounting, including A/R, A/P, GL, and financial statements. Strong mathematics, analytical, and research capabilities.
✔ Well organized and detail oriented with a proven ability to manage time effectively, streamline processes, and improve work flow.
✔ Enjoys challenges and learns quickly.
✔ Works well independently as well as collaboratively in a team setting.
✔ An excellent communicator who easily establishes trust and rapport with coworkers, management, and public; demonstrated skill in solving problems and resolving disputes.

EDUCATION

CALIFORNIA STATE UNIVERSITY, Northridge, CA
Bachelor of Science in Business Administration; Completion May 2002
Emphasis in Accounting; GPA in major—3.8

Member, Beta Alpha Psi, Honorary Accounting Fraternity
Member, California Society of CPAs, Student Division
Treasurer, Alpha Beta Gamma Fraternity

EXPERIENCE

Accounts Receivable/Payable Clerk • Aug. 1999 to Present (*Part-Time*)
SUNSET BREEZE HOTEL, Santa Monica, CA
• Work closely with Sales Manager and Controller of 225-room hotel in overseeing accounts receivable and payable functions, utilizing proprietary computer software program.
• Process lodging receipts submitted by front-desk clerks; prepare bank deposits.
• Tactfully resolve discrepancies with guests and corporate accounts.
• Prepare billings for corporate and tourism accounts, averaging $30,000 monthly, on timely basis to ensure steady cash flow.
• Verify accuracy of invoices and process payments, averaging $250,000 monthly.

Sales Associate • Sept. 1997–Aug. 1999 (Part-Time and Seasonal)
TODAY'S MAN, Santa Monica, CA

Camp Counselor • Summers 1996, 1997
BIG PINES SUMMER CAMP, Big Bear Lake, CA

COMPUTER SKILLS

Applications include Windows, Microsoft Office (Word, Excel, PowerPoint, Access), Lotus 1-2-3, QuickBooks, Quicken, and proprietary accounting software. Proficient using Internet and email.

Shannon O'Reilly

124 East 51st Street North
Metamora, IL 61111
(309) 555-1212/email@email.com

"Shannon is one of the sharpest students we've ever had in our office. There is
<u>nothing</u> she can't learn!" (Dan Mathers, Operations Manager, Mathers Manufacturing)

<u>Objective</u>

Seeking entry-level **Data Entry/Office Support** position.

<u>Profile</u>

- Proficient office skills include keyboarding (50+ wpm), data entry, customer service, billing, and answering multiple phone lines.
- Diplomatic in relating to coworkers and the public; balances a positive, outgoing personality with professionalism and courtesy.
- Completes assignments with a high level of speed and accuracy.
- Possesses a sound knowledge of the rules of English grammar.
- Computer literate; knowledgeable in all Microsoft Office products; able to learn and apply new software quickly.

<u>Experience</u>

Data Entry & Customer Service Associate/Student Co-op   3/01 to Present
MATHERS MANUFACTURING—Peoria, IL
Performs a wide range of office support functions, working within a time-sensitive environment.
Enters and continually updates account information onto database. Answers phone inquiries and
provides direct support to corporate accounts. Cross-trained to enter and retrieve inventory
control data for the production department as needed.

- One of two selected to process payments and apply credit for the company's largest account.
- Attended several training classes for both customer service and in-house computer system.
- Cited for completing assignments with a high level of speed and accuracy.

Office Clerk, part time as needed   1/00 to Present
O'REILLY LUMBER—Metamora, IL
Calculates employee vacation and sick time, orders office supplies, and tracks inventory levels.

- Designed and implemented the company's first inventory-control database.

<u>Education</u>

Diploma, METAMORA HIGH SCHOOL—Metamora, IL   5/02

ADMINISTRATIVE SUPPORT

CAROLYN SMITH
123 10th Street
Marion, SC 27666
512/555-1212 / Email@email.com

RECEPTIONIST • OFFICE ADMINISTRATION • CUSTOMER SERVICE

Summary of Qualifications
- Excellent qualifications for Receptionist, Office Administrative, or Customer Service positions
- Experienced in answering and directing calls through a busy multiple-line telephone system
- Extremely sociable and able to put visitors immediately at ease
- Organized, efficient, and precise—strong communication skills
- Skilled in completing time-critical projects
- Decisive and direct, yet flexible in responding to constantly changing assignments
- Able to coordinate multiple projects and meet deadlines under pressure
- Enthusiastic, creative, and willing to assume increased responsibility

Special Skills
- Microsoft Office: word processing, spreadsheet, database, and graphic applications
- Familiar with medical terminology
- Progressive experience in customer service

Education
- Graduate: Any High School, Any City, ST—Relevant courses included:
  - Microsoft Office: Word, Excel, Access; and PowerPoint
  - Office Administration
  - Customer Service

Relevant Skills

RECEPTIONIST:
- Resolving customer service problems
- Answering a high volume of incoming telephone calls
- Setting and confirming appointments
- Mail processing
- Multitasking

OFFICE ADMINISTRATION:
- Collecting and recording statistical and confidential information
- Assembling and organizing bulk mailings and marketing materials
- Data entry with 10-key by touch and typing at 85 wpm
- Ensuring smooth and efficient flow of functions
- Experience in prioritizing time-critical assignments

CUSTOMER SERVICE:
- Consumer advocacy experience
- Knowledgeable in problem resolution

CONFIDENTIALITY:
- Handling extremely confidential records

Relevant Experience

ADMINISTRATIVE RECORDS CLERK
Dana Garber Hospital, Marion, SC   2 years
Accomplishment:
- *Developed a new grade-reporting format saving $10,000 annually*

RECEPTIONIST—METRO VICE-NARCOTICS-INTELLIGENCE DIVISION
Marion Police Department, Marion, SC   1 year
Accomplishment:
- *Created a new visitor-tracking report saving $5,000*

REFERENCES AND FURTHER DATA UPON REQUEST

VICTOR SMITH

105 South Street
Kansas City, MO 64101

816-555-1212
email@email.com

ADMINISTRATIVE ASSISTANT

*— Seeking to help an organization reach its financial and customer service goals
by contributing to efficient, smooth-running office operations —*

Three summers of administrative support positions in temporary assignments. Regularly requested by name for return engagements. Known for ability to get up to speed quickly on new tasks and do them right the first time. B.A. degree in English. Bilingual in English and Spanish. Additional skills include:

- Providing attentive customer service
- Organizing and prioritizing tasks
- Multitasking in deadline-sensitive environments
- Taking the initiative to solve problems
- Contributing to positive office-team dynamics
- Microsoft Word (typing speed is 65wpm), Excel, PowerPoint

Efficient & Effective

EDUCATION

WASHINGTON UNIVERSITY, St. Louis, MO
Bachelor of Arts in English   2002

- Two years' office support experience as part of work-study assignments in the Office of Alumni Affairs.
- Assistant Editor of the *Campus Daily News*. Proofread and edited articles, organized the production team, and consistently produced the paper on schedule.

WORK EXPERIENCE

OFFICETEMPS, St. Louis, MO   Summers 1999–2001
  Selected Assignments

The *St. Louis Post Dispatch*, St. Louis, MO, **Office Support Staff**, Classified Advertising Division

- Using MS Word, word-processed weekly sales & marketing reports.
- Coordinated submissions by account executives and ensured that deadlines for ads were met.
- Researched area demographics using the Internet and created an Excel spreadsheet to present data.

"Whenever we have a work overload in Classifieds, we ask OfficeTemps to send Victor because he is very deadline-conscious and will pick up and complete assignments that are new to him." — Assistant Manager, Classified Dept.

Beth Israel Surgical Associates, Richmond Heights, MO, **Receptionist**

- Greeted surgical patients in English or Spanish, answered questions, and helped put them at ease.
- Booked appointments using Meditech software and confirmed upcoming appointments over the phone.

"Victor reduced the number of 'no-shows' by a third through his persistent and organized approach to calling patients." — Dr. Siddique

Sullivan Manufacturing, St. Louis, MO, **Data Entry**

- Entered 1200 names and contact information into an MS Access database.

"We like to have you assign Victor when we have an administrative overload, because he gets the job done accurately and I don't have to allocate staff time to redo his work." — Office Manager reporting back to OfficeTemps

WARREN JAMES WILSON

265 Charlotte Street • Boone, NC 28600 • (828) 555-1212 • email@email.com

Seeking Integrated Advertising Communications Internship

■ Advertising   ■ Public Relations   ■ Marketing

Creation & Strategic Planning of Complete Advertising Campaigns . . . Market Research . . . Graphic Design . . . Public Relations Plan Development . . . Public Relations Crisis Management . . . Writing for Media . . . Presentation and Public Speaking . . . Consumer Behavior . . . Selling

◆ Primary research experience includes conducting surveys on buyer behavior and opinion polls to test advertising ideas.
◆ Secondary research experience on interpretation of demographics (SMRB), advertising rates (SRDS), histories, and statistics on variety of individual businesses.
◆ Computer friendly: E-mail, WordPerfect, Aldus PageMaker, MacWrite, MacDraw, PowerPoint, Microsoft Picture Publisher, Microsoft Publisher, Microsoft Works.
◆ Creative; critical thinking skills; adaptive team player with good problem-solving abilities; persuasive.

Related Coursework:

• Advertising Management
• PR Management
• Principles of Marketing

• Media Sales
• Nonverbal, Interpersonal, & Mass Communications
• Theory & Practice of Persuasion

• Broadcast Production
• Electronic Publishing
• Print Newswriting, Journalism

B.S., Advertising & Public Relations (double major), with **Minor in Marketing**, expected December 1998
Appalachian State University, Boone, NC
• Dean's List ~ Awarded Dan B. Remian Memorial Scholarship for Outstanding Leadership, 1997
• Executive positions in Alpha Phi Omega:
coordinated special events; planned/executed formation of intramural athletic teams
• Varsity Football (all-conference)

Graduate, Simpson Senior High School, Hallsville, NC, 1994
• Who's Who Among High School Students
• Active in student government and school organizations;
Varsity football, baseball, soccer (all-conference)

HIGHLIGHTS OF SUMMER & PART-TIME EXPERIENCE

Assistant Sales Manager • A-1 USA Sports, High Point, NC • 1993–1997
Daily operations; Acting General Manager in absence of owner. Directly responsible for indoor/outdoor advertising, accounting, customer relations, opening/closing; screen printing; ordering and receiving merchandise; strategic product placement.
• Directed move into new store location and handled grand opening of new store.

Production Manager • Housecolor Painters, High Point, NC • 1996
Directed crew of 5 house painters, including scheduling, goal setting, conflict resolution, for company based in Lansing, MI. Responsible for meeting deadlines, payroll, collections. Worked closely with customers on needs determination and discrepancies. Handled all advertising for district (High Point, NC).
• Grossed 3d-highest sales in nation out of 85 crews nationwide in first year. Earned gross income of $52,000 in 3 months.
• Beat deadline on every job.

Sales Associate • Abercrombie & Fitch Outfitters, Winston-Salem, NC • 1995–1996
• Exceeded ever-higher personal sales goals every month.

Waiter/Cook • Bill's Seafood Restaurant/Cheeseburgers in Paradise, Boone/Blowing Rock, NC • 1997–1998
• Tips averaged 7% above other staff and doubled sales of specials within 3 weeks of hire; set 2 daily sales records.

Referee & Coach • Hallsville Soccer Association, Hallsville, NC • 1992–1994
Taught teamwork, the value of team play, benefits of competition, and self-esteem and determination to youngsters ages 6–16. Settled parental complaints and uprisings.

Mark Dalglish

3443 Morley Drive
Chico, California 95973
(916) 555-1212 • email@email.com

AGRICULTURIST

SUMMARY OF QUALIFICATIONS

◆ B.A. in Agriculture with extensive experience in greenhouse techniques, viticulture, marketing, production, agricultural science, and horticulture.
◆ Demonstrated knowledge of government agencies and agricultural resources.
◆ Strong communication, interpersonal relations, leadership, and management skills.
◆ Ability to work and communicate effectively with farmers and provide instructional assistance.
◆ Proficient in teaching IBM and Macintosh computer skills, techniques, and procedures.

EDUCATION AND TRAINING

B.A., Major: Agriculture—Sonoma State University, 2001
Graduated with Honors
Community College Teaching Credential: Computer Technology—Butte College, 1999
Fully certified Crop Insurance Specialist—USDA Farm Service Agency, Sacramento, 1998
Annually updated classroom and on-the-job crop-loss training with USDA Farm Service Agency

AGRICULTURAL EXPERIENCE

◆ Irrigated, fertilized, pruned, and harvested crops.
◆ Identified pests through orchard trapping to stop exportation of apple-maggots to other counties.
◆ Authored written and computer reports for mapping, trap placement, and pest location.
◆ Planned and accomplished vegetable and seedling growth project in 40-acre family farm greenhouse.
◆ Managed working farm for 8 years—used integrated pest-management techniques.

EMPLOYMENT HISTORY

Agriculturist Intern   U.S. Department of Agriculture, Chico, California   1995–present
◆ Related mutually with Agricultural Stabilization Conservation Service, Soil Conservation Service, University of California Farm Advisors, and county agricultural commissioners. Notified farmers of USDA financial assistance availability for agricultural conservation programs, and verified farmers' eligibility for aid.

Program Assistant   Farm Service Agency, Woodland, California   1992–1995
◆ Supervised crop-loss adjusters during training to assure that procedures were followed correctly.
◆ Scheduled training, formulated and submitted reports on hours and dates, and types of crops.

Agricultural Technologist   Colusa County Agricultural Department, Colusa, California   1990–1992
◆ Conducted on-the-job training for new U.S. Department of Agriculture crop-loss adjusters.

Instructor   Contra Costa Unified School District, Concord, California   1989–1990
◆ Developed and implemented class curriculum for cities of Concord and Danville, California. Educated students, teachers, aides, and parent volunteers on Macintosh and IBM computer systems.

ARCHITECTURE COVER LETTER

Frank L. Wright

123 NW Madison St. • Kewanee, IL 61443   (888) 449-2200 • Email: email@email.com

— ARCHITECTURAL DESIGN —

Art
Masonry
Client Relations
Electrical Systems
Infrastructure & Design
Building Safety Regulations
Marketing Architectural Services
Asbestos Abatement Management
Industrial & Residential Design Concepts
Dale Carnegie Leadership Training Course

Mr. Adam Johnson
Overland Construction
555 Jordan Street
Willmington, IA 12345

Dear Mr. Johnson:

At the suggestion of Carl Whitman, I am submitting my resume for your consideration as a possible candidate as an Architectural Design Engineer. Let me start by saying that I have had an interest in architecture from the first time I laid eyes on pictures of the Great Pyramids in my schoolbooks. And although I will probably never have the opportunity to play a role in designing one of the seven wonders of the new millennium, I have formed a strong foundation from which to build my skills into successful professional experience.

As you can see from the seminars listed above, I have taken every possible opportunity to add more training, skills, and knowledge to my architectural repertoire. All of these courses and seminars were ones that I chose to complete independently, outside of my academic studies in architecture.

The enclosed resume also lists several of the key projects I have been involved in during my internship and current position with J.T. & Associates, Ltd. The wide range of projects includes designs for both new construction and additions, and has covered a wide range of architectural styles. I have also had the opportunity to research special window options and assist in the layout of a complex medical facility with special ventilation and steel-beam-support requirements.

Additionally, I have worked as a Team Leader for Asbestos removal and have a solid knowledge of all related state regulations. As a crew supervisor, I often met with the State Fire Marshall to ensure compliance in both procedures and safety equipment.

If you have an opening for a creative and enthusiastic design professional, please contact me to discuss additional information. Thank you for your time, and I look forward to hearing from you soon.

Sincerely,

Frank L. Wright

(Resume enclosed)

ARCHITECTURE

Frank L. Wright

123 NW Madison St. • Kewanee, IL 61443   (888) 449-2200 • Email: email@email.com

— ARCHITECTURAL DESIGN —

QUALIFICATIONS SUMMARY

- Enthusiastic and dedicated Architectural Design Engineer with a solid foundation of both academic knowledge and hands-on training.
- Fully knowledgeable of local building codes, Illinois and Iowa construction regulations, and asbestos removal requirements; certified and experienced in asbestos removal.
- Skilled team leader; effective liaison, negotiator, and problem solver. Able to relate comfortably and effectively to people at all levels.
- Computer skills: Auto CAD, Softplan, Arris, Excel, Quattro Pro, MS Word, Access, WordPerfect, DOS, Windows 95/98, Mac, Internet, and E-mail.

EDUCATION AND TRAINING

Bachelor of Science in Architecture   2002
STATE OF IOWA UNIVERSITY—Spring Falls, IA

Professional Seminars:
Marketing Architectural Services • Electrical Systems • Infrastructure & Design • Client Relations • Building Safety Regulations • Masonry • Industrial & Residential Design Concepts • Asbestos Abatement Management • Dale Carnegie Leadership Training • Art

PROFESSIONAL EXPERIENCE

Intern Architect/Architectural Engineer, RICHLAND ARCHITECTS—Lee, IA   2000 to Present

Review and analyze architectural blueprints for both residential and commercial building projects. Assist in preparing illustration revisions, interact with clients in communicating project progress, and gather resource information for senior architects. Assemble proposal packets for clients containing all drawings and cost information. Participate in both client and internal meetings to exchange information and finalize construction details.

- Selected to assist the company's lead construction engineer on several residential and commercial projects.
- Recruited by management to become a full-time company employee as a result of dedication, professionalism, and skills.

Asbestos Removal Team Leader, J.T. & ASSOCIATES LTD.—Mason, IL   1997 to 2000

Directed asbestos removal projects for commercial and educational facilities throughout the state of Illinois. Supervised and trained a team of eight in all aspects of setup, removal, clean-up, and disposal. Resolved critical and safety issues with clients and employees. Collaborated and interacted with state officials to ensure proper regulation compliance. Routinely inspected all safety equipment and ordered new supplies. Served as the main liaison between the company and clients to communicate issues of concern.

- Commended by management on outstanding professional abilities and customer relation skills; recipient of the "Employee of the Year Award."
- Started as a Team Member, promoted to Team Leader.

PROFESSIONAL AFFILIATIONS/CREDENTIALS

Registered Architect—State of Iowa
Certified in Asbestos Removal—State of Illinois
AMERICAN INSTITUTE OF ARCHITECTS, Member

(Continued)...

Frank L. Wright

- Page Two -

— SAMPLE PROJECTS —

LEE SCHOOL DISTRICT 120—Lee, IA   2002

Gymnasium
New construction project for a 3500-square-foot gymnasium addition equipped with a special rubber-coated floor, an acoustic angled ceiling, and a second-level balcony. Assisted in both design and construction aspects for this seven-month project.

IOWA MEDICAL GROUP—Cole Hill, IA   2001 to 2002

Medical Clinic
Addition of a 10,000-square-foot Pediatric Clinic including special ventilation systems and the installation of reinforced supports for overhead x-ray equipment. Selected to revise all intermediate-phase blueprints for the project.

CITY WATER MANAGEMENT—Oak View, IA   2001

Heavy Equipment Maintenance and Storage Building
Complete design and construction of a 15,000-foot combination equipment maintenance and storage facility with three industrial hydraulic lifts, five vehicle maintenance stalls, and a large internal support-free warehouse.

NORTHMOORE COUNTRY CLUB—Hillsdale, IA   2001

Club House
Special construction of a modernistic main administrative office and dining facility for an exclusive member golf club. Oversaw special research for all skylight and decorative window options. Assisted in reviewing and adjusting blueprints to meet client expectations.

THE NEW WAVE—Jones, IA   2000

Retail Store
Construction of a 5000-square-foot retail store with two loading docks. Prepared all materials for client meetings, assisted with materials research to determine costs, and assisted senior architects with minor revisions.

ATTORNEY COVER LETTER

Karen D. Hays, Esq.

10 Washington Street
Salem, MA 01970

(978) 555-1212
email@email.com

"Ms. Hays was an important contributor to our team. Her work was carefully and thoroughly executed. She also made several suggestions for improving our 'sales' techniques. I believe her legal and marketing skills will make her a valuable addition to any law office." (William Shepherd, Attorney-at-Law)

"Fine analytic abilities...answers were clear and concise." (Property)

"Your analysis was solid and evidenced a thorough understanding and application of case law and Federal Rules of Civil Procedure. Your paper was very well organized and written." (Civil Procedure)

"This was an excellent essay. Your analysis was clear and your discussion of the relevant cases was outstanding." (Constitutional Law)

"This was a strong job of legal analysis. You saw the issues posed by the examination problems and your treatment of them reflected a good grasp of the relevant law and the ability to do thoughtful and convincing legal analysis." (Criminal Justice)

June 21, 2002

Jon Slater, Attorney-at-Law
10 Lynde Street
Salem, MA 01970

Dear Mr. Slater:

William Shepherd, for whom I worked as a Law Clerk, suggested I call you about the possibility of joining your legal team. My goal is to contribute to the growth and reputation of a well-regarded general practice law firm such as Slater and Associates.

I offer superior analytical and writing skills and a four-year background in legal settings. I have experience in Real Estate, Civil, Juvenile, and Family Law as well as Will, Estate, and Probate Law. My skills include online and traditional research, interviewing clients, document preparation, and ensuring regulatory compliance.

I enjoy developing positive, productive relationships with clients in order to better serve their legal needs and encourage repeat business. I maintain an interest in marketing that I cultivated during my undergraduate studies and look forward to supporting a law firm's business development initiatives.

The quotes on the left provide an indication of my ability to help generate new business, analyze, write, and "think like a lawyer."

I would welcome the opportunity to talk with you in person about how I might contribute to the continued success of your firm. I will call next week to discuss a possible meeting time. Thank you for your time and consideration.

Sincerely yours,

Karen D. Hays, Esq.

Enclosure

KAREN D. HAYS, ESQ.

10 Washington Street, Salem, MA 01970 ■ (978) 555-1212 ■ email@email.com

Seeking a position as...
ATTORNEY—GENERAL PRACTICE

Juris Doctor committed to generating new and repeat business by providing skilled legal services and building strong client relationships. Four years of varied legal experience. Bachelor of Science degree in Marketing. Polished, professional demeanor. Areas of strength:

- *Research using Westlaw and CaseBase*
- *Legal analysis*
- *Legal strategy development*
- *Negotiation*

- *Interpersonal skills*
- *Public speaking*
- *Written and oral communication*
- *Regulatory compliance*

EDUCATION

NEW ENGLAND SCHOOL OF LAW, Boston, MA
Juris Doctor 2001

BABSON COLLEGE, Wellesley, MA
Bachelor of Science in Marketing 1996

LEGAL EXPERIENCE

Law Clerk, The Law Offices of William Shepherd, Attorneys-at-Law, Danvers, MA 1999–2001
Real Estate Mortgage and Conveyance Practices
- Helped generate new business by writing and implementing a new telephone script for use in responding to initial inquiries from potential clients.
- Researched titles and drafted deeds.
- Discharged documents and trust provisions.
- Negotiated lien discharges and conveyance materials with the I.R.S., the F.D.I.C., and municipal tax assessors.
- Assisted attorneys in the administration of home equity mortgage refinance options for a major bank.
- Prepared documents for recording procedures and mortgage closings.

Intern, LOWELL DISTRICT COURT, Lowell, MA 1998
Civil and Juvenile Law
- Directly assisted the 1st Magistrate.
- Conducted research and wrote opinions.
- Interviewed petitioners.

Legal Assistant, SHARON WILLIS, Attorney-at-Law, Peabody, MA 1997
Family Law and Will, Estate, and Probate Law
- Assisted attorneys in drafting documents, pleadings, and outside correspondence.
- Interviewed parties involved and made recommendations.

LICENSURE AND MEMBERSHIPS

Licensed to Practice Law in the Commonwealth of Massachusetts by The Board of Bar Overseers
Licensed Notary Public
Member: Massachusetts Bar Association, Boston Bar Association, American Bar Association
Member: Toastmasters International

ATTORNEY

GREG KALABIC
5625 Ashland Avenue ▪ Roseville, MN 55113 ▪ 651.555.2399 ▪ Email@email.com

---

ATTORNEY AT LAW: CORPORATE SERVICES/HEALTH CARE SPECIALIZATION...

Environments:

Health Care Practitioners & Providers
Underwriters

Health Benefits Companies
Manufacturers & Suppliers

Representation:

Fraud & Abuse Investigations, Counseling, & Compliance
Legislation
Bioethics Counseling

Litigation
Regulatory Compliance
Transactions

PROFILE
21 years of experience in managing the delivery and financing of complex health care services. Expert advisor and negotiator; capable of working long hours under pressure. Skilled in dispute resolution and conflict management. Motivated to win, but able to roll with the punches.

EDUCATION
ADMITTED TO THE MINNESOTA STATE BAR, 2001

WILLIAM MITCHELL COLLEGE OF LAW—St. Paul, MN
JURIS DOCTOR (2001)
Specialty Studies:
- Formation and structure of health services: joint ventures, corporations, partnerships, and limited liability companies.
- Development of mutually beneficial joint ventures: analysis of tax, antitrust, and regulatory issues, and negotiation/documentation evidencing transaction and ongoing relationships.
- Agreements between providers and third-party payors: HMOs, PPOs, IPAs, PHOs, PSOs, and other managed-care organizations.
- Legal rights and responsibilities of health services.
- Compliance programs for federal and state statutes and regulations, including fraud and abuse (antikickback), Start I and II, Codey, Medicare, and Medicaid.
- Multifaceted legal and financial activities involved in new construction of health care facilities.

Student Leadership Roles:
- Student Bar Association ▪ Law Review Contributor ▪ **2d Place**, The Negotiation Competition

UNIVERSITY OF MICHIGAN—Ann Arbor, MI
MASTER OF HEALTH SERVICES ADMINISTRATION (1989)
BACHELOR OF BUSINESS ADMINISTRATION: Business Economics/Public Policy (1986)

LEGAL EXPERIENCE
PRATT & HUGHLEY, P.A—St. Paul, MN   June–August 2001
SUMMER ASSOCIATE: CORPORATE SERVICES
- Apprenticed under mentor attorney practicing Business, Health Care, and Employment Law.
- Assisted in providing legal counsel to diverse corporations encompassing manufacturing, wholesale, retail, service firms, consultants, and land-use developers.
  - ✓ Received "Outstanding" midsummer and end-of-summer reviews evaluating legal research and writing, analysis, oral presentation, and overall attitude and responsibility.
  - ✓ Commended by supervisors as "an accomplished advocate with a bulldog's tenacity."

(Continued)

ATTORNEY (CONTINUED)

HEALTH CARE EXPERIENCE

COMMUNITY HEALTH PLAN—St. Paul, MN   1989–1998
EXECUTIVE DIRECTOR/CHIEF EXECUTIVE OFFICER

- Administrative responsibility and authority for the direction and management of a $62-million growth-oriented health plan with a staff of 420. CHP served 60,000 members in St. Paul through its own clinic facilities and a contracting provider network.
- Administered comprehensive insurance operations, including finance, membership, billing, claims, and information systems.
- Negotiated/launched government contracts for Medicaid and Medicare.
- As CEO of a community-oriented subsidiary health plan, reported to a local board of directors and to executive management of a parent corporation. Maintained board relations, local management, human resources, licensure, and autonomous operations.
  - ✓ Expanded staff model HMO operations to five suburbs.
  - ✓ Built complementary provider network model to expand service area.
  - ✓ Increased market share from 10% to 36%.
  - ✓ Tripled revenue through growth and customer partnership programs.
  - ✓ Streamlined operations expenses by 21% simultaneously with above-revenue growth.
  - ✓ Achieved full NCQA (National Committee on Quality Assurance) accreditation within first application and review process.

BLUE CROSS/BLUE SHIELD OF MICHIGAN—Detroit, MI   1985–1989
VICE PRESIDENT, ALTERNATE DELIVERY SYSTEMS

- Developed one of the largest Independent Practice Association (IPA) model HMO programs in the United States. Directed the recruitment of 7000 physicians throughout 27 Michigan counties.
- Coordinated, staffed, and directed all operations, plus provider and marketing/sales activities.
  - ✓ Achieved growth level of 225,000 members during tenure.
  - ✓ Initiated start-up organization plans and budgets.

BLUE CROSS/BLUE SHIELD OF IOWA—Des Moines, IA   1980–1985
VICE PRESIDENT OF HMO OPERATIONS (BCBSI)
CHIEF OPERATING OFFICER (HMO IOWA)
PRESIDENT (HMO CENTRAL)

- Achieved growth and financial objectives through targeted marketing/sales activity, effective provider contract negotiations, mergers, and through development of a "sister" health plan.
  - ✓ Launched the first Medicaid Risk contract in the United States.
  - ✓ Negotiated two mergers, and developed HMO Central, an Illinois-based health plan.

PROFESSIONAL AFFILIATIONS

- American Bar Association
- Minnesota State Bar Association
- American Association of Health Plans Member   1982–present

COMMUNITY PRESENCE

- St. Thomas Academy Mock Trial Team Coach   2000–present
- Roseville Area Chamber of Commerce Board of Directors   1989–1991
- United Way of Greater St. Paul   1989–1998

References, Letters of Recommendation, and Writing Samples Furnished upon Request.

BROADCASTING

JOHANNA MARTIN

161832 South 600 West
Sun City, Idaho 83401
(208) 555-1212 / email@email.com

BROADCAST NEWS & REPORTING

QUALIFICATIONS
- Four years of successful broadcast news and reporting on campus.
- Proficient knowledge of linear and nonlinear equipment and DVC Pro Cameras.
- Successful writing, editing, shooting, producing, reporting, and enterprising stories.
- Able to lead, motivate, and promote team building among coworkers.
- Creative, enthusiastic, outgoing, dependable, hard working, and dedicated.

EXPERIENCE

KIDX/CAMPUS NEWS 8, Idaho Falls, Idaho
Intern Anchor • Intern Reporter • Intern Producer
October 2000 to Present

Anchor and produce weekend newscasts—the weekend news program on campus. Daily assignments include enterprising the lead story and presenting "live" news coverage. Fill in live on camera and deliver the news on weekends.

KDIE/NEWS 59, Twin Falls, Idaho
Intern Reporter • Photographer
May 1999 to August 2000

Field reported for nightly newscasts in addition to shooting video, writing and editing packages, VOs, VO/SOTs, and teases generated for air.

CNN, Atlanta, Georgia
Environment Unit Intern
September 1998 to December 1998

Researched potential environmental stories for daily CNN news broadcasts as well as for weekly Network Earth program, organized satellite interviews, produced CNN feature news story, participated in editing and postproduction sessions.

EDUCATION

Idaho State University, Pocatello, Idaho
Bachelor of Arts Degree in Communications, 2001

Georgia State Junior College, Atlanta, Georgia
General Education Courses, 1998–1999

REFERENCES

References upon Request

CHEF

ARMONDO SANTERELLI
123 First Street, Norfolk, Virginia 23501
(804) 555-1212 • e-mail: email@email.com

Seeking Position as...

SOUS CHEF—LINE CHEF—PASTRY CHEF
Outstanding Culinary Arts skills for the benefit of hotel or country club restaurants worldwide

Fluent in English, French, Italian, Spanish, and German
A Team Player with Excellent Communications and Interpersonal Skills

---

A highly astute, energetic, and team-spirited Sous Chef, Line Chef, or Pastry Chef seeking an opportunity upon graduation from the Broadmoor Hotel School of Culinary Arts in June, 2002. As a graduate of this highly acclaimed school of Culinary Arts directly associated with the 5-star and 5-diamond Broadmoor Hotel in Colorado Springs, Colorado, my experience makes me uniquely well qualified to immediately **contribute to the culinary reputation of any hotel or country club worldwide**.

CORE STRENGTHS

Dependable, prompt, and creative	Quality control
Kitchen management	Sanitation compliance assurance
Staff training and supervision	Experience in fast-paced and high-volume environments
Customer service/customer interaction	Wine stewarding

Special Skills: Ice Sculpting, Menu Development, Signature Specialties, and Wine Service
Fluent in English, Spanish, French, Italian, and German

EDUCATION

BROADMOOR HOTEL SCHOOL OF CULINARY ARTS, Colorado Springs, Colorado
Graduate Diploma: Chef—Sous Chef—Pastry Chef, summer, 2002 (Present GPA: 4.0)
(Selected Curriculum: Kitchen Management, Sanitation Compliance, Customer Service, Wine Stewarding)

PIKES PEAK COMMUNITY COLLEGE, Colorado Springs, Colorado
Associate of Arts (Honors): Romance Languages, 1999 (GPA 4.0)

EMPLOYMENT HIGHLIGHTS

BROADMOOR HOTEL, Colorado Springs, Colorado
Assistant Chef (while in training)
Located in Colorado Springs, Colorado, this hotel has consistently been rated as a 5-Star and 5-Diamond facility for its dining experience. While attending the School of Culinary Arts, I have been privileged to rotate in all six restaurants with duties ranging from general food preparation through the creative art of ice sculpting. Certified Wine Steward (ASWSA).

- Introduced a new pastry item that has become a favorite of hotel guests and local residents of the area.
- Trained kitchen staff members in preparation of high-volume meals for convention facilities.
- Designed signature menu items that significantly enhanced sales and repeat clientele.

PROFESSIONAL AFFILIATIONS

American Association of Culinary Arts

References and Supporting Documentation Furnished upon Request

MICHAEL LEVIN

366 South 200 West • Jones Valley, Idaho 83402
(208) 555-1212 / email@email.com

CIVIL ENGINEER

QUALIFICATIONS SUMMARY

- ⊗ Experienced in analyzing topographic aerial photographs for data points.
- ⊗ Competent in hydraulics and hydrology.
- ⊗ Adept at conducting and evaluating experiments and models.
- ⊗ Effective problem-solving and decision-making skills.
- ⊗ Enjoys goal-oriented, team environments.
- ⊗ Adept at managing multiple projects simultaneously.
- ⊗ Computer literate in AutoCad, DesignCad, Excel, Word, Windows, PowerPoint, GIS, Internet, and Email.

EDUCATION

Bachelor of Science Degree in Civil Engineering, Idaho State University, Pocatello, Idaho. 1999.
Special project: evaluated numerical model for flood-routing capabilities for the Snake River.

University of San Diego, San Diego, California. General Education Courses. 1994.

WORK EXPERIENCE

INTERN, City of Idaho Falls—Street Department. Idaho Falls, Idaho. June 1996 to December 2001.
Conducting physical hydraulic model tests; obtaining water velocity measurements; preparing client reports; completing hydraulic and hydrologic analyses; collecting field data, including soil and water samples.

SUMMER INTERN, Yellowstone National Park. Wyoming. June 1995 to August 1995.
Assisted in the U.S. Geological Survey. Performed GPS surveys of hydrothermal pools.

LABORER, City of San Diego—Street Department. San Diego, California. June 1992 to August 1994.
Assisted in surveying and repairing streets, and operated equipment.

MEMBERSHIPS & AWARDS

- ⊗ American Public Works Association (APWA)
- ⊗ American Society of Civil Engineers
- ⊗ Outstanding Performance Award, City of Idaho Falls, 2000.
- ⊗ Laborer of the Year Award, City of San Diego, 1994.

References Furnished upon Request

MARGARET SUNBAUER
278 Fairborn Street
Hallsville, TN 38800

December 15, 2001

Mr. John Landers
A&R Associates
255 Stemson Street
Nashville, TN 29856

Dear Mr. Landers:

Your client has the opportunity to enter a new, potentially lucrative resort market in the Southeast, nobody knows his corporate name, and aggressive rivals are breathing down his neck—that's his nightmare.

His dream? He is at the helm of a highly competitive market leader, a resort destination considered first in its field, with a reputation for customer service, innovation, and making dreams come true. His is the first name that springs to mind.

I can do that for him.

I am a recent graduate with an MBA in Corporate Communications and broad sales, marketing, and public relations experience in mature, high-growth, and transitioning resorts. I can point to outstanding marketing and PR communication successes during this last decade with the renowned Sunset Bald Inn; my graduate studies have honed my skills in developing internal as well as external corporate communication strategies.

Have you a client in need of my skills? I am open to relocation anywhere in the Southeast.

I look forward to further conversation.

Best regards,

Margaret Sunbauer

(888) 555-7893
myemail@aol.com

MARGARET SUNBAUER

278 Fairborn Street
Hallsville, TN 38800
(888) 555-7893
myemail@aol.com

PUBLIC RELATIONS/MARKET POSITIONING/CORPORATE COMMUNICATIONS

Print & Broadcast Media Relations

Special Event Planning

Marketing

Advertising & Sales Promotion

New Business Development

Public Presentations

Corporate Communications MBA with 10-year career providing innovative marketing, advertising, and communications strategies driving new business development in resort market. Specialty in special event promotions.

Managed publicity, public relations, and special events during one of the most progressive periods of 4-diamond, 5-star resort's 70-year history—the multimillion-dollar expansion and renovation that turned the hotel from a small seasonal inn to a full-service grand resort. Member of team charged with updating resort's vision and identifying core customer segments.

PROFESSIONAL EXPERIENCE

SUNSET BALD INN, RESORT & SPA, Hallsville, TN   1992–Present
4-Diamond, 5-Star, world-class resort. 510 rooms; 2 golf courses; 7 pools.

DIRECTOR OF SPECIAL EVENTS
(1995–Present)

DIRECTOR OF PUBLIC RELATIONS & SPECIAL EVENTS
(1992–1995)

- Conceived and developed 18 theme weekends (list available) and the renowned 6-week Christmas and Fall Festivals—boosted occupancy to record levels over winter and holiday weekends and smoothed transformation of hotel into year-round operation.

- Generated History Project and served as hotel historian—oversaw archival development and Memory Exhibit. Developed profitable offspring, e.g., hardbound SBI History Book. Designed and created 12 permanent historic exhibits for public areas of the inn. Captured national recognition on *Today* and *Good Morning America* television shows.

- Launched and orchestrated Sugarplum Competition (largest in country), featured on national television and now a corporate icon.

- Created and hosted 4-week Staff Holiday Chorus, generating record daily crowds, featured in *Southern Living*.

BALD ROCK PARK, Bald Rock, TN   1991–1992

DIRECTOR OF MARKETING

- Directed design, media buying, and development of advertising programs; publicity, public relations, and special event promotions; admission ticket sales; design and printing of promotional material; and media relations. Tripled guest count within a year.

MARGARET SUNBAUER

(888) 555-7893 • myemail@aol.com

(Continued)

THE HEARN CORPORATION, Hallsville, TN   1989–1991

DIRECTOR OF SALES
& PUBLIC RELATIONS

- Directed group tour sales, publicity, and public relations for the Hearn castle.

- Orchestrated Grand Opening of 500-seat Park Restaurant. Managed banquet sales and promotion.

- Full accountability for media relations. Represented company at national conventions; served as hostess for special events.

- Triggered film industry's initial and now ongoing interest in property as movie site, generating revenues of $6 million within 2 years.

EDUCATION

M.B.A., Corporate Communications, University of Tennessee-Hallsville, 2001
B.A., Advertising, Louisiana State University, Baton Rouge, LA, 1989
Additional study at University of Berlin, Germany (1 year)

ADDITIONAL

Community service: Board of Directors, Community Food Bank; Clean Air Campaign.
Certified Toastmaster
Extensive travel; fluent in German.

COMMUNICATIONS—MARKETING/PUBLIC RELATIONS COVER LETTER

Erich Starrett

123 Fourth Street / Peoria, Illinois 61111 / 309-555-1212 / email@email.com

July 27, 2001

Josiah B. Jeremiah
Jeremiah Placement Services
486 Ninth Avenue West
Peoria, IL 61222

Dear Mr. Jeremiah:

Thank you for taking the time to speak with me this afternoon regarding a position as a corporate public relations and marketing liaison. As per your request, I have enclosed a copy of my resume.

As you will note, I have created promotional campaigns that have received positive media coverage and facilitated considerable growth. I have written newspaper and radio advertising and feature articles, appeared in television and radio ads, managed a busy, rapidly growing business, and provided customer support within a highly competitive industry.

Perhaps equally important, I am originally from Peoria and, having returned a few years ago, I am committed to this area. A great believer in community involvement, I have developed a fund-raiser for the Peoria Symphony Guild, traveled to Illinois high schools with an original production, and cofounded a local nonprofit organization. Such activities provide high visibility and valuable contacts that will make me an asset to your client's company.

In short, I am a born communicator. I enjoy developing creative advertising and promotional strategies, as well as building relationships and strategic alliances among diverse and often disparate groups. I believe that my qualifications are a unique match to this position and would welcome the opportunity to meet with you to discuss my qualifications in greater detail.

Thank you for your time and professional courtesy in reviewing the enclosed materials. I look forward to hearing from you in the near future.

Sincerely,

Erich Starrett

Enclosure

Erich Starrett

123 Fourth Street / Peoria, Illinois 61111 / 309-555-1212 / email@email.com

Corporate Liaison—Communications

Profile of Qualifications

Accomplished communicator with solid oral, written, and presentation skills. Widely experienced in public relations, event planning, advertising, and management. History of developing effective promotional strategies and building alliances among diverse community, business, and political groups.

Educational Background

B.A. in Communications/Public Relations, 2001
BRADLEY UNIVERSITY—Peoria, IL

A.A. in Theater
AMERICAN ACADEMY OF DRAMATIC ARTS—Pasadena, CA

Academic Highlights:
Group leader in the development of advertising and promotional strategies for Mansion in May, a two-week fund-raiser for the Peoria Symphony Guild. Solicited the participation of numerous organizations and businesses. Integrated the Peoria Ballet Company for an authentic Maypole dance to open festivities and wrote related cover story for *Arts Alive* magazine.

Led a team of three in the development of an integrated marketing plan, with the goal of raising the public profile for Options Center for Health and Education. Wrote copy for radio and newspaper advertisements.

Professional Experience

Independent Antique Dealer   1999–Present
Peoria, IL/Los Angeles, CA

Purchase and sell antiques, concentrating on jewelry and American art.

Sales Representative/Jeweler   1991–1998
JOHNSON'S JEWELERS—Peoria, IL (1995–1998)
BEST JEWELRY—Peoria, IL (1991–1995)

Provided direct customer support in the sales and repair of fine jewelry. Wrote over 1000 appraisals of items ranging from diamonds to antique carvings. Acquired Registered Jeweler status through the American Gem Society, as well as Certificates in Diamond Grading and Colored Stones from the Gemological Institute of America. Wrote and performed in radio commercials for Bremers.

(Continued...)

Erich Starrett

General Manager   1986–1991
MRS. R. A. SPERRY'S PANTRY—Glendale, CA

Hired as wait staff; promoted to General Manager within four months. Oversaw all operations including budgeting and personnel supervision, and served as the lightning rod for questions and problems to both staff and clientele. Pioneered the restaurant's successful participation in a number of promotional events including "Taste of Glendale" and "Taste of Los Angeles." Designed creative booths and represented the organization to the public. Voted one of the Best New Restaurants in Los Angeles by *L.A. Magazine*.

Special Assignments

- Simon Wiesenthal Center for Holocaust Studies, Los Angeles, CA, yearlong assignment in collaboration with producer Sam Egan. Wrote a 40-minute documentary for in-house presentation on the history of the Third Reich newspaper *Der Sturmer* and the subsequent capture of its editor by a U.S. soldier.

- Wrote advertising copy, restaurant reviews, and feature articles highlighting San Fernando Valley businesses for *On the Boulevard in Van Nuys, CA* magazine.

- Appeared in television commercials for Sapporo Beer (Japan), Liberty Mutual Insurance, Dial-a-Joke, and York Peppermint Patties.

Community

- Cowrote and performed in the original production, *The Best Years of Your Life*. Toured Illinois high schools with the People's Theater.

- Lakeview Wilds, Inc., Peoria, IL: Cofounded and served as president and vice president for this nonprofit organization dedicated to preserving natural green space in Peoria County. Wrote newsletters, brochures, and press releases, planned and staged fund-raisers, and represented the organization to the public and the City Council.

COMMUNICATIONS—NONPROFIT

JENNIFER WARREN
jwarren@email.com

5555 Cherry Blossom Lane
West Hills, CA 91343

Residence: (818) 555-1234
Mobile: (818) 555-4321

Recent College Graduate, Qualified for Positions in
FUND-RAISING/COMMUNITY OUTREACH—NONPROFIT SECTOR

Highly organized and hardworking with proven success in fund-raising and community outreach programs. Excellent networking and presentation skills with ability to organize events, raise money, and enhance community awareness. Committed team player who works well individually as well as in collaborative settings. Highly skilled in recruiting and motivating volunteers.

—Core Competencies—

Project Management • Event Organizing & Coordination • Recruiting • Educating • Publicity
Taskforce Modeling • Community Liaison & Outreach • Consensus Building • Media & Public Relations
Budgets • Oral & Written Communications • Public Speaking • Presentations

EDUCATION

UNIVERSITY OF CALIFORNIA, Los Angeles, CA (UCLA); 2001
B.A. in Communications; Emphasis in Nonprofit Organizations; GPA: 3.4

Relevant Course Work: Volunteer Management, Fund-raising for Nonprofit Organizations, Public Relations, Media Relations, Community Outreach Programs

Honors: Recipient, Dean's Community Service Award

Campus/Community Activities: President—South East Asian Student Association, Intramural Softball and Bowling, Staff Member—*Daily Bruin* (Campus Newspaper).

EXPERIENCE

Volunteer Fund-raiser and Recruitment Specialist, South Asian Task Force   1997 to Present
SOUTHEAST ASIAN FAMILY EDUCATION (SAFE), Los Angeles, CA
Worked closely with Project Director of nonprofit organization that provides educational services in the Southeast Asian community at the local, national, and international levels. Established key contacts with community and religious organizations and leaders, set up presentations and information booths on college campuses, organized and arranged fund-raising drives, recruited and coordinated volunteer efforts, planned and implemented special events, handled media relations.
* Organized benefit concert that raised $15,000 to fund educational projects in India for underprivileged children.
* Increased awareness of need for after-school programs in South Asian community through special events, presentations, and articles.
* Devised and conducted numerous outreach events for schools and on-campus clubs.
* Increased local volunteer recruitment by 100%.
* Obtained corporate donors to fund translation of educational materials into three South Asian languages.

WORK HISTORY

Administrative Assistant   2000 to 2001—*Part-Time, Concurrent with University Studies*
ALL VALLEY PROPERTY MANAGEMENT, Mission Hills, CA
Performed variety of administrative and clerical functions including bookkeeping, filing, data entry, typing, and handling telephone inquiries regarding rental properties.
 • Redesigned filing system, enhancing productivity.
 • Consistently diffused client complaints.

Sales Associate   1996 to 2000—*Part-Time & Seasonal, Concurrent with Studies*
THE GAP, Fashion Square, Sherman Oaks, CA
Assisted clients with selections, providing high level of customer service.
 • Consistently met or exceeded sales goals.
 • Recognized as "Employee of the Month."

FOREIGN LANGUAGES

Punjabi, Hindi (speak fluently)
Spanish (reading/writing knowledge)

COMMUNITY ACTIVITIES/AFFILIATIONS

Member, National Asian Women's Health Organization
Member, South Asian Network

COMPUTER SKILLS

Proficient in Windows, Microsoft Word, Excel, PowerPoint, Access, WordPerfect, Lotus Works, Internet, E-mail
Light skills in Web site development; working knowledge of FrontPage, Macromedia Flash

Corporate Communications

ANDREW STEWART
123 SW Madison Street ■ Kewanee, IL 61433
(888) 449-2200 ■ emial@email.com

Public Relations

January 24, 2002

STANLEY COMMUNICATIONS COMPANY
P.O. Box 12345
Turner, IL 12345

Allow me to introduce myself:

In response to your advertisement for a Corporate Communications Assistant, I believe you will find my background and skills to be an excellent match.

Believe it or not, I worked my way into my current position as Writer/Editorial Assistant for a prestigious newspaper publication company from the bottom up. I started out as the Mascot; dressed in yellow tights and wrapped up in a newspaper. Definitely not the most dignified position I've ever held, but it does show that I'm willing to do whatever the job requires.

Having recently obtained my B.A. in Corporate Communications to round out my skills and knowledge, I would like to find a position in a corporate setting where my strong communication skills could be of value. As you will see on the enclosed resume, I have developed many comparable abilities through my long-term employment with *The California Press*.

If you have an opening for an enthusiastic communications professional with my background and skills, please contact me. Although I would prefer to avoid the mascot gig again, I would certainly be eager to discuss any related communications or PR positions that would match my abilities.

Thank you, and I look forward to hearing from you soon. I promise you won't be disappointed!

Sincerely,

Andrew Stewart

(Resume enclosed)

Corporate Communications

Public Relations

ANDREW STEWART
123 SW Madison Street ■ Kewanee, IL 61433
(888) 449-2200 ■ emial@email.com

CORE STRENGTHS
Writing ■ Editing ■ Publishing
Negotiating ■ Public Speaking ■ Training

QUALIFICATIONS SUMMARY

- Accomplished, enthusiastic, and dedicated Communications/Public Relations professional. Solid academic credentials complemented by hands-on experience.
- Polished communicator with excellent negotiation, training, conflict resolution, and written/oral presentation skills; able to relate comfortably and effectively to people at all levels and from diverse backgrounds.
- Advanced computer skills include MS Word, Excel, Access, WordPerfect, Lotus 1-2-3, PowerPoint, Internet, and E-mail.

EDUCATIONAL BACKGROUND

B.A. in Corporate Communications (2002)
UNIVERSITY OF CALIFORNIA—San Diego, CA
A.A.S. FONTAINE COMMUNITY COLLEGE—Lewiston, CA (1990)
Academic Highlights: Warren Johnson Academic Scholarship Recipient ■ Elected Vice President of the University's Student Public Relations Association ■ Served as Chairperson and President of the Association for Student Activity Programming ■ Annual Fund Phonathon participant ■ WXYZ College Radio DJ/News Reporter

PROFESSIONAL EXPERIENCE

Public Relations Assistant Intern (1999 to 2002)
NELSON & BRIGGS COMPANY—Bronsonville, CA
Performed a wide range of PR functions for the company including research/fact finding on current internal labor negotiations information to include in outside press releases. Posted current company information and employee-related topics on the corporate Internet site and edited existing information. Typed and distributed all press releases to the local media.
- Commended for thorough research and excellent written communication skills during labor negotiations, which had favorable results.

Writer/Editorial Assistant (1987 to 1999)
THE CALIFORNIA PRESS/OBSERVER—San Diego, CA
Served as the main point-of-contact for resource information and editorial subject matter for this large communications publication with a distribution of 175,000. Researched and wrote articles on various current business topics, prescreened all articles submitted for possible publication, and supported staff members in locating vital resource information.
- Started as company mascot, promoted through the positions of Advertising Sales Representative, Events Coordinator, and then Writer/Editorial Assistant.

EVALUATION COMMENTS

"Andrew Stewart possesses exceptional proficiency at both communications and customer relations. Also, his charismatic personality complements his fine work ethic, which I can assure you is both energetic and assertive. I feel **Andrew has all of the confidence, motivation, courage, and skills necessary to excel at any endeavor in life.**"

—Ed Sims, PR Manager
NELSON & BRIGGS CO.

"Andrew's positive attitude is a great testament to his outlook on life. He is able to find the positive in every situation. I have been in the communication's industry for 17 years [and] must say that **Andrew is one of the best professionals I've ever had the privilege of meeting, based on the extra effort he put forth.** He is able to maintain a steady pace in the workplace without having to be prodded, even though the pressures are very great."

—Reese Olson, Editor
THE CALIFORNIA PRESS

"He is flexible and always willing to accept and embrace change."

—Mike Smith, Manager
NELSON & BRIGGS CO.

References Available on Request

ANDREW SCOTT STEVENS

7237 High Street ◆ Columbus, Ohio 43229
Phone (614) 555-1212 / E-mail: email@email.com

TRAINING—FEDERAL POSTAL SERVICE

> *Energetic, industrious graduate combining achievements in academic, extracurricular, and employment areas.*
>
> **Strategically educated in the planning, developing, and executing of effective training strategies. Able to increase work performance by organizing and effectively communicating organizational practices, procedures, and polices.**
>
> Quickly learn and master new responsibilities and challenges; able to meet or exceed organizational objectives.
> Dedicated to providing exceptional support; relate easily to all levels of staff and management.
> Often recognized by colleagues for strong work ethic, integrity, and commitment to success.
> Excellent communicator with a proven understanding of small- and large-group dynamics.

EDUCATIONAL ACHIEVEMENTS

Bachelor of Arts in Communication
The Ohio State University—Columbus, Ohio
Minor in Corporate Training

Relevant Course Topics:

- Communication of Ideas & Attitudes
- Organizational Communication
- Telecommunications & Electronic Media
- Persuasive Communication
- Presentational Speaking

- Program Development & Implementation
- Organizational-Needs Analysis
- Team Building & Consultation
- Training in the Digital Age
- Cost-Effective Training Models

PROFESSIONAL EXPERIENCE

COMPUTER IMPACT—Columbus, Ohio (www.impact2000.com)
Training Coordinator
- Successfully marketed software training program and maintained database for 3000+ clientele while offering strong sales support to computer sales team in a high-volume retail environment. (January 1999 to Present)

CITY OF URGON, DIVISION OF WATER—Ugon, Illinois (www.udow.com)
Messenger
- Fully accountable for timely and efficient sorting and delivery of mail for entire Utilities Complex including Water, Electric, and Sewage & Drains Divisions. Organized and maintained stockroom. Received office supply shipments on daily basis and distributed supplies as required. Interacted with all levels of City Officials and support personnel. (August 1997 to December 1999)

E' MOTION COMMUNICATIONS—Urbana, Illinois (www.e-motion.com)
Customer Service Assistant
- Performed diversified customer support activities within high-volume call-service environment. Served as initial line of communication answering inquiries for new and existing clients. Networked with sales & marketing departments while helping customers resolve product-related and billing concerns. (June 1994 to August 1997)

MOVING SUBS—Urbana, Illinois (www.movingsubs.com)
Food Production Associate
- Responsible for wide variety of activities involved in sandwich preparation in high-volume deli, carryout restaurant. Emphasis in work-flow management, operational efficiency, and maintaining quality standards. (June 1991 to August 1993)

EXCELLENT REFERENCES FURNISHED UPON REQUEST

COSMETOLOGIST COVER LETTER

PAULINE S. NOTA

P.O. Box 1234
Auburn, Maine 04210
Telephone: (207) 555-1212 / email@email.com

COSMETOLOGIST

26 November, 2001

Joanne Pelletier, Hiring Manager
The Hair Palace
999 Riverside Plaza
Lewiston, Maine 04240

Dear Ms. Pelletier:

Congratulations on the Grand Opening of The Hair Palace! Based on your newspaper ad, your facility appears to be absolutely beautiful! It is exactly the type of environment in which I am seeking to put to use my recent training, hands-on experience, and interpersonal skills. I feel confident that I could very quickly build a very impressive list of clients in the field of cosmetology to the mutual benefit of an employer.

As requested in your newspaper advertisement, I am submitting this cover letter, enclosed resume, and three letters of reference. Please consider this documentation as my formal application for your position of Cosmetologist. I feel confident that I could very effectively perform all duties required of this position while offering you the following:

- Recent State of Maine Cosmetology License
- Associate's Degree in Cosmetology Science
- Several Years' of Experience Working in a Hair Salon
- Extensive Experience in Interacting with Clients
- Immediate Availability

Furthermore, with my current flexible schedule, I could interview and/or begin in your position at any time. I may be contacted by telephone at my home number 555-1212 during the morning hours or in the afternoon at 555-0000. I look forward to meeting with you to further discuss this position, my qualifications, and your specific requirements for becoming a team member of The Hair Palace staff. I look forward to hearing from you!

Very truly yours,

Pauline S. Nota

Enclosure

PAULINE S. NOTA

P.O. Box 1234
Auburn, Maine 04210
Telephone: (207) 555-1212 / email@email.com

COSMETOLOGIST

QUALIFICATIONS

- **Licensed State of Maine Cosmetologist**
- **Associate's Degree in Cosmetology Science**

- **Certificates Earned & Experience in the Following Areas:**
  - Hair Color—Corrective
  - Hair Cuts & Styling (Razor & Scissors)
  - Permanent Curls & Waving
  - Scalp Massage Treatments
  - Facial Massages
  - Beauty Aid Selections

- **Assisted Various Platform Artists (While Training) Including:**
  - Gino Scabelli of New York
  - Jack Myers of Tennessee

WORK HISTORY

Receptionist, Paulette's Styling Salon, Auburn, ME, 1993–Present
Hair Stylist Asst., J. C. Penney Salon, Auburn, ME, 1989–1993
Hair Stylist Asst. & Appointment Scheduler, Charlotte, NC, 1979–1989
Appointment Scheduler, Joline's Beauty Boutique, Auburn Mall, Auburn, ME, 1973–1979

EDUCATION

Licensed Cosmetologist, State of Maine, 2001
- Mr. Johnson's School of Hair Fashion (Auburn, ME)
- Associate's Degree Program
- Completed Additional 300 Hours of Instruction for Licensing
- Graduated with the Highest GPA in Class

Nexus Educator Conference, 2001
- Certificate of Achievement
- 5-Step Education Program

AFFILIATIONS
Member, National Cosmetology Association, 2000–Present

REFERENCES ARE AVAILABLE UPON REQUEST

DENTAL ASSISTANT COVER LETTER

CLAIRE JAMES

12 Willow Terrace • Springfield, NC 28801 • (828) 555-1212

July 13, 2001

Attn: Alice Cooper
William J. Silvers, D.D.S.
11 Brucemyer Street
Anytown, NC 28803

Dear Ms. Cooper:

Please accept my enclosed resume in application for the Dental Assistant position in your new office, which I understand from Donna Myers will be opening in August. You and I met about a month ago at her office, and I mentioned my interest in the position at that time.

I am currently an Assistant Telecommunication Supervisor with the Xavier County Sheriff's Department; in effect, I am one of the people you would talk to when you dial 911 in emergency situations. I work all shifts, and I do love this job. However, I have been married for two years now and rarely see my husband. Hence, I have worked hard to earn the 2-year certification as a Dental Assistant from Xavier. I am looking for a position that, while requiring accuracy, attention to detail, and rapport-building skill, will also offer the possibility of regular hours.

I am certified at the expanded, advanced duties level, including x-ray qualification. I can also bring strong experience to the position. At first glance, my 7 years' experience answering 911 calls may seem a far cry from a dental office, but I don't believe that it is. In both places, I would be working as a member of a team whose express purpose is to assist people who may be feeling discomfort in some degree; both require balancing a number of tasks at the same time while maintaining a helpful and calm manner; both require the ability to answer more than one telephone line, maintain accurate records, and be able to find them quickly; both require computer proficiency and the ability to learn new software.

I would appreciate the opportunity to talk with you in greater detail about the position. I will call you some time next week to answer any questions you may have, and possibly finalize an appointment date.

I look forward to seeing you again.

Sincerely,

Claire James

enc.

DENTAL ASSISTANT

CLAIRE JAMES   12 Willow Terrace • Springfield, NC 28801 • (828) 555-1212

*New graduate seeks **Dental Assistant** position requiring strong CUSTOMER SERVICE,
CLERICAL, PUBLIC RELATIONS, and COMMUNICATIONS abilities.*

XAVIER COMMUNITY CAREER INSTITUTE
- **Associate's Degree, Dental Assistant Certification**, May 2001
- **With Expanded Duties; X-Ray Certified**

Core strengths include:

- ❏ Exceptional customer relationship skills. Work well and calmly in stressful, changing situations.
- ❏ Outstanding multiline telephone skills in high-intensity environment.
- ❏ PC proficient, including Microsoft Windows, Internet, and specialized DCI software (computer-aided dispatch).
- ❏ Type approximately 70 words per minute accurately. Excellent spelling and grammar.
- ❏ Excellent filing and bookkeeping skills—successful experience in high volume, time-sensitive working environments.
- ❏ Quick and able student—recognized twice for exceptional speed in learning new systems.
- ❏ Excellent work ethic; attentive to detail; high personal standards.

PROFILE OF EXPERIENCE

1993–Present   **Assistant Telecommunication Supervisor**
XAVIER COUNTY SHERIFFS DEPARTMENT, Hanover, NC
Respond to emergency and routine calls from the public, manning 12 lines. Track locations of deputies at all times for dispatch. Record-management responsibilities include accessing appropriate DMV, Wanted, and Missing Persons records and ensuring accurate, current filing of records of Stolen Property and Missing and Wanted Persons.
- ❏ Sheriffs Meritorious Service Medal
- ❏ Twice Employee-of-the-Month

1988–1992   **Printer Systems Operator**
UNITED STATES AIR FORCE, Texas, Florida, Maryland, and England
Collected and plotted a variety of printer signals (voice, Morse code, electronic). Classified position—Top Secret Clearance.
- ❏ Good Conduct Award.
- ❏ Sammy Award for exceptional speed in copying Morse code.
- ❏ Learned a significant number of different collecting systems in relatively short time.

ADDITIONAL TRAINING

- ❏ Certification, DMV Computer Operation, Department of Criminal Information, 1994–Present
- ❏ Querying, Accessing, & Data Entry, Department of Criminal Information System.
- ❏ Air Force Technical Training, Pensacola Naval Air Technical Training School, 1989. Military intelligence collection techniques.

Volunteer, Special Olympics

JOHN P. CLOONEY

458 Broad Lane • Suffern, NY 10901
(845) 555-1212 • email@email.com

DISC JOCKEY • ENTERTAINMENT SPECIALIST

- An energetic music entertainment professional with extensive experience in creating unique entertainment experiences for all types of affairs, including weddings, Sweet Sixteen parties, bar & bat mitzvahs, birthdays, anniversaries, and corporate events.
- Able to develop strong rapport with clients establishing a solid trust, and able to set both a fun and relaxed atmosphere at any event.
- Adept planning capabilities and accustomed to developing multiple projects on short notice, maintaining total responsibility for quality.

EDUCATION

SUNY Rockland Community College—Suffern, NY
Associate of Art • Music Theory • GPA 3.9 • May 2001

AREAS OF EXPERTISE

- **Client Relations**
- **Staff Training**
- **Entertainment Management**

- **New Business Development**
- **Cross-Marketing Promotions**
- **Cost Controls**

PROFESSIONAL EXPERIENCE

CLOONEY ENTERTAINMENT—Suffern, NY • 1999 to Present
GENERAL MANAGER/LEAD ENTERTAINER

- Direct day-to-day operations of this music entertainment firm providing DJ and Karaoke services for weddings, Sweet Sixteen parties, bar & bat mitzvahs, birthdays, anniversaries, and corporate events for up to 600 guests with 12 DJs and a crew of 25 dancers.
- Consult with clients on appropriate entertainment packages and song lists to develop programs to meet each individual's budget and personal preference.
- Coordinate marketing initiatives with local wedding planners, photographers, videographers, catering halls, and trade show promoters to increase market penetration.
- Train new dancers, DJs, and crews on policies, procedures, technology implementation, and entertainment coordination to ensure superior levels of service.

Selected Accomplishments:

- **Coordinated operations for this firm from the ground up—obtaining funding, developing business plans, hiring staff, and creating successful marketing programs.**
- **Increased business from zero to over $25,000 monthly within 7 months by establishing solid marketing campaigns and hiring the area's best DJs and dancers.**
- **Reduced inventory expenses by 37% by renegotiating rates with suppliers for props.**

DOCTOR OF OSTEOPATHY COVER LETTER

Kathleen McCoy, D.O.

123 Fourth Avenue West • Galesburg, IL 12345
(332) 555-1212 / email@email.com

September 8, 2002

Jeffrey Long, Director of Placement
Mt. Placid Medical Center
Mt. Placid, IL 63333

Dear Mr. Long:

During my last year as a family practice physician I attended an annual Harvard Review Course, which was a 50-hour psychiatric update.

As a result of that course, I was eager to use what I had learned with troubled patients, rather than refer them to psychiatrists, an option that is often not practical—particularly in this world of cost-conscious HMOs.

And so I embarked on what has proven to be a personal and professional quest: first, to reduce the number of patients I referred to other physicians and, second, to learn as much as I could in the field of psychiatry. I eventually left family practice to study psychiatry, and I have recently completed my residency in the field.

In my practice, I have cared for clients with a variety of mental health disorders, including very difficult-to-treat children and geriatric patients. I have access to any number of experts in the field, and so if I don't know how best to treat a patient, I contact someone who does. I have never thought of medicine as a routine, and I relish every opportunity to expand my knowledge so as to better serve my patients.

Your ad in *Medical Review* regarding an opening for a board-certified psychiatrist caught my eye, and I am hereby throwing my hat in the ring. I would welcome the opportunity to meet with you for a personal interview and look forward to hearing from you.

Sincerely,

Kathleen McCoy, D.O.

Enclosure

DOCTOR OF OSTEOPATHY

Kathleen McCoy, D.O.

123 Fourth Avenue West • Galesburg, IL 12345
(332) 555-1212 / email@email.com

Synopsis

Board Certified Psychiatrist...
with experience treating patients of all ages and socioeconomic backgrounds with a wide range of disorders, including acute psychiatric illness, chronic mental illness, and treatment-resistant mood and thought disorders. Qualified speaker and trainer with a background in family medicine, as well as a commitment to educating family practitioners and other health care professionals to identify and treat mental health disorders.

Education & Credentials

Board Certified, American Osteopathic Board of Neurology and Psychiatry
(6/01–present)

Licensed to practice medicine in Illinois and Iowa

D.O., College of Osteopathic Medicine and Surgery—Des Moines, IA (6/83)
Sigma Sigma Phi Osteopathic Honor Society

B.A., Biology, University of Northern Iowa—Cedar Falls, IA (5/79)
Beta Beta Beta Biology Honor Society

Psychiatric Resident, Kirksville Osteopathic Medical Center—Kirksville, MO
(7/98–6/01)

Intern, Pontiac Osteopathic Hospital—Pontiac, MI (7/83–7/84)

Psychiatric Rotations (1993)
St. Joseph Hospital—St. Joseph, MO, chronically mentally ill and forensic units; Mercy Hospital, Des Moines; work with neurologist Jason Leaderer, M.D. at Ottumwa Regional Medical Center; and University of Missouri at Columbia with Richard Bestman, M.D. and Jane Salomon, D.O. for Consultation-Liaison psychiatry.

Professional History

Psychiatrist, Community Mental Health Center—St. Louis, MO (1994–Present)
Staff Physician, Missouri Hospital—Louis, IL (1995–Present)
Staff Physician, Southern Hospital—Troy, IL (1994–Present)
Staff Psychiatrist, West District Hospital—Lambert, IL (1994–Present)
Medical Director/Board Member, Red Cross—Galesburg, IL (1992–1993)

Continued...

Kathleen McCoy, D.O.

Staff Physician, Southern Indiana Health Center—LaCrosse, IN (1991–1993)

Staff Physician/Consulting Physician, Inpatient Addiction Treatment Unit, Indianapolis Neurological & Psychiatric Associates/Indianapolis Regional Specialty Clinic,—Rosewood, IA (1991–1993)

Staff Physician for Inpatient Addiction Treatment Unit, Clarinda Treatment Complex—Clarinda, IN 1991–1993)

Medical Examiner, Center County, Sparksburg, IN (1983–1986)

Family Practice Physician, Sparksburg, IN (1983–1986)

Staff Physician, Memorial Hospital—Central, IN (1983–1985)

Continuing Education (1986–2001)

Advances in the Treatment of Depression & Anxiety, Stephen M. Stahl, M.D., Ph.D.—Chicago, IL

Upper Midwest Osteopathic Health Conference, Iowa Osteopathic Medical Association

Psychiatric Neuroscience: A Primer for Clinicians, Harvard Medical School

Child & Adolescent Psychopharmacology, Harvard Medical School

Comprehensive Update & Board Preparation—Psychiatry, Harvard Medical School

Psychiatry—A Comprehensive Update & Board Preparation, Harvard Medical School

Upper Midwest Osteopathic Health Conference, Iowa Osteopathic Medical Association

Comparison of SSRIs in the Treatment of Depression, Jeffrey Goffreis, M.D. from Finland—St. Paul, MN

Upper Midwest Osteopathic Health Conference, Iowa Osteopathic Medical Association; three-day OMT Practical Session

Directions in Behavioral Health, Pfizer Pharmaceuticals—Naples, FL

Additional: Routinely participate in educational teleconferences on a wide range of topics

Professional Affiliations

American Osteopathic Association

Diplomat, National Board of Examiners: Osteopathic Physicians & Surgeons

American Osteopathic College of Neuropsychiatry

Charter Member of the American Osteopathic Academy of Addictionology

WILLIAM H. (BILL) WILKS

email@email.com

123 Second Street • Saybridge, Connecticut 55342 • (702) 555-1212

Drama Teacher—Community Theatre Director

FORMAL EDUCATION

Bachelor of Arts—May 1998
Speech and Drama
University of Kansas, Lawrence

TEACHING CREDENTIALS

K–12 Certificates:

Alabama	*Florida*
Colorado	*Kansas*
New York	

PERSONAL PROFILE

- Proven professional in planning, budgeting, coordinating, and scheduling.

- A practical problem solver using analytical, communication, and creative skills.

- Award-winning teacher.

- Experience with comedy, drama, Shakespeare, melodrama, and musicals.

- Intense educator, with the ability to motivate students to achieve their potential.

- Well-organized and goal-oriented director with proven ability to create high-caliber theatrical events.

- Outstanding participant in community affairs, utilizing a fair and balanced approach to the needs of the arts.

PORTFOLIO, PRODUCTION HIGHLIGHTS, AND PUBLISHED REVIEWS AVAILABLE AT TIME OF INTERVIEW

PRACTICAL EXPERTISE

- ➤ Able to achieve major increases in revenues:
  - ➤ Designed marketing plan that increased sales by 47%
- ➤ Community interaction:
  - ➤ Served on the Boards of United Way, County Art Council, and BBB
- ➤ Expense control:
  - ➤ Under expense budget by $22,000 at season end 2001
- ➤ Effective negotiator, moderator, and mediator:
  - ➤ Negotiated first long-term union contract in theatre's history

CREATIVE EXPERTISE

- ➤ Directing:
  - ➤ "Colorado's Best Summer Stock Director" - Durango
- ➤ Choreography:
  - ➤ "The finest high school choreographing ever" - Manhattan
- ➤ Writer:
  - ➤ "His work will always play here" - Peoria
- ➤ Actor:
  - ➤ "Even with his Midwest 'twang,' the Globe's best male lead" - San Diego
- ➤ Teaching:
  - ➤ Honored as "Teacher of the Year" 2000–2001

EMPLOYMENT HISTORY

Director
Diamond Circle Theatre, Durango, Colorado   **Summers 2000–2001**
Direct professional actors in "The Tavern" melodrama and oleo skits for this summer stock Theatre in this mountain tourist community. Manage all marketing and community relations. Negotiated first long-term union contract for stagehands. Direct responsibility for working within an assigned budget.

Theatre & Speech Instructor
XYZ High School, Manhattan, Kansas   **September 1998 to Present**
Director and choreographer of three productions per class year. Classroom instructor of Theatre and Speech (2 Drama Classes and 2 Speech Classes) with a waiting list of students. Faculty Advisor to Thespian Club and Drama Club. Teacher of the year award.

Guest Director
Joe Jefferson Players, Mobile, Alabama   **2000**
Directed the first musical ever produced by this 85-year-old theatre company.

Actor
Old Globe Theatre, San Diego, California   **1998–1999**
Played numerous lead and supporting parts including comedy, drama, Shakespeare, melodrama, and musicals. Assisted with choreography.

REFERENCES AND FURTHER DATA UPON REQUEST

ELECTRICIAN

Kara Freemann
3057 Marina Road * St. Cloud, MN 56301 * (320) 555-3772 * email@email.com

JOURNEYMAN ELECTRICIAN . . .

- ... committed to continued development of career as a professional electrician.
- ... contributing journeyman licensure, an associate degree, and three years of apprenticed experience.
- ... offering a strong work ethic, high standards, exceptional employer loyalty, and acceptance of change.
- ... willing to learn and handle any task at hand; able to represent employer with professionalism at all times.

LICENSES

Journeyman Electrician, Minnesota State Board of Electricity (2001)
Special Boiler's License, State of Minnesota (1995)

EDUCATION

ST. CLOUD TECHNICAL COLLEGE—St. Cloud, MN
AAS Degree in Construction Electrician Program (2001)
Minnesota State Board of Electricity Accreditation

EXPERIENCE

CRAWFORD ELECTRIC—St. Cloud, MN   1996–present
Indentured Electrical Apprentice (1998–present)
- Work under the mentorship of owner/president holding Master Electrician and Contractor licensures.
- Under supervision, plan, lay out, install, repair, and maintain traffic control systems and commercial/residential circuits, wiring, and outlets in union and nonunion settings.
- Follow wire diagrams, read blueprints, and comply with state and local building codes.
- Specialize in industrial electrical maintenance and preventive maintenance; and repairing motors, transformers, generators, and electronic controllers.

Shop Assistant (1996–1998)
- Gained knowledge of general procedures and a vast electrical parts inventory for this large commercial electric contractor. Delivered parts to job sites, unloaded trucks, and helped maintain inventory.

L & P SERVICES—St. Cloud, MN   1994–1996
Maintenance Engineer/Production
- Cross-trained with this textile laundry production service. Aggressively assumed increased responsibility.
- Operated a PLC-controlled automated wash floor. Handled special work orders for fan and light installations.
- Performed preventive maintenance and repairs on production equipment.
- Welded using wire feed, cutting torch, solder, and stick weld. Operated hand and power tools.

UNITED STATES AIR FORCE—Mountain Home AFB, ID   1990–1994
Integrated Avionics Components Specialist/Honorable Discharge
- Performed ongoing maintenance of avionic systems and equipment at aircraft flight line and workshop levels.
- Inspected, removed, installed, assembled, and disassembled electric aircraft components.
- Prepared and used aircraft support equipment, manufactured and repaired electrical looms and antenna cables, performed 240-volt testing, serviced aircraft earthing systems, and prepared technical equipment for transport.

SUCCESSES, CONTRIBUTIONS, & HONORS

- Balanced full-time studies (15–19 credits) with 40-hour-per-week employment; maintained a 3.75 GPA.
- Donated 500 hours of pro bono, professionally supervised electrical wiring services with Habitat for Humanity.
- Performed community outreach work on behalf of the Minnesota Electrical Association.
- Recognized as L & P's "Employee of the Month" five times—awarded for reliability, attendance, and work quality.
- Honored by the U.S. Air Force with three Achievement Medals and a Humanitarian Ribbon.

Jennifer Snell

4729 Roland Avenue ■ Houston, TX 77063 ■ (713) 555-1212 ■ email@email.com

Objective:

Structural Engineering Position / Project Management

Profile	<ul><li>Experience working on a wide range of projects including the design of steel, wood, concrete, and masonry structures.</li><li>Knowledge of Concrete Code (ACI 318-89), Masonry Structures Code (ACI 530-88/ASCE 5-88), and BOCA; ASD 9th edition and LRFD first edition.</li><li>Software: Microstation, AutoCAD, RISA-2D & RISA-3D, and Microsoft Office.</li><li>Effective as project leader or as a supportive team member.</li></ul>

Education   **Bachelor of Science**, Civil Engineering   5/01
UNIVERSITY OF HOUSTON—Houston, TX

EIT: Passed Fundamentals of Engineering exam   6/01

Attended Wood Seminar on glulam and LVL beams, and wood shear walls

Experience   **Project Intern/Design Engineer**   8/98 to Present
DEAN JONES & ASSOCIATES, INC.—Houston, TX

Began as intern; progressed to engineering and project leadership responsibilities. Cited for a positive attitude, enthusiasm, the ability to learn quickly, and a willingness to take on extra work. Projects have included:

- 30,000-square-foot fitness center: designed and detailed the structure in coordination with an architect.
- Remodel for police headquarters: both gravity and lateral design responsibilities as well as on-site supervision.
- Houston Prison: examined an existing structure to determine if it could accommodate proposed additions.
- 60,000-square-foot fitness center: part of a team to conduct lateral frame analysis. Designed concrete one-way slab, beams, and girders.
- Cardiac rehabilitation facility: designed wood load-bearing walls; analyzed wind loads and related factors for shear wall analysis.
- Library: designed storm water retention basin; used Rational Method to design storm sewer layout. Prepared a Cut-and-Fill Analysis and worked closely with Project Manager during the construction phase.
- 450-foot roadway/sewer extension: developed plan and profile sheets, calculated invert and rim elevation for sanitary system, and used Rational Method to design storm sewer layout.

Activities   Volunteer: Heart Fund, American Cancer Society, and Make-A-Wish Foundation
Member: SEOF Association, ERTR Engineering Group

References Furnished upon Request

MIKE DESA

123 Third Avenue • Summerville, South Carolina 29483
(888) 555-1212 • email@email.com

Electrical Engineer, seeking an **Internship position**

SUMMARY OF QUALIFICATIONS

Recent academic credentials qualify me for an **Internship Position** as an **Electrical Engineer**. Background encompasses demonstrated knowledge of commercial and industrial HVAC systems. Excellent communication skills with clients, crews, and subcontractors, providing leadership by example. Exceptional work ethic, committed to guiding all projects through successful completion.

AREAS OF STRENGTH

- Site Leadership
- Job Scheduling & Estimating
- Cost Reduction & Containment
- Service-Level Standards
- Contract Adherence
- Crew Supervision

LICENSES AND CERTIFICATIONS

Currently sitting for the Electrical Engineer license, State of Colorado
HVAC Universal License—States of Colorado and Wyoming
Commercial Driver's License—State of Colorado
Current "Top Secret-SBI" Security Clearance

EDUCATION

B.S., Electrical Engineering, University of Wyoming, May 2001 (GPA 3.8)
Graduate, Cheyenne High School, Cheyenne, Wyoming

WORK EXPERIENCE

HVAC Mechanic
DEPARTMENT OF DEFENSE, Warren Air Force Base, Wyoming   1989–Present

- Contracted by the government to maintain operation of industrial HVAC systems.
- In charge of all aspects of system diagnostics, preventative maintenance, and repair.
- Responsible for job-order changes, blueprint interpretation, and occupational safety.

[*Note:* This position allowed me the time to complete my college degree.]

Journeyman Welder & Pipe Fitter
LOCAL 192, Cheyenne, Wyoming   1995–Present
LOCAL 698, Rapid City, South Dakota   1985–1989

- Complete repairs for organizations, municipalities, schools, hospitals, and banks.
- Numerous time-critical assignments.

REFERENCES AND FURTHER DATA UPON REQUEST

ENVIRONMENTAL ENGINEERING

FELICIA ARMANI

34040 Scott Street
San Francisco, California 94134

(510) 555-1212

Day: email@email.edu
Evening: email@email.com

ENVIRONMENTAL ENGINEERING

Environmental Management Systems/Project Planning
Quality Engineering / Research and Development/Consultation

Focused and highly motivated with hands-on experience in environmental engineering, project management, technical, and business development. Excellent organizational, problem solving, team building, leadership, budget management, and negotiation skills. Develop and deliver diversified support training administration to corporate networks. Effective interpersonal, multicultural communications, and team-based management style. Bilingual in English and French. Demonstrated strengths in:

Engineering Documentation/Technology Integration/Quality Assurance
Occupational Safety and Health Administration (OSHA)/Customer Satisfaction

EDUCATION

MBA   Marketing, (In Progress—Anticipated December 2001)
University of California, Berkeley, California

BA   Environmental Engineering, 1998
University of California, Berkeley, California

Additional Training and Certifications

- ISO 14001 Environmental Management Systems Internal Auditor, 1998
- ISO 9001 Quality Management Systems Internal Auditor, 1998
- SA 8000 (Social Accountability) Induction Training, 1998
- Business Communications, Related Seminars, and Self-study Programs

INTERNSHIP

☑ Project Development/Environmental Health and Safety Manager Assistant, 1996–1998
Challenged with series of diversified environmental engineering projects for international construction, government, and pharmaceutical companies.

FELICIA ARMANI

PROFESSIONAL EXPERIENCE

UNIVERSITY OF CALIFORNIA, Berkeley, California, 2000–Present
Environmental Department Research Assistant
Conduct comprehensive research and manipulate environmental data for university contracts.

- ☑ Charged with design and development of San Francisco International Airport ISO 14000 Environmental Management Systems project.
- ☑ Managed and wrote project proposals through field assessment, research, data compilation, and project specifications to contract negotiation.
- ☑ Researched current U.S. business environment issues and presented results.
- ☑ Prepared findings on soil treatment technologies.

BUREAU VERITAS QUALITY INTERNATIONAL (BVQI), Paris, France, 1997–1999
Environmental Department Assistant
Recruited to accredited, global service-based organization, implementing third-party cutting-edge management system certification programs for 27,000+ corporations with 580 offices in 150 countries. Company supports design and development of ISO 9000 and other equivalent standards.

- ☑ Redesigned strategy for operating fully functional internal management systems conducive to environmental activities.
- ☑ Facilitated review and subsequent acceptance of planning and design of environmental, health, and safety audits for certification contracts.
- ☑ Streamlined administrative affairs including preparing and negotiating contracts.
- ☑ Directed marketing efforts to enhance new business development.

CORE COMPETENCIES AND ACHIEVEMENTS

Project Management/
Engineering:
- Pivotal in engineering series of construction, government wastewater systems.
- Directed environmental systems design projects.
- Achieved and surpassed corporate objectives for system performance functionality, reliability, and quality integration and project management.

Consultation/Training:
- Planned and facilitated well-received internal audits, ISO, OHSA, and environmental legislation consultancy and training.
- Standardized performance expectations and improved consistency and quality of staff performance.

Technical:
- Advanced profit performance through a series of online technology integration projects, marketing strategies, and media placement.
- Computer proficiency in Microsoft Office Suite 2000, PowerPoint, Front Page, Dreamweaver 3, Fireworks 3, and Flash 5.
- Multifunctional experience in e-commerce architecture and systems.

AFFILIATIONS

Member, SFSU-Graduate Business Association Event Committee
Student Visa valid until May 2002

TIMOTHY M. GRAHAM

12 Granite Avenue
Broomfield, CO 80021

E-mail: TMG@aol.com
Phone: (303) 555-9812

COLLEGE GRADUATE
SEEKING POSITION IN ENVIRONMENTAL ENGINEERING

EDUCATION

University of New Hampshire, Durham, NH
Masters in Science: Environmental Engineering (Marine/Aquatic Engineering), 1998
    * Member: UNH Environmental Club, 1997–98
    * Member: UNH Campus & Community Clean-Up Task Force, 1997–98

Boston University, Boston, MA
Bachelor of Science: Biology, 1996
    * Member: BU Students for a Clean Harbor, 1993–96

INTERNSHIPS—Undergraduate and Graduate

ENVIRONMENTAL ASSOCIATES, INC., Dover, NH   1997 and 1998
Environmental Engineering Assistant
- Worked with clients in developing golf courses in environmentally sensitive areas
- Liaison between senior environmental engineer and EPA, State EPA, and other regulatory agencies
- Researched and troubleshot actual and potential environmental problems

JOHNSON AND CAGE, 1NC., Newington, NH   1995 and 1996
Environmental Engineering Assistant
- Worked with clients in developing office buildings in environmentally sensitive areas
- Performed extensive research and prepared in-depth environment feasibility report based on findings
- Awarded "Mast Valuable Intern," 1996 from a group of 16 interns

EMPLOYMENT WHILE FINANCING EDUCATION

Pizza Delivery (20 hours a week), Ginos Pizza, Durham, NH   1997–1998
Waiter/Host (20 hours a week), Boston Ale, Brookline, MA   1993–1996
Usher—Weekends Red Sox Baseball Games, Fenway Park, Boston, MA   1993–1996

brian lawrence
email@email.com

6701 Margarita Avenue • Valley Glen, California 91405
(818) 555-5432 • Mobile (818) 555-2345

"Brian stood out in every way. He was courteous, efficient, prompt, professional, highly motivated, and very eager to learn. He also showed a tremendous amount of initiative."

C.R.,
Assistant Director
The Haunted Castle

"I found Mr. Lawrence willing to take the initiative, resourceful, conscientious, and highly motivated."

F.B.,
Vice President
Zebra Spot Productions

"I was very impressed with Brian's student film production. I fully expect to see his name among the credits of tomorrow's blockbuster films."

R.M.,
Director
The Longest Shadow

college senior—experienced in film production & coordination

- Film & Television major with direct experience and in-depth understanding of the production process.
- Skilled in identifying tasks and following through to completion.
- Well organized with proven strengths in handling multiple responsibilities in a fast-paced environment with critical deadlines.
- Possesses excellent verbal and written communication skills; works well with broad range of temperaments.
- Learns quickly and enjoys challenges.
- Proactive in tackling projects and resolving problems.

experience includes:

Script Breakdowns • Production Schedules • Story Boards
Preproduction • Postproduction
Coordinating Production Material • Budget Management
Scriptwriting • Editing (Digital & Linear)

education

CALIFORNIA STATE UNIVERSITY, Northridge, CA
B.S. in Film & Television; May 2002
Dean's List, 5 semesters; 3.5 GPA; 3.8 GPA in major
Teaching Assistant, Film Production; Spring 2001

producer/director credits

Producer/Director
THE CONFLICT
Oversaw all aspects of production on student film from development through postproduction. Hired crew, obtained equipment, cast talent, coordinated shooting schedule, directed actors, managed budget, etc.
- **Received first place in regional student film competition**

FILM AND TELEVISION (CONTINUED)

internships

Production Assistant, The Haunted Castle   (May–Sept. 2001)
ZEBRA SPOT PRODUCTIONS, Los Angeles, CA
- Provided direct assistance to producer on location.
- Facilitated communications between location shots and studio.
- Assisted with coordinating international travel.
- Compiled, summarized, and submitted detailed expense reports including currency conversions.
- Managed executive calendar, scheduled appointments, handled correspondence, directed calls.

Publicity Intern   (Feb.–May 2001)
GRANITE PRODUCTIONS, Hollywood, CA
- Assisted publicist and talent with interviews, press, and media.
- Contributed ideas to promotional campaign for popular cast member. Organized appearance on TV news show to promote upcoming film release.

Production Assistant, *The Longest Shadow*   (Summer 2000)
SUNSET STUDIOS, Hollywood, CA
- Coordinated voice-over recording sessions, script breakdowns, and updating.
- Scheduled executive and production meetings. Produced and distributed agendas for producer approval meetings.
- Arranged international and domestic travel.
- Maintained business and personal calendars for two producers through all phases of production.

additional work history

Server   (Seasonal & Part Time 1998–2000)
WILD BILL'S GRILL, Sherman Oaks, CA
Provided high level of customer service at popular dining establishment.

computer skills

Windows, Microsoft Word, Excel, PowerPoint, Access, Outlook, WordPerfect, Quicken, QuickBooks, WordPerfect, Lotus 1-2-3, Adobe Photoshop, Telnet, E-mail, Internet, HTML, Web Page Design

Dorothy Nieto

email@email.com

46 San Pedro St.
Powell, Ohio 43065
Home: 740-555-1212

Financial Services • Equities Trader

Analytical **financial services** professional with combined formal education, internship, and employment experience. Demonstrated communication abilities complemented with excellent organizational skills and project management attributes resulting in repeated successful endeavors. **Exceptional work ethic, joined by integrity, commitment to success, and dedication to clients.**

- **Stocks & Bonds**
- **Corporate Investments**
- **Personal Investments**
- **Advanced Equities**
- **Blue Chips**

- **Labor Relations**
- **Accounting Principles**
- **General Ledgers**
- **Business Valuations**
- **Policies & Procedures**

- **Financial Auditing**
- **Financial Reporting**
- **Cash Management**
- **Financial Software**
- **Budget Analysis**

Professional Survey

QQQ Financial—Columbus, Ohio
[*Provides investment and financial services to individuals and businesses providing expertise in investment banking, securities brokerage, trading, investment management, retirement planning, estate planning, and trust services.*]

Intern (February 1999–Present)
Support management of high-volume asset portfolios for financial managers and floor traders. Handle incoming phone calls and research information on specific bonds, stocks, mutual funds, options, securities, and assets. Currently studying to obtain Series 7 and Series 63 licenses required for all brokers.

Ferdinand Yost Foundation—Columbus, Ohio
[*Nonprofit organization actively involved in funding various community outreach programs.*]

Part-Time Front Desk Agent (January 1998–January 1999)
Orchestrated nightly operations; accountable for maintaining start and finish time for various programs and projects. Focused on operational activities including monitoring telecommunications, building security, and maintenance. Facilitated mass mailings, both electronic and traditional. Participated in training and development of associates.

Education & Affiliations

Franklin University—Columbus, OH
Candidate, **Bachelor's in Financial Services**—2002

University of Luxemburg—Europe
International Economics—Summer 1999

Student Vice President—Franklin University, 2001
Student Treasurer—Franklin University, 2000
President—Franklin University Stock Market Club, 2001
Past President, Student Board—Beta Theta Phi Fraternity, 2001
Vice President—Franklin Financial Careers Society, 2000
Member—Columbus Brokers and Traders Club, 1999, 2000

FINANCE

Greg Fantin
30 Devonshire Place
New Haven, CT 06222
(888) 555-1212

FINANCE PROFESSIONAL
Relationship Management Skills • Complementary Sales Abilities
Organizational Development • Leadership Qualifications
IBM/Mac Expertise (Excel, Word, Windows)

EDUCATION

UNIVERSITY OF MASSACHUSETTS • Amherst, MA
- *Bachelor of Science, Finance* (1998)

CERTIFICATE DES ETUDES FRANCAIS • Paris, France
- *Degree in French Studies* (1997)
- Successfully completed year-long program (UMASS-accredited)

PROFESSIONAL EXPERIENCE

1995–Present   THE CAR STORE OF CONNECTICUT • New Haven, CT
Assistant Operations Manager (part-time, 1997–Present)
- Provide financial support and consulting to one of state's largest independently owned/operated cellular/digital telephone stores through accurate budgeting, forecasting, and reporting of financial analysis.

Service/Installation Specialist (part-time, 1995–97)
- Professionally handled customer installations, performing all service functions for growing customer base of 1800 (80% individual, 20% corporate accounts).
- Directly responsible for sales and marketing efforts to individual prospects; contributed $2K–$4K/month in new sales installations and contracts (summers/winter breaks while in college).

1993–95   CALDOR • Orange, CT
Accounting Associate
- Assisted with management of Accounting Department, training new personnel on electronic processing systems.
- Handled bank deposit verification, conducted inventory control, and processed purchase orders.

FINANCIAL INVESTMENT ADVISOR COVER LETTER

Nancy B. Cunningham

808 Livingston Way
Brunswick, Maine 04011
Email: email@email.com

Phone: (207) 555-1212   Pager: (800) 222-3333

---

5 December, 2001

James F. Aitken, CPC
RO-LAN Associates, Inc.
725 Sabattus Street
Lewiston, Maine 04240

Dear Mr. Aitken:

As a recent MBA graduate, I am seeking a position that will allow the further development of my financial investment background. My ultimate goal is to earn the (CFP) Certified Financial Planner credential within the next couple of years. For this reason, I need to remain in a financial field as I prepare for the required training and exams.

Currently, I am working as a Financial Planner Trainee with a local company. I enjoy my work there very much but feel the need to accelerate my training and learning to achieve the CFP credential. In my present position, there are others with more seniority than I who are being groomed for the CFP exam to be administered this spring. This means that my growth opportunities will become more limited in the next year. I have discussed this with my immediate supervisor, Cheryl Poppell, who is aware of my situation. In fact, she has indicated that she understands and would be happy to provide an excellent work reference for me, should I decide to leave the company and take on another position.

For this reason, I am submitting my resume to you in consideration for any position that you and your agency would handle in my field as a Financial Investment Advisor or in a similar environment. For your information, my salary requirements are quite flexible at this time, taking into consideration possible career advancement opportunities. I would also be willing to relocate or commute, for the right position. My availability to begin a new position would be contingent upon having given a two-week notice to my current employer. I feel this could be negotiated, somewhat.

In the interim, I want to thank you in advance for all your help! To get started, I could be available to meet with you in person (if necessary) any day of the week after 4:30 pm. I will call you this coming Monday to discuss this and hopefully to schedule a tentative time to meet with you. If you need to reach me prior to then, please feel free to contact me at any time via email. Thanks again! I look forward to working with you—to our mutual benefit!

Respectfully yours,

Nancy B. Cunningham

Enclosure/Attachment

FINANCIAL INVESTMENT ADVISOR

Nancy B. Cunningham

808 Livingston Way
Brunswick, Maine 04011
Email: email@email.com

Phone: (207) 555-1212

Pager: (800) 222-3333

Financial Investment Advisor

Qualifications ....
- ➤ MBA—Finance .... Recent Graduate with High Honors
- ➤ Financial Internships .... Major Recreational and Manufacturer Companies
- ➤ Financial Advisor Trainee .... Recognized as "Trainee of the Month"
- ➤ Successfully Completed Series 7 and Life & Health Licenses .... State of Maine

Education ....

MBA—Finance   **May 2001**
BA—Management   **May 2000**
Simmons College, Boston, MA
- ➤ Received Masters Degree with High Honors
- ➤ Served as President, Young Financial Managers of America Group, 2000–2001

Related MBA Projects:

- ➤ *Recreational Organization—3-month (plus) project*—Evaluated & formulated a strategic financial plan and made recommendations for varied ski resorts in New England. Documented and presented recommendations and assisted in the actual implementation of the plan. Received highest grade in class.

- ➤ *Major Manufacturing Company—3-month (plus) project*—Analyzed existing financial management of a well-established and transitioning golfing club manufacturer. Introduced a more up-to-date marketing plan and strategic objectives for the company. Produced a comprehensive report and presented to their Board of Directors for approval (received approval on the spot). *Received highest grade in class.*

Current Position ....

Financial Advisor Trainee
Northeast Investment Group, Hallowell, Maine   **July 2001–Present**
- ➤ Successfully passed required testing to acquire necessary credentials to assist clients.
- ➤ Gained knowledge of the inner workings of the firm and the finance industry.
- ➤ Sharpen marketing skills, participate in workshops, and keep current on financial trends.
- ➤ Maintain varied client accounts and continue to cultivate new clients monthly.
- ➤ Received "Trainee of the Month" Award for September, October, & November of 2001.

Other Skills ....

- ➤ <u>Language Skills</u>: Fluent in French, Spanish, and German.
- ➤ <u>Computer Literate</u>: Microsoft Word, Excel, and Access; Real World, FCI, FNAS, Quicken, Quick Books; research experience with CD-ROMs, Lexis-Nexis, World Wide Web, Internet, and InfoTrac.

JOHN CARTIGLIA

17 Riley Drive Phone:
Lewiston, Maine 04240

(207) 555-1212
email@email.com

CAREER PROFILE:

Student—Funeral Director
(New England Institute of Applied Arts & Sciences)
Three years' experience in varied areas relating to current studies. Assist with basic entry-level clinical procedures, facility sterilization & maintenance, transports, vehicle operation and maintenance. Gather documentation, assist in file maintenance, and interact with print media when necessary. Assist with viewings and greet visitors. Familiar with funeral arrangements for formal military burials, as well as civilian burials (varied denominations and sizes).

OBJECTIVE:

Seeking a 6-month internship position with a local funeral director.
Need to complete required clinical experience in order to finish studies and receive degree. Ultimate goal is to receive State of Maine Funeral Director's License and find a permanent position within the state of Maine.

EDUCATION:

New England Institute of Applied Arts & Sciences (Boston, MA)	**2001–Present**

Associates Degree in Science Program—Graduation Pending, Fall 2002
(Studies near completion pending required 6-month clinical internship.)
- Dean's List Student

Harvard Medical School (Boston, MA)	**2000–2001**

- Studies of Anatomy

University of Maine (Auburn, ME)	**1999**

- Preparatory Studies (Science, Biology, Physiology, & Anatomy)

Lewiston High School (Lewiston, ME)	**Diploma, 1999**

- Vocational Training/Emergency Medical Tech/Advanced First Aid

WORK EXPERIENCE:

Peterson's Funeral Home (Auburn, ME)	**1998–1999**

- Clinical Assistant/Assisted with funerals

Fortin's Funeral Parlor (Lewiston, ME)	**1997–1998**

- On Call, Transporting/Assisted with funerals.

EMT (Emergency Medical Tech)	**On Call, 1998–1999**

References Furnished on Request

DOTTIE GARDNER

94342 Parkway Court   (718) 555-3232
Queens Village, New York 11428   email@email.com

GUIDANCE COUNSELOR

Highly motivated professional educator with combined adult training and staff development education and experience. Solid background in career counseling, social work, team building, program design, and presentation. Broaden curriculum development functions across academic disciplines to enhance quality of education. Empower and support cross-cultural individuals and groups. Consistently rated "outstanding" in training evaluation instruments.

Selected Coursework

- Social Work
- Adult Education
- Crisis Counseling
- Career Counseling
- Vocational Guidance
- Professional Development
- Human Behavior
- Group Facilitating
- Suicide Prevention

Advocate adult theory of learning style, create safe environment for students to take risks, provide support, and emphasize professional responsibility.

EDUCATION

Candidate for MSW, Adelphi University, Garden City, New York, Expected May 2002
BBA, Management, Central Illinois University, Troy, Illinois, 1991

LICENSURE AND CERTIFICATION

Licensed Professional Counselor, 2000

COUNSELING EXPERIENCE

Columbia University, New York, New York, 1999–Present
Career Development Intern

Explore vocational and career options to assist clients personally in planning and organizing job searches. Create action plans for career transition and reentry adults. Develop curriculum and formulate directory of resources. Produce PowerPoint presentations, synthesize instructional manuals, and aid in selection and approval of appropriate literature and textbooks.

- ☑ Originated pilot career design projects for women and minorities.
- ☑ Counseled job searchers on career choices and community resources.
- ☑ Rated "superior" as instructor for increasing productivity and allowing students to practice job-search and interview skills.

Central Illinois University, Troy, Illinois, 1991–1999
Assistant Professor/Instructor

Educated students in Business Ethics, Professional Development, Business Law, Professional Responsibility, and Constitutional Law.

- ☑ Partnered with ASU and community organizations to expand and manage homeless coalition program to reduce effects of substance abuse in Troy.
- ☑ Educated substance abuse counselors in human behavior and ethics.

Colleen Davis

618 Fifth Avenue East * Grand Forks, ND 58202 * 701-555-0975 * email@email.com

December 16, 2001

Mary Grandy, M.D.
Director of Medical Education
Trinity Health Care
One West Burdick Expressway
P.O. Box 5020
Minot, MD 58702-5020

Dear Dr. Grandy:

Your associate, Dr. Jerry Westrup, advised me that he has sent you my resume so that you may consider me as a 2002 participant in Trinity Health Care's Clinical Laboratory Science internship program. I have enclosed another copy of my resume for your convenience. Please contact me if I can provide you with other documentation that will help with your decision making.

On May 23, 2003, I will graduate from the University of North Dakota's School of Medicine and Health Sciences with a Bachelor of Science Degree in Clinical Laboratory Science. I am currently completing my third year of Honors Program curriculum at UND, and am confident that my education has prepared me well for a senior internship.

Dr. Westrup and others have spoken highly of Trinity's training program. It is precisely the type of challenge I seek. In return, I offer a solid foundation of relevant knowledge. Unlike other applicants who may have a more general background, mine includes four years of combined experience in medical research and health care settings. My background would allow me to be a highly productive member of your clinical program.

The opportunity to work with your program would be a real asset in jump-starting my career, and I would appreciate your serious consideration of my qualifications. I appreciate your time, and look forward to hearing from you.

Sincerely,

Colleen Davis

Enclosure: resume

HEALTH CARE—INTERN

Colleen Davis
618 Fifth Avenue East * Grand Forks, ND 58202 * 701-555-0975 * email@email.com

QUALIFICATIONS
- Eligible Fall 2002 for SENIOR-YEAR CLINICAL INTERNSHIP WITH CLINICAL LABORATORY SCIENCE PROGRAM AFFILIATE.
- Over four years of experience in health care and research settings.
- Earned Certified Nursing Assistant credentials in 2000.
- Skill in dealing with sensitive populations and confidential situations in a professional and concerned manner.
- Dedication to the field; several immediate family members in medical technology spurned long-time interest.

EDUCATION
UNIVERSITY OF NORTH DAKOTA—Grand Forks, ND   1999–present
SCHOOL OF MEDICINE AND HEALTH SCIENCES
BACHELOR OF SCIENCE: CLINICAL LABORATORY SCIENCE (expected Spring 2003)
Program accredited by the National Accrediting Agency for Clinical Laboratory Sciences (NAACLS).

- **Completing third year of Honors Program curriculum** with a cumulative 3.68 grade point average.
- Exposed to the theoretical and practical aspects of clinical laboratory science in medicine:
  Hematology * Microbiology * Parasitology * Mycology * Immunology * Immunohematology
  Biochemistry * Chemistry * Hemostasis * Urinalysis.
- **Involvement:** Medical Laboratory Science Club * Student Activities Committee * Women's Hockey Club.

CLINICALS
UNITED HOSPITAL AND GRAND FORKS CLINIC—Grand Forks, ND   2000–present
- **Generalist experience provided rotation:** Blood Bank * Hematology * Microbiology * Chemistry * Urology.
- Perform and interpret tests on blood and body fluids to monitor health, aid in the diagnosis of disease, and help with the recovery of patients.
- Use state-of-the-art biomedical instruments and Interface with computers to perform and generate accurate, reliable laboratory tests.

HEALTH CARE & RESEARCH EXPERIENCE
ALTRU HEALTH SYSTEM—Grand Forks, ND   1997–present
CERTIFIED NURSING ASSISTANT: MEDICAL ONCOLOGY UNIT/ALTRU HOSPITAL   (2000–present)
- Provide medical and personal care focused on patients' achievements of peak physical functioning.
- Honored with award for perfect attendance.

FILM CLERK: RADIOLOGY DEPARTMENT/ALTRU HOSPITAL   (1999–2001)
- Epeditiously and accurately matched, dispatched, and transported film file and reports.

BILLING CLERK: SPECIALTY HOME SERVICES/ALTRU CLINIC   (1997–1999)
- Handled entire range of billing and collection services: gathering billing information, verifying, editing, submitting claims, and posting payments.

NATIONAL INSTITUTES OF HEALTH (NIH)—Washington, D.C.   Summer 2000
SHADOW INTERN: FDA LAB TEAM
- Studied vaccines, with a special focus on Group B Streptococcus.

EMPOYMENT WHILE FINANCING EDUCATION
Banquet Supervisor (15 hours a week), University of North Dakota Dining Service   1997–2000
Customer Service (10–20 hours a week), Hardee's Family Restaurant, Grand Forks, ND   1996–1997

Excellent Professional and Character References Provided upon Request.

JENNIFER GRAHAM

376 Lisbon Street – New Gloucester, Maine 04260 – (207) 555-4444

Objective:

Medical Billing Internship Position

Education:

Medical Terminology & Medical Coding Certificate	**2001**

Mid-State College, Auburn, ME
- Dean's List Student—GPA: 3.9
- Preparing to Sit for the Certified Clinical Account Technician Exam 03/02

Other Related Training:
- Certified Nurses Aide—CNA (1998)
- Certified Emergency Medical Tech—EMT (1998)

New Gloucester High School, New Gloucester, ME	**Diploma, 1999**

- Class Valedictorian/College Preparatory Courses
- Received Full Scholarship to Junior College

Internship:

Medical Billing **(Internship Through Mid-State College)**	**08/01–11/01**

Central Maine Clinical Associates, Lewiston, ME
- Assisted in Medical Billing Department
- Worked with BX, BS, and HMOs
- Became proficient with ICD-9 and CPT-4 Codes
- Placed collection calls to small accounts
- Maintained a good rapport with insurance carriers

Work History:

St. Mary's Regional Hospital, Lewiston, ME **(Full-Time) Business Office**	**06/99–08/00**

- Filled in as needed in covering the phones, general office duties, filing, data entry, mail prep, and varied courier duties.

Filene's Bargain Basement, So. Portland, ME **(Part-Time) Retail Sales**	**08/98–06/99**

- Customer Service & Cashier

Per Diem, CNA & EMT (Varied Locations)	**06/98–Present**

HEALTH EDUCATOR

NICK KOLB
105 Flatlands Avenue, Brooklyn, NY 11236
Phone: (718) 555-5678 / Cell: (917) 555-2701
Email@email.com

PUBLIC HEALTH EDUCATOR

Perceptive, results-oriented and team-minded Public Health Educator seeking to favorably contribute related strengths and knowledge to a community-based organization while attaining post-graduate training. Assesses organizational/constituent needs, formulates solutions, implementing steps towards favorable outcomes. Competencies include:

Infectious Disease Control	Outstanding Written/Oral Abilities
Domestic Violence	Cultural Sensitivity
Workshop/Program Development	Bilingual—Spanish

EDUCATION

BROOKLYN COLLEGE, C.U.N.Y., Brooklyn, NY
Master in Public Health: Present GPA 3.61
Curriculum, Fall 2001: Human Resource Management in Health Care, International Health

UNIVERSITY OF VIRGINIA, Charlottesville, VA
Bachelor of Arts: Foreign Affairs (Concentration in Latin America) 2000

PROFESSIONAL EXPERIENCE

CHINESE AMERICAN PLANNING COUNCIL, Brooklyn, NY   2001–Present
Skills Instructor
Engaged to advance ESL proficiency in Asian/Chinese adults. Created curriculum incorporating daily writing, grammar, vocabulary, and computer proficiency. Encouraged individuals' personal growth through the development of language skills.

➪   Increased job placement rate by 12% within the first quarter of employment.

ESCUELA BILINGUE HONDURAS, Comayagua, Honduras, Central America   2000–2001
ESL Instructor
Hired upon recommendation by both the U.S. Minister and Ambassador to Honduras to broaden English language skills among 29 fourth-grade students. Developed ESL studies program and organized class trips.

➪   Advanced English grades within a 10-point range in one semester.
➪   Revamped program structure promoting English language usage outside the classroom.

EMBASSY OF HONDURAS, Washington, D.C.   1999
Assistant Educator (Research and Tourism)
Recruited upon University recommendation to provide valuable information about infectious disease, inoculations, vaccinations, and health risks of the Honduran government. Directed detailed inquiries to the Center for Disease Control and local health departments. Held public forums on sex education, various birth control, and STD prevention. Assessed property damage/community needs following Hurricane George, and provided detailed accounting of findings to government agencies.

CENTRO DOMINICANO DE ASESORIA E INVESTIGACIONES LEGALES
Santo Domingo, Dominican Republic   1998
Domestic Violence Workshop Leader
Accepted by SUNY for participation in the Cultural Exchange Program. Educated survivors on anti-abuse laws, medical treatment, and personal development. Accompanied attorneys on community outreach meetings with religious and social service organizations.

➪   Developed and instituted *"Happiness"* workshop empowering survivors to develop emotional and financial independence.

HOSPITALITY COVER LETTER

JORGE MONTANEZ

116 Montview Avenue
Chicago, IL 60608
Residence: 773-555-1212
Cell: 773-555-2121
email@email.com

August 19, 2002

Mr. Ron Klein
TMP Personnel
250 Lake Boulevard
Chicago, IL 60608

Dear Mr. Klein:

If you are searching for a dynamic Assistant Manager for an up-scale restaurant anywhere in the United States, you will be interested in my background. While earning my Bachelor of Science in Hospitality and Tourism Management, I held several positions that significantly enhanced my ability to manage food and beverage operations and deal with a demanding clientele.

You may be familiar with Cappuccino-To-Go, a concession business I launched in 2000 and sold at a profit in 2002. During that entrepreneurial venture, I learned how to grow profit margins, market the business, hire and train staff, and maintain organized and reliable operations. Similarly, as Assistant Manager of a top-flight restaurant, I would focus on helping the restaurant run smoothly, managing staff successfully, and growing the bottom line.

As a bartender at Seasons here in Chicago, I was a valuable member of the restaurant team. I set the up-beat, festive tone, dealt effectively with customer complaints and problems, and added to total bar revenues by successfully selling appetizers and meals in addition to beverages.

Even my time as a manager at City Parking gave me experience that will be useful in an Assistant Restaurant Manager's role. My responsibilities there required a high degree of organization and customer management skills, as well as an ability to motivate and retain staff.

I am flexible as to location within the United States, but would particularly like to be part of a growing restaurant that is creating a "buzz" in its community. I may be reached any time on my cell phone (773) 555-1212 should an opportunity arise for someone with my qualifications. Thank you.

Sincerely,

Jorge Montanez

Enclosure

JORGE MONTANEZ

116 Montview Avenue

Chicago, IL 60608

email@email.com

Residence: 773-555-1212

Cell: 773-555-2121

HOSPITALITY MANAGEMENT

Record of successfully creating repeat business and revenue growth.

Strengths: Customer Service ▪ Sales & Marketing ▪ Up-Selling

- Entrepreneurial, high-energy professional with experience in both food and beverage and activity-based hospitality.
- Profit-driven with P&L management experience.
- Proven ability to manage, motivate, and retain staff.
- Natural skills in relating to the public, creating an upbeat, sophisticated ambiance, and defusing conflicts as they arise.
- Experienced in use of spreadsheet and database tools for hospitality applications. Skills: MS Word, Excel, and Access.
- Conversational Spanish.

EDUCATION

THE EVELYN T. STONE UNIVERSITY COLLEGE, ROOSEVELT UNIVERSITY, Chicago, IL
Bachelor of Science in Hospitality and Tourism Management (BSHTM)   2002

Selected Coursework

- Financial Accounting
- Front Office Management
- Personnel Management
- Food and Beverage Management
- Hospitality Sales
- Food and Beverage Controls

- Urban Tourism
- Wines, Liquors, and Beverages
- Multiunit Foodservice Management
- Computer Applications for the Hospitality Industry
- Marketing for the Food Service Industry
- Multicultural Issues

WORK HISTORY

CAPPUCCINO-TO-GO, Chicago, IL, Owner, Manager (2000–2002)

Developed and operated a concession gourmet coffee and pastry business to serve commuters. Full P&L responsibility.

- Grew business from zero to $80K in annual revenues in two years.
- Obtained permits and ordered supplies.
- Hired, managed, and trained four employees to operate the concession.
- Planned and implemented marketing plans, e.g., creating promotions to introduce customers to new menu items.
- Negotiated the sale of the business at a profit.

SEASONS RESTAURANT, Chicago, IL, **Bartender** (1999–2000)

Tended bar and prepared/served food at a fast-paced restaurant serving nouveau American cuisine. Tasks included inventory management and receipt reconciliation.

- Consistently met goals for pour cost.
- Attended to details of service and presentation for a demanding clientele.
- Successfully up-sold food items to beverage customers.
- Significantly increased the number of repeat customers.
- Described by the restaurant manager as an "easy person to manage," based on ability to respond quickly to the profit and customer-service requirements of the business.

JORGE MONTANEZ   773-555-1212

WORK HISTORY (Continued)

CITY PARKING, Chicago, IL, **Manager** (1998–1999)

Accountable for on-site operations at a premier restaurant, including scheduling staff, reconciling receipts, interfacing with city traffic control officers, and resolving customer complaints.

- Exercised tact and courtesy in dealing with a demanding VIP clientele.
- Trained and motivated staff, maintaining a good record of staff retention in spite of relying upon a typically transient working population.

CLUB MED, Mexico, **Windsurfing Teacher, Host** (1997–1998)

- Contributed to developing an innovative step-by-step curriculum that enabled new windsurfers to experience progressive mastery of the sport.
- Achieved a high level of client retention as a result of strong customer focus, which included remembering individual names, skill levels, and learning requirements.
- Provided 24/7 hospitality services to guests concerning lodging, dining, and activities.

CERTIFICATIONS

Certified by the Boardsailor Instructors Group in Windsurfing
Bartending

INTERESTS

Gourmet food, hiking, biking, sailing, windsurfing.

HUMAN RESOURCES

Heather Auberry

6517 Holly Lane ■ Minneapolis, MN 55101 ■ (612) 555-2401 ■ email@email.com

PROFILE

- High level of ambition to continued human resources career path as intern. HRIR degree (2002) and experience.
- Organized, creative problem solver, with an ability to manage conflicts towards win/win solutions.
- Offer a mature perspective, open mind, and balanced humor to work effectively with people at all levels.
- Committed to maintaining confidentiality, proactive towards change, and capable of efficient multitasking.
- Technology: HRnetSource™, HR Intranet Solution™, HRA Professional, HRMS®, and SHRM® Learning Systems.

EDUCATION

UNIVERSITY OF MINNESOTA CARLSON SCHOOL OF MANAGEMENT—Minneapolis, MN
BACHELOR OF SCIENCE IN BUSINESS (May 2002)—Current GPA 3.8
MAJOR: HUMAN RESOURCES & INDUSTRIAL RELATIONS

INDEPENDENT SENIOR RESEARCH THESIS: "**Wisdom in the Workplace,**" November 2001

RELEVANT EXPERIENCE

TARGET CORPORATE OFFICES—Minneapolis, MN   Fall 2001
Carlson Mentoring Network: Job Shadowing, Team Relations/Human Resources
Observed the interviewing, hiring, training, benefits administration, and staff evaluation processes within the Target organization. Performed support tasks for the development of Target's first computerized applications scanning and sorting system.

SOCIETY FOR HUMAN RESOURCES MANAGEMENT—U of M Twin Cities Chapter   2001–present
Vice President
Coordinated human-resource-focused events, attended the Minneapolis Area Personnel Association meetings as university liaison, arranged for human resources speakers, and assisted with fundraising for human resources professional awareness within the university community.

AVANT COMMUNICATIONS—Minneapolis, MN   1998–2001
Personnel Development Assistant
Designed and developed a performance appraisal tracking system. Organized and maintained personnel records. Created job description handouts. Worked closely with local temporary services and college placement offices. Organized an open house as part of Avant's recruitment program. Assisted with employee interviews, and helped coordinate new-hire orientations.

CITY OF HOPKINS RECREATION DEPARTMENT—Hopkins, MN   Summers 1998–2001
Pool Manager
- Scheduled and supervised staff for a citywide municipal pool recreational program. Wrote and implemented curriculum.

HONORS & ACTIVITIES

- Carlson School of Management Mentoring Network
    Mentored under Target's Human Resources Director. Participated in job shadowing, a leadership speakers series, and networking business events.
- Society of Human Resources Management *Outstanding Student* recipient, 2 semesters
- Honors Association Emerging Leadership Program

MARK DALGLISH

5151 Fairview Circle Drive
Los Angeles, California 90047
(310) 555-5555 / Mobile (310) 555-1234 / email@email.com

BACHELOR OF SCIENCE IN INDUSTRIAL ENGINEERING

Strong Understanding of Convergence of Technical, Operating, and Management Objectives

Technical Skills

Production Planning	Product Structures	Labor Standards
Control Systems	Process Capability Analysis	Document Control Systems
Documentation & Procedures	Quality Inspections	Lean Manufacturing
MRP & ERP Systems	Production Control/Planning	Six Sigma
Floor Time Studies/Standards	Time & Value Analysis	SPC

Competencies

Oral/Written Communications	Research & Analysis	Time Management
Team Building & Leadership	Mathematics	Consensus Building
Creativity	Attention to Detail	Flexible/Adaptable

EDUCATION

UNIVERSITY OF CALIFORNIA, Irvine, CA; 2001
B.S. Industrial Engineering   GPA: 3.6

Activities: President—UCI Engineering Society; Social Chair—Alpha, Beta, Delta Fraternity

INTERNSHIPS/WORK HISTORY

Engineering Intern   June–Aug. 2001
METALWORKS INTERNATIONAL, Irvine, CA
Gained valuable hands-on experience participating in analysis of plant control systems.

Shipping/Receiving/Warehouse Clerk   Sept. 2000–May 2001 (Part-Time)
TXL AEROSPACE LABS, Irvine, CA

Additional part-time and seasonal employment in fast food and retail   1998–2000
(Details provided upon request)

COMPUTER SKILLS

Operating Systems: DOS, Windows, UNIX
Applications: Microsoft Office (Word, Excel, PowerPoint, Access), Auto CAD, Computer Associates/PRMS
Software for B.O.M.

INSURANCE SALES COVER LETTER

JAMES WILLIAM OLDFEATHER

265 Charlotte Street • Asheville, NC 28801
(828) 555-1212 • email@email.com

December 15, 2001

Mr. Robert Michaels
Bolls Abner Mutual Financial Network
36 Boston Road
Asheville, NC 28800

Dear Mr. Michaels:

Your advertisement in Sunday's edition of the *Asheville Citizen* tells me that you are looking for a top-flight Insurance Sales Representative. You may very well have found him.

My enclosed resume will tell you that I have documented sales success in both retail and banking environments, a newly acquired degree in insurance from FNU (a new degree program that several Florida colleges have implemented), and the required licensure. I am ready to go to work.

What it does not tell you is that I grew up in the insurance business—my grandfather began (and my father has continued) Wichita's oldest insurance company, Oldfeather Insurance, currently a million-dollar agency representing over a dozen major insurance companies, both personal and commercial lines. This background sparked my keen interest in investment and financial planning at an early age, an interest I have followed with both training and achievement. However, I've discovered that the banking industry is not my environment of choice, and the merger of Atlantic Bank and First Federal Finance in 1999 (with concomitant layoffs looming) seemed an excellent time to return to my roots.

I'll call you in a few days to answer any questions you might have and possibly gain an appointment for further discussion. Thank you for taking the time to review my resume, and I look forward to talking with you.

Best regards,

James W. Oldfeather

JAMES WILLIAM OLDFEATHER

265 Charlotte Street • Asheville, NC 28801
(828) 555-1212 • email@email.com

*Recently graduated banking expatriate seeks novice position in **Insurance Sales and Financial Services** . . .*

B.S., Business Management, with concentration in Insurance, Magna Cum Laude
December 2001
Florida National University, Miami, FL

■

A.A., Business, Broward College, Ft. Lauderdale, FL, 1996

■

Life & Health Insurance Licensed in Florida and North Carolina
Series 3 & Series 66 License

Courses in finance, math, accounting, business law, government, with specialty insurance coursework in:

Financial Foundations	*Client-Centered Selling*
Small Business Consulting Skills	*Customer Retention*
Investment Sales Training	*Total Account Development*
Mutual Funds Sales Operations	*Mutual Funds Regulatory Compliance & Sales*
Variable Annuity Sales & Operations	*Fixed Annuity Sales & Operations*

■ Gregarious, focused, multitasking diplomat with genuine commitment to customer service; scrupulous. Organization, prioritizing, accuracy, and documentation abilities are legendary.

■ 3 years' financial services experience in banking environment, honing client relationship, follow-up, and presentation shills. Steadfast and resilient in a volatile market.

■ Computer proficient: Money, Word, Excel, Evergreen Mutual Fund Architect, Quicken, Client Master 2000 CPA Software, Accounting Expert Inventory Program

---

PERSONAL INVESTMENT COUNSELOR   1996–1999
FIRST ATLANTIC BANK & TRUST   Asheville, North Carolina

Member of 10-person financial center team comprised of customer relations manager, teller manager, and 7 tellers. Only loan officer and financial services representative on site. Implemented sales and service strategies while ensuring NASD regulatory compliance of new products regarding signage and teller communication.

• Top performance in sales of prime equity lines, core deposit accounts, small business loans, and financial products. #1 in team package sales for 1998.

• Consistently met or exceeded monthly Loan, Investment Brokerage, and Product goals. Always met contact goal of 200 telephone contacts every month.

• Recipient, Stellar Service Award for customer service.

SALES ASSOCIATE   1994–1996
ELECTROLUX   Ft. Lauderdale, FL

Highly successful sales and service of vacuum cleaners door-to-door. Used a cross-reference directory to learn prospect's name and length of residence *before* the cold call. Handled service, repair, and troubleshooting.

• **Among Top 5 Sales Representatives** in district, despite working only part-time while attending college. Sold 90% of all demonstrations (triple the national average).

INTERIOR DESIGN

Katherine K. Jones

41265 Wilcox Circle ◆ Idaho Falls, Idaho 83406 ◆ (208) 555-1212 ◆ (208) 555-2121 Cell ◆ Email: email@email.com

CAREER OBJECTIVE

Residential, Showroom, and Office Interior Design

PROFESSIONAL SUMMARY

- Over six years' experience in family-owned interior design business.
- Successful in selling a variety of interior design products by establishing good rapport with clients, determining their needs, and making recommendations on products based on competent knowledge.
- Have established clientele including contractors, businesses, and private individuals.
- Won Best Decorated Home—Builder's Show 2000.
- Organized, scheduled, and marketed events and shows for automobiles and RVs.
- Decorated campers, trailers, and motor homes for trade shows.
- Redesigned a 30,000-square-foot showroom and won Second Place in Display Competition.

PROFESSIONAL SKILLS

- Expertise in coordinating wallpaper, window treatments, floor coverings, tile, accessories, and overall design.
- Highly motivated, resourceful, and can get the job done.
- Excellent customer service and public relations.
- Prompt, reliable, dependable, and willing to learn.
- General office skills including answering multiline telephone system, copy and facsimile machines, and various office machines.
- Computer literate—experience in Word, Excel, DesignCad, AutoCad, Illustrator, Quark, PhotoShop, Internet, and Email.

WORK EXPERIENCE

INTERIORS BY DESIGN, Idaho Falls, Idaho. May 1995–Present (Part-Time).
Family-owned business.
Designer Trainee. 1997–Present. Produce floor plans and designs for homes, offices, and commercial space. Work with clients to determine color schemes, lighting, window treatments, accessories, wallpaper, and overall design.

Salesperson. 1996–1997. Sold a variety of wallpaper, carpet, linoleum, furniture, and accessories. Made office visits and in-home visits to assess customer needs. Placed orders and tracked sales.

Inventory Stocker/Receptionist/Cashier. 1995–1996. Answered multiline phone system, directed calls, balanced cash drawer, and made bank deposits. Regrouped and organized wallpaper and accessories to make them easier to locate.

EDUCATION

Idaho State University, Pocatello, Idaho. Attended three years. 1998–Present.
Pursuing Bachelor of Arts Degree in Interior Design.

Skyline High School, Idaho Falls, Idaho. Graduated May 1998.

BROOKE GARROU
INTERIOR DESIGN COACH

143 Buena Vista Avenue • Orland, California 95963

(530) 865-3241 • indesign@mindspring.com

CAREER PROFILE

High-energy, passionate design coach encouraging self-expression and creativity. Empower clients to trust their creative side, take risks, and create interior living environment supporting who they are and all their commitments in life. Originate spaces utilizing all senses where clients can play and bring individual creative self-expression to life in their own homes.

AREAS OF EXPERTISE

- Creative Services
- Strategic Planning

- Merchandise Resources
- Interior Design Market Research

- Special Events
- Parties and Promotions

EDUCATION

Master's Program • Graphic Design • Academy of Art College • San Francisco, California, EDG May 2002
Certified Proactive Co-Active Coach (CPCC) • Coaches Training Institute • San Rafael, California, 2001
Bachelor of Arts • Interior Design • University of California • Chico, California, 1994

DESIGN COACH SUCCESSES

- Coached client in what was standing in way of supporting having romance in marriage. Engaged client in conversations to uncover what was missing in house to support having passion in life. Resulted in client's recommitting to honest relationship and providing space to invite closeness in marriage while nurturing individuality within house and in separate home offices.

- Developed plan to confront reasons for executive's avoidance and resistance to action. Supported client in taking weekly action to design supportive office. Resulted in inspiration to change unproductive office to one of joy, contentment, productivity, and financial success.

- Designed imaginative workspaces for marketing firm with limited budget to reflect vision and mission statement. Saved $8000 by researching resources for affordable quality furniture and decorator items.

PROFESSIONAL EXPERIENCE

Interior Design Coach • INNOVATIVE DESIGN • Orland, California   2001–Present
Originated innovative interior design coaching concept to engage clients in inquiry about how living environment influences them. Incorporate training in fine arts consultation, interior design, and coaching to empower people to create environments in which they are fully supported and inspired.

Design Assistant • CREATIVE INTERIOR DESIGN • Chico, California   1999–2001
Recognized for artfully decorating model units of luxurious-living penthouse apartments and condos. Created customized furniture and interior design solutions to facilitate personal commitments of clients. Built resource relationships with vendors and manufacturers.

Art Consultant • ROMAN ALAYA GALLERIES • San Francisco, California   1997–1999
Represented modern sculpture, acrylic, photography, and charcoal art from over 1200 Bay Area artists. Consulted with clients in education, selection, and care of fine art for home interior design, including works by Picasso, Miro, and Chagall.

AFFILIATIONS

Coachville • Member and Participant   2001–Present
Redding Design Center • Member   1999–Present

INVENTORY CONTROL

PETER PARISH
27 Richard Rd., Unit 47, Harriman, NY 10926
Phone: (845) 555-1212 • Cell: (845) 555-4321 • email@email.com

---

INVENTORY CONTROL • WAREHOUSE MANAGEMENT

• A results-oriented warehouse management professional with extensive experience in inventory control and staff development. • Detail-oriented individual with demonstrated success in managing diverse priorities to meet deadlines while reducing inventory costs. • Possesses strong staff development, project management, and presentation skills geared toward consulting and new business development. • Computer experience includes Titan Warehousing System, Lotus 1-2-3, and an extensive knowledge of the Internet.

EDUCATION

• **Dominican College—Orangeburg, NY**
Bachelor of Science • Business Management • GPA 3.75 • May 2001

RELEVANT PROFESSIONAL EXPERIENCE

Pavion Limited—Nyack, New York   2000 to Present
INVENTORY CONTROL SPECIALIST

• Promoted through a series of progressively responsible positions with this multi-million-dollar cosmetics manufacturer with nationwide distribution.
• Managed inventory control procedures, accounting for up to 10,000 in-house items and the production of 40,000 items on a monthly basis.
• Developed and implemented inventory rotations schedules to maintain superior levels of merchandise quality.
• Established two new distribution facilities, trained employees on daily operations and procedures, and coordinated timely transfer of finished products to warehouse.
• Supervised day-to-day activities of 36 employees on three assembly product lines and detailed all manufacturing activities in daily production reports.

ADDITIONAL EXPERIENCE

• **Mike's Deli & Pizzeria**—Montgomery, NY   1999 to 2000
PIZZA CHEF
• **Deli Central**—Central Valley, NY   1997 to 1999
OWNER/GENERAL MANAGER
• **The Pizza Place**—Nyack, NY   1989 to 1997
GENERAL MANAGER

IT ENGINEER

JOHN ROMANO
email@email.com

5012 Bay Canyon Drive
Beverly Hills, California 91405

Residence (310) 555-4545
Mobile (310) 555-4546

INTERNSHIP—SYSTEMS ENGINEER/ANALYST

Broad Knowledge of Computer Hardware / Software Systems and Technology

- Computer Science major with hands-on experience as well as technical/academic training. Proven ability to complete complex and challenging assignments under pressure in a team-based environment. Skilled communicator able to convey technical information to nontechnical team members. Excels in research, analysis, and problem solving.
- Understanding of architectures, applications, and processes.
- Enjoys challenges... Learns quickly... Attention to Detail... Able to multitask.

COMPUTER SKILLS

Hardware: PC and Macintosh, LAN, WAN, Client Server Technology, Windows Networking.

Operating Systems, Platforms, & Languages: DOS, Windows (NT, 9x, 2000, XP), OS/2, HTML, UNIX, Linux, Java, C, C++, Visual Basic, Visual C, COBOL, SQL, CICS, Perl, CShell, Windows System Programming (including Winsock, COM components), TCP/IP protocols.

Applications: Microsoft Office (Word, Excel, PowerPoint, Access, Outlook), Lotus Suite, other popular programs.

EDUCATION

CALIFORNIA STATE UNIVERSITY, Northridge, CA
Major: Computer Science
B.S. Expected 2003

PROFESSIONAL EXPERIENCE

Freelance Computer Consultant   1998 to Present
Design hardware systems and configure software to meet needs of diverse users. Projects ranged from single computers to LAN and WAN networks.

Sales Engineer   Summers 1999, 2000, 2001
COMPUTER CITY, Los Angeles, CA
Consult with customers for major hardware/software reseller to determine specific needs. Design customized systems, provide recommendations, troubleshoot problems. Frequently requested by repeat clients and referrals.

—Letters of Commendation Provided upon Request—

DENNIS MULEY

6654 Havens Run Road
Columbus, Ohio 43222

email@email.com

Home: (614) 555-1212
Cellular: (614) 555-2121

INFORMATION TECHNOLOGY PROFESSIONAL
COMPUTER APPLICATIONS PROGRAMMER...DATABASE ANALYST

Committed new Information Technology graduate combining formal education with simultaneous fast-track experience in the financial services industry. Capable of profitably managing technology projects from concept to completion. Compatible team player through complete project lifecycles from determination of user requirements through testing and final implementation. Recognized as a resourceful contributor, offering productivity in fast-paced, high-volume environments. Outstanding problem-solving and research abilities. Articulate communicator who works productively with subordinates, peers, and key management.

AREAS OF STRENGTH & SKILL SETS

- 2-Tier & N-Tier Architecture
- SQL & Stored Procedures
- System User Training
- Creative Problem Solving
- Business Process Optimization

- COM Components & ADO
- Strategic Planning & Analysis
- Interdepartment Communications
- Large-Scale Project Management
- Policies & Procedures/Technical Manuals

TECHNICAL SUMMARY

- Application Development Tools:	- Visual Basic 6.0 – Visual C++
- Operating Systems:	- Windows 2000 – Windows 98 – Visual C++
- Databases:	- Oracle 8i – Microsoft SQL Server
- Programming Languages:	- Visual Basic 6.0 – C – C++ – SQL
- Office Productivity Software:	- Microsoft Word Microsoft Excel – Microsoft Access – Lotus Notes
- Presentation Software:	- MS PowerPoint – Crystal Reports 8.0

EDUCATION • TRAINING

DeVRY INSTITUTE OF TECHNOLOGY, Columbus, Ohio   October 2001
Bachelor of Science, Information Technology; Concentration: Client/Server Architecture & Development
- Completed 1-Year Accelerated Program; Graduated Magna Cum Laude

CAREER PROGRESSION

MANHATTAN MORTGAGE CORPORATION – Columbus, Ohio   February 1999 to present
[Mortgage division of the Yankee Corporation, with operations in Columbus, OH; Deerfield Beach, FL; San Diego, CA; & Edison, NJ; and generates annual revenue of $100+ million.]

Default Loan Services System Administrator
- Empowered with full responsibility for administration of Fortracs, the company's loan default tracking system, an off-the-shelf product customized for Manhattan Mortgage users, which facilitates the processing of default loans; system operates on Windows NT and uses a Citrix environment to handle network traffic and data volume.
- Received a "Spot Award" for conducting a "mini preaudit" six weeks prior to the annual GAD audit in the foreclosure area, which contributed to raising the real audit grade from a "C" to a "B."

KATHIE TERWILLIGER

777 Rebekah Ave. ✶ Pekin, IL 61554

(309) 555-1212 ✶ email@email.com

Seeking to pursue a **Journalism** career. Qualifications include extensive training and hands-on experience in lead development, research, analysis, interviewing, editing, and story development. Strong and concise writing skills. Background includes personnel supervision and public/customer relations. PC literate.

EDUCATIONAL BACKGROUND

Bachelor of Science in Journalism, Jonah University—Pekin, IL   8/02

ACADEMIC HIGHLIGHTS

Conducted an independent study for the Department of Athletics. Researched 12 private universities to determine methods of athletic fund raising. Prepared a report analyzing the results and sent a copy to each of the institutions. The study was hailed as "very valuable to all of the collegiate institutions that participated."

RELATED EXPERIENCE

THE HERALD, Jonah University Newspaper—Pekin, IL   1/00 to 5/02

Reporter/Editor

Began as researcher; progressed rapidly to full responsibility for scheduling, staffing, editing, and planning, while maintaining a full load of writing assignments. Covered a wide range of special events including VIP speakers and sporting competitions.

- Managed to secure an interview with Vice President-elect Cheney during a brief stopover in the area. The interview was subsequently quoted in local newspapers.
- Launched a weekly column analyzing political events.
- Played a key role in expanding the readership of the paper by approximately 20%.

ADDITIONAL EXPERIENCE

JABEZ CLINIC—Peoria, IL   2/98 to present

Materials Coordinator (5/99 to Present)

Selected to create a new position concurrent with Materials Management Clerk responsibilities. Develop cost estimates, and place orders valued at $100,000+ per week. Analyze costs and collaborate with the Director in developing strategies to reduce costs and improve productivity. Serve as the liaison between the clinic and the corporate office.

Materials Management Clerk (2/98 to present)

Process and distribute a wide range of materials. Communicate regularly with hospital staff and management, and participate in team projects as needed.

MR. B'S SUPERSTORE—Peoria, IL   4/89 to 11/92

Video Department Supervisor

Oversaw all departmental operations including P&L, purchasing, scheduling, productivity improvement, customer service, inventory control, staff supervision, and computer updates. Developed advertising campaigns and wrote copy for in-store promotions.

— REFERENCES & WRITING SAMPLES ARE AVAILABLE ON REQUEST —

LANDSCAPE ARCHITECT

BRIAN MAJESTY

52 Kirkland Street ✸ Cambridge, MA 02138 ✸ 617-555-1212 ✸ email@email.com

LANDSCAPE ARCHITECT

Seeking to contribute to landscape design that adds value to natural and built sites while minimizing environmental impacts and project costs...

Skills
- Drafting
- AutoCAD 14 and 2000
- Site analysis and planning
- Appropriate selection of plant materials
- Oral/written/artistic communication
- Modeling using collage, sculpture, drawing, video, and multimedia

Academic and Project-Based Knowledge
- Design of gardens, courtyards, parks, and plazas
- Rural, suburban, industrial reclamation, recreational, and urban design
- Designing for compatibility with area architecture, history, natural systems, culture, and landscape

EDUCATION

TEMPLE UNIVERSITY AMBLER, Ambler, PA
Bachelor of Science in Landscape Architecture   2002
Selected Coursework

- Field Ecology
- Woody Plants
- Site Design Studio
- Landscape Engineering I, II, and III
- Geology
- Soils

- Western Landscape Tradition
- American Land Tradition
- Park Design
- Management & Restoration
- Design Build Studio
- Herbaceous Plants

LANDSCAPE DESIGN EXPERIENCE

DEPARTMENT OF PARKS AND RECREATION, Hamilton, MA   Summers 2000 and 2001
Intern
Participated in the Rails-to-Trails initiative funded by the Massachusetts State Legislature. Worked with two licensed landscape architects to design and model a park area in the town center through which the trail runs.
- Selected five species of trees indigenous to the area and planned their placement.
- Helped design seating areas and select bench materials and style to be compatible with the landscape.
- Researched different natural path materials and made recommendations.
- Used AutoCAD 2000 to help plan the layout for the one-half-acre town center park.
- Selected hardy ground covers for nonpath areas.

THE SUZUKI FAMILY, Hamilton, MA   Spring and Summer 1999
Garden Planner (Volunteer)
Designed and built a small fishpond for a neighbor's sloping land.
- Created a garden with tiered pools bordered by 10 varieties of shade-loving perennials.
- Stocked the lowest pool with Japanese koy and planted water plants.

Portfolio available upon request

Robert J. Brown

email@email.com
123 Fourth Street, St. Albans, West Virginia 25177
(304) 555-1212

Law Enforcement Officer—GS-7

FORMAL EDUCATION

Bachelor of Science
(June 2001)
Criminology
(Minor in Psychology)
Regis University

Associate's Degree
(May 1993)
Police Science
Pikes Peak Community College

CAREER PROFILE

- Fresh academic credentials for law enforcement Officer positions
- Outstanding experience in instructing others in law enforcement programs
- Proven performance record in all major aspects of law enforcement
- Physically fit with high endurance capabilities
- Professional in planning, budgeting, coordinating, and scheduling
- A practical problem solver using analytical, creative, and communication skills
- Experienced in fast-paced and high-volume environments
- Strong leadership and organizational skills

SECURITY CLEARANCES

Held a "Top Secret, SBI/SCI" Security Clearance

PROFESSIONAL MANAGEMENT EXPERIENCE

Deputy Chief of Field Training—Recertification Section
Organization for Secure Community in Europe/S.A.I.C.
Kosovo National Police Academy
Vecutrin, Kosovo   11/1997 to 11/1999
- Managed, planned, accessed, and analyzed training programs
- Conducted field studies to determine adherence to protocols
- Modified courses to reflect professional police standards
- Trained other iternational instructors for the Academy

Highlights:
- Developed course materials and instructed classes in:
  - Investigations • Interviews • Community Policing
  - Domestic Violence • Crime Scene Investigations
  - Evidence Collection and Preservation
  - Theft and Aggravated Theft
  - Statement-Taking from Victims, Witnesses, and Suspects

Human Rights Investigator
United Nations
Bosnia-Herzegovina   5/1995 to 11/1997
- Worked with 17 investigators and 6 language assistants
- Determined if cases had substance for investigation
- Evaluated cases and matched to investigators for case follow-up
- Trained investigators
- Implemented policies and procedures
- Wrote reports extensively
- Briefed dignitaries on investigation progress

Highlights:
- Managed high-profile cases
- Extensive interaction with high-ranking police and governmental officials
- Worked closely with international top-ranking police officials

Platoon Sergeant
United States Army
Various Duty Stations   5/1993 to 5/1995
- Responsible for the safety and welfare of 6 subordinate soldiers

REFERENCES AND FURTHER DATA UPON REQUEST

LAW ENFORCEMENT

DONNA PHILLIPS

171 Orchard Way ■ Galt, California 95632 ■ (209) 555-0011 ■ email@email.com

---

LAW ENFORCEMENT OFFICER
Ability to maintain control while emphasizing respect for others

---

Highly effective communicator, leader, and team member with staff and inmates. Work well under pressure and thrive on challenging opportunities. Complete oral and written projects on time. Enthusiastic motivational spirit and passion for encouraging others to achieve goals.

EDUCATION & TRAINING

AA, Delta College, Stockton, California, 2001
ADMINISTRATION OF JUSTICE

R.A. McGee, Basic Correctional Academy (BCOA), Galt, California, 2001
CORRECTIONAL OFFICER

PEACE OFFICERS STANDARDS AND TRAINING (POST) / PC 832 BCOA COURSES

✓ Chemical Agents	✓ First Aid/CPR	✓ Count Procedures
✓ Effects of Force	✓ Post Trauma	✓ Special Housing Unit
✓ TASER and Stun-Gun	✓ Time Keeping	✓ Inmate Work Incentive
✓ Sexual Harassment/Orientation	✓ Defensive Driving	✓ Preservation of Evidence
✓ Side-Handle Baton Certification	✓ Disturbance Control	✓ Principles of Negotiation
✓ Ruger Mini-14 Semi Automatic Rifle	✓ Officer/Hostage Survival	✓ Control Room Procedures
✓ Firearms Safety and Familiarization	✓ Weaponless Self-Defense	✓ Transportation of Prisoners

---

SPECIALIZED ACCOMPLISHMENTS

- Ensured safe living and working environment, including safety, health, and welfare of inmates and staff members.

- Supervised inmates during participation in recreation or hobby programs to ensure conformance to established safety guidelines.

- Conducted search of inmate cells, property, and persons. Logged results in search log.

- Practiced prevention of riots or arson constituting immediate jeopardy to institutional security, and possibility of escapes or death of other persons.

- Made discretional decisions using tact and diplomacy while dealing with inmates, correctional staff, government agencies, and members of public.

- Accomplished custodial and correctional functions with minimal reliance on use of force.

- Communicated with staff and inmates as a team to resolve institution issues.

BASIC CORRECTIONAL OFFICERS ACADEMY AWARDS

- Awarded Top Gun designation from class of 700 cadets.
- Recognized for Highest Academic Achievement.

EMPLOYMENT HISTORY

BUSINESS MANAGER, *Johnson Toyota*, Lodi, California   1991–2001

Directed finance and insurance department for one of area's largest automobile dealerships. Investigated credit applications for contract approval. Sold life, disability, and auto insurance.

555 Main Street
Kent, Ohio 43550

Cell: 705-555-1212
email@email.com

Marian Smith

Librarian...Media Specialist

Talented, proactive professional with 15+ years of progressive experience in the field of education, including a comprehensive internship in Library Science with a high-profile public school system. **Dedicated to exceptional service**, with the ability to cultivate strong positive rapport and nurture relationships by performing beyond expectation. **Solid project management skills** with an effective combination of directing multiple priorities and generating innovative strategies to meet and exceed objectives. **Outstanding communication, savvy**, extremely personable, capable of working both independently and in a productive team effort. Areas of knowledge and expertise include:

- **Resource Center Management**
- **Liaison with Classroom Teachers**
- **Maintenance of Media Inventories**
- **Organization of Book Fairs**

- **Cataloging Procedures**
- **Selection of Appropriate Titles**
- **Computerized Library Systems**
- **Newsletter Preparation**

Education / Certifications

KENT STATE UNIVERSITY, SCHOOL OF LIBRARY SCIENCE, Kent, Ohio
Master of Library Science Degree; Majors: Special, Academic, and Public Librarianship
Expected in Spring, 2001

CENTRAL STATE UNIVERSITY, DEPARTMENT OF EDUCATION, Wilberforce, Ohio
Bachelor of Science in Elementary Education, 1985

CERTIFICATIONS

- **Permanent Life Certification** with the State of Ohio, Department of Education in the area of **Educational Media School Library**, Grades Pre-K to 12 (Pending)
- **Permanent Public School Teacher Certification** with the State of Ohio, Grades Pre-K to 12

Professional Experience

COLUMBUS BOARD OF EDUCATION—Columbus, Ohio   1982 to Present
[Metropolitan school system employing 15,000 faculty and serving 63,000 students.]

Librarian Internship (6/2000 to Present)
Report to Head Library Media Specialist within school district's library program, serving four schools, grades Pre-K to 12. Observe and assist library staff in all library operations, as assigned, which includes the following:

- Selecting, ordering, organizing, and systematizing all materials for Library Resource Center, the central library for the Columbus, Ohio Public School System, which has 500,000+ volumes.
- Serving as a key resource person to assist educators in planning and implementing units of study. Coordinating media skill instruction for classes/groups while working in a cooperative team effort with teachers. Planning and instructing individuals and groups on locating and using various resources in the media center. Working cooperatively with university and public libraries.
- Evaluating and reviewing sample textbooks and library materials. Making recommendations to school librarians and consulting with teachers concerning the best titles for the districtwide curriculum, and coordinating the ordering and shipment of titles to respective schools.
- Overseeing automation and technical services and operations. Maintaining all appropriate records and files related to the media program. Utilize Wide Area Network (WAN) and Local Area Network (LAN) for accessing resources outside of the state of Ohio.
- Compiling and maintaining media inventories. Gathering and organizing relevant statistics and preparing reports to satisfy accreditation standards of North Central Association of Colleges and Schools.
- Training and enlisting assistance from media and student assistants, as well as parent and community volunteers.
- Administering all cataloging procedures, including classification, accession, recording, and filing.
- Development and administration of media budget.

Marian Smith, Page Two

Professional Experience

COLUMBUS BOARD OF EDUCATION ...continued

Classroom Teacher, 6th Grade (Lakeview Middle School)   1982 to 2000
- Managed all classroom activities and strategies, including instruction, developing lesson plans, testing, and evaluations, for all curriculum areas; have taught all primary grades throughout tenure, on a rotational basis.
- Played an active role in curriculum development and enrichment programs, and served on various administrative committees.

Key Projects & Accomplishments:
- Participated in learning project, integrating technology in the classroom; authored study project with four other staff members and presented to parents, district staff, and board of education.
- Led weekly grade-level planning meetings and served as grade-level representative in principal's round-table discussions.
- Served as Team Leader Representative with parent committee and principal, to brainstorm on various topics such as curriculum, discipline, district testing, and various school events for students and parents in the district.
- Supervised four student teachers completing undergraduate and graduate programs; consulted with university advisors concerning student teachers' progress.

CREATIVE PUBLICATIONS, Mountain View, California   1974 to 1982
International publishing company providing educational support materials, two nontraditional mathematics programs (MathLand: K–6; MathScape: 5–8) and training for the educational market.

North Eastern (New England) Regional Manager and Sales Consultant   1975 to 1982
South Eastern Sales Consultant   1974 to 1975
- Supported company's sales efforts throughout Florida, Georgia, and New England. As the New England sales consultant, hired, trained, and managed up to 7 new sales consultants for territory's rapid growth.
- Assisted local and state school districts with grant writing, needs assessments, and staff development requirements, in preparation for adopting company's products into regular curriculum.
- Trained sales consultants on new products, tracking, and communication forms.
- Assisted in the development of an outline of workshops for all major products.

Key Accomplishments:
- Took over New England territory in 1975 and received "Fireman's Hat" award at national sales meeting, for regaining customer confidence and recapturing 95% of territory business.
- Exceeded annual defined goals by up to 33%, consistently within designated budgetary limits.
- Successfully collaborated with Boston Public School district in promoting use of *MathLand and MathScape* in 25% of all the schools; the usual percentage of "nonstandard" curriculum adoptions was 10%.
- Developed and implemented a system for tracking territorial sales and usage of *MathLand, MathScape,* and *Algebra: Themes, Tools, Concepts,* and compiled user-group directory.
- Assisted in citywide approved materials lists, including the NYSTL and the Teacher's Choice programs in NYC.

Excellent References Will Be Furnished upon Request

TRACEY EVANS

12130 East Locust Circle • Two Cities, Idaho 83401 • 208.555.1212 • 208.555.2121 Cell
Email: email@email.com • www.traceyevansl2.com

LOBBYIST

A highly persistent, dedicated, and aggressive advocate with a passion for winning environmental, health, Internet privacy, and sales tax issues.

QUALIFICATIONS

- **High performer, visionary, resourceful, energetic, aggressive, and persistent.**
- **Excellent written and oral communications—collaboration, public speaking, networking.**
- **Spearheaded efforts that raised $10,000 for a Red Cross fund raiser on campus.**
- **Led campus research committee on Internet privacy and sales tax issues.**
- Experienced in writing press releases, news-related stories, and proposals.
- Good rapport with a variety of advocate groups, profit and nonprofit organizations.
- Demonstrated **organization and planning skills**; will get the job done.
- Resolved a long-standing issue through intelligent redesign and presentation of facts to the right people who make changes to policy.
- Understands and interprets trend analysis.
- Assisted in developing a multifaceted strategy to get a major piece of social legislation passed in Idaho.
- Proficient in WordPerfect, Quattro Pro, Presentations, Word, Excel, PowerPoint, Windows, Email, and Internet.
- Fluent in reading, speaking, and writing in Spanish.

EDUCATION

University of Idaho, *Bachelor of Science Degree in Political Science*, Moscow, Idaho.
    Graduated June 2001. High Honors.
    Dual Minor: Business Law and Economics.
    Active in numerous clubs, fraternities, and campus organizations.

Rigby High School, Rigby, Idaho. Graduated May 1997. High Honors.
    Active in Debate, Yearbook Club, and Government.

EMPLOYMENT

LEGISLATIVE ASSISTANT. Senator Mike Robertson, Moscow, Idaho. May 2000 to May 2001 (part-time).
- Track and analyze bills via the Internet, and present information to the Senator.
- Conduct polling and statistical analysis on voter issues.
- Provide interpretations of trend analyses.
- Assist in press releases and conferences.

(Continued)

TRACEY EVANS
Page 2

EMPLOYMENT (CONTINUED)

LEGISLATIVE CORRESPONDENT. Senator Mike Robertson, Boise, Idaho.
May 1998 to August 1999 (Summers).
- Coordinated, fielded, and tracked incoming calls and correspondence.
- Assisted in press releases and conferences.
- Produced direct mail and broadcast mail solicitations.

FIELD REPORTER. Idaho Press, Idaho Falls, Idaho. May 1997 to September 1997 (Summer).
- Reported on local, state, and national political news.
- Reported on local civil and administrative litigation.

HOBBIES & INTERESTS

Reading, golf, history, basketball, fishing, boating, hunting, and model airplanes.

PROFESSIONAL ASSOCIATIONS

Associate Member, Idaho Environmental Law Student Committee.
Associate Member, Idaho Tax Reform Student Committee.
Member, Boy Scouts of America.
Member, Elks Club.

REFERENCES

Available upon Request

MANUFACTURING

JUAN ROCHA

139 Garden Street, Apt. 6A ■ Chicago, IL 60608 ■ (773) 555-1212 ■ email@email.com

---

Seeking an entry-level position in...

MANUFACTURING—*Materials Planning*

✓ B.S. Degree in Management with a Certificate in Materials Management.

✓ Hands-on work experience in fast-paced manufacturing environments.

✓ Working knowledge of MS Word, Excel, e-mail, and ERP/MRP II.

✓ Ability to identify components and raw materials from engineering and production specifications.

✓ Strong oral and written communication skills with experience facilitating cross-functional communication in manufacturing settings.

✓ Organized, with the ability to priortize and multitask.

EDUCATION

UNIVERSITY OF ALABAMA AT HUNTSVILLE, Huntsville, AL
Bachelor of Science in Management   2002

■ Maintained a 3.3 GPA in major.
■ Completed a specialized part-time certificate program in materials management while completing a full-time course of study for a B.S. degree.

UNIVERSITY OF ALABAMA AT HUNTSVILLE, Huntsville, AL
Certificate in Materials Management   1998–2002
Selected Coursework

■ *Purchasing Techniques for Effective Buying*   ■ *Managing Supply Chains for Competitive Advantage*
■ *Managing and Improving Warehouse Operations*   ■ *Advanced Traffic Management*
■ *Managing Inventories for Increased Profitability*   ■ *Advanced Purchasing Techniques*

APICS (American Production and Inventory Control Society), Birmingham, AL
Purchasing and Materials Management Workshop   2002

WORK HISTORY

ILLINOIS TOOL MANUFACTURING, INC., Chicago, IL
Material Supply Support   Summers 2000 and 2001

■ Assisted Materials Manager in coordinating movement of materials between warehouse and production areas.
■ Serve as liaison between purchasing, engineering, production, and warehouse to coordinate scheduling.
■ Troubleshooter for logistical problems.
■ Made suggestions about warehouse layout that were implemented, resulting in increased efficiency.

BIOPRODUCTS, Chicago, IL
Manufacturing Technician   Summer 1999

■ Cleaned, prepared, and assembled equipment parts.
■ Moved product through specified process steps following approved SOPs (Standard Operating Procedures).
■ Received a bonus for exceeding personal productivity goals by 10%.

TECHNICAL PRODUCTS GROUP, Chicago, IL
Mechanical Assembler   Summer 1998

■ Followed engineering drawings to assemble data storage equipment.
■ Awarded an "Achievement Certificate" for achieving higher than 95% accuracy on parts assembled.

Lorilie
G.E.O.R.G.E

123 SW Madison St. ◻ Kewanee, IL 61443
Ph. (888) 449-2200 ◻ email@email.com

– International Marketing –

Leadership/e-Commerce/Multilingual/Motivation

Qualifications Summary

Highly motivated and goal oriented International Marketing Professional with solid academic qualifications, proven leadership abilities, and hands-on experience. Expertise in e-Commerce issues relating to global marketing techniques. Skilled communicator fluent in speaking, reading, and writing English, Spanish, German, and French. Polished communication, negotiation, customer relation, sales presentation, problem solving, and conflict resolution skills.

Education and Training

B.A. in International Marketing, SOUTHERN UNIVERSITY—Madison, IL (GPA 3.98)   2002

◻ Elected to serve as Senator for the UNDERGRADUATE STUDENT GOVERNMENT ASSOCIATION
◻ Spearheaded a new position as Secretary for the COLLEGE OF BUSINESS & MARKETING SENATE
◻ Nominated for the NATIONAL PRESIDENTIAL INTERNSHIP PROGRAM
◻ President/Member of the INTERNATIONAL MARKETING ASSOCIATION
◻ Who's Who Among University Students, 2002
◻ President's List/Deans' List
◻ Selected to participate in an International Business Trip to Amsterdam; attended an Executive Seminar, met with top executives from international companies, and discussed global business issues.

A.A.S. in Marketing and e-Commerce, CENTRAL COLLEGE—Clark, IL (GPA 3.80)   1998

◻ Member of the Special Events Committee
◻ Elected Vice President of the College e-Commerce Program
◻ Marketing Honors Program
◻ President's List / Deans List

Professional Experience

CONNER PLASTICS—New Windsor, IL   2001 to 2002
Marketing Intern
Communicated with various purchasing representatives in Germany, France, Belgium, Italy, and Mexico to ensure accuracy of account and order information. Assisted Sales Team in promoting add-on products by calling existing customers. Managed numerous special projects for the Marketing Director. Coordinated shipping information for international deliveries. Tracked all individual account information and entered data on computer system.
◻ Commended by management for excellent telephone sales skills as a result of successfully securing a record 21 add-on sales in one day.

TRINITY MEDICAL CENTER—Clark, IL   1994 to 1996
Receptionist/Blood Drive Coordinator
Served as the main point-of-contact for visitors requesting information. Distributed reports and records for various departments. Performed data entry of patient addresses.
◻ Selected to serve as the Blood Drive Coordinator for the facility as a result of excellent communication, networking, personnel interaction, and marketing abilities.

THE HEART CONNECTION CHILDREN'S CANCER CAMP—Elm Grove, IL   Summers 1995 to 1996
Administrative Secretary/Counselor

– Excellent References Available on Request –

MARKETING

Andrea Justin

1135 Michigan Avenue
East Lansing, MI 48823
(517) 555-0588

SUMMARY OF QUALIFICATIONS

- Marketing Degree from Michigan State University
- Tom Hopkins Seminar Attendee
- 2 years' experience selling telephone service and publishing materials
- High level of ambition to begin career

EDUCATION

Michigan State University

East Lansing, Michigan   March 1999

Earned a Bachelor of Arts in Marketing in under the prescribed four-year course schedule, while financing my own education. My final two years I was totally self-supportive, working an average of 30 hours per week.

Tom Hopkins Seminar

Detroit, Michigan   February 10, 1999

The seminar "How to Master the Art of Selling" shall improve my inherent sales abilities. Learning various personnel skills for applicable situations will be an invaluable asset to my career.

WORK EXPERIENCE

United Parcel Service, Lansing, Michigan   November 1997 to present

Working at UPS enabled me to earn enough to support myself in school. I earned over $12,000 per year, an impressive accomplishment for a college student. As well, I maintained the highest production average at our center.

Sprint Telephone Division, Lansing, Michigan   1996

Sold local telephone feature services to the consumer market in Lansing. This experience paved the way for my future career path in sales. After three months at Sprint, I was the sales leader among the part-time college students and enjoyed the interaction with the customer. The only reason I left was to move on to UPS, where the part-time earning potential was greater.

American Collegiate Marketing, Lansing, Michigan   1995

This position was my introduction to sales, where I worked in a call center selling magazine subscriptions. Though I enjoyed the sales environment, my desire was to sell closer to customers in a more direct manner.

SKILLS/INTERESTS

Beyond my formal education, I have a working knowledge of MS Word, Excel, Outlook, and Explorer. I also enjoy playing golf, tennis, and fishing.

MARKETING

MARK STAPLES

Residence
7555 Old Schoolhouse Rd.
New City, NY 10956 (845) 555-1212

Mailing Address
1212 West 57th St.
Buffalo, NY 10001 (716) 555-2323

email@email.com

A recent MBA graduate seeking a position in...

MARKETING/BRAND/PRODUCT MANAGEMENT OR MARKET RESEARCH
Utilizing Outstanding Market Research, Teamwork, and Analytical, Organizational Skills

---

A results-oriented professional with experience in positions requiring superior interpersonal, communication, and problem-solving skills. Demonstrated ability to function effectively under all types of circumstances while maintaining a clear perspective of goals to be accomplished. Excellent leadership, time management, and decision-making abilities.

CORE STRENGTHS

- **Marketing Management**
- **Product Management**
- **Brand Management**
- **Market Research & Analysis**
- **Product Development**

- **Advertising/Public Relations**
- **Consumer Goods**
- **Consumer Products**
- **Medical Products Devices**
- **Quantitative & Qualitative Research**

Computer Skills: Windows: MS Word, Excel, Access, PowerPoint, FrontPage, Outlook, Internet Explorer, Netscape, SPSS.
Macintosh: WordPerfect, ClarisWorks, MS Office 98, Lotus 1-2-3.

EDUCATION

MBA, University at Buffalo, Marketing Management, May 2001
BS, Binghamton University, Management—Marketing concentration, May 1999

EMPLOYMENT HIGHLIGHTS

MARKETING RESEARCHER   1999 to 2001
Rehabilitation Research Center, Buffalo, NY

- Handled the evaluation of new product submissions for this multi-million-dollar organization specializing in the transfer of assistive technologies and medical products into the consumer marketplace.
- Evaluated secondary market potential to determine critical sales mass targets that could be reached, and formulated sales projections. Identified and benchmarked competing products to determine unique selling points of submitted product.
- Provided recommendations to clients on market segmentation, product positioning, promotion, distribution, and pricing strategies.
- Prepared consumer panel surveys and focus group questions used to evaluate various assistive products.
- Analyzed consumer data using SPSS and wrote consumer evaluation reports based on qualitative and quantitative data gathered from consumers in order to determine commercial viability of product.

MARKETING INTERN   Summer, 2000
ACME, Inc., Buffalo, NY

- Evaluated marketing potential, target markets, secondary markets, and competing products for the new product division submitted to this firm specializing in market research and commercialization.
- Increased efficiency of new product evaluation process by more than 50%, enabling shorter response times to clients.
- Updated Web site information; registered Web site on search engines, significantly improving search result placement.
- Organized and executed three targeted direct mail campaigns, resulting in increased exposure of client products.

MBA GRADUATE

MARK LUDWIG

517-555-2491

RESUME OF QUALIFICATIONS
328 WESTERN MILL
OKEMOS, MICHIGAN 48821

SUMMARY OF QUALIFICATIONS

EDUCATION

Master of Business Administration, 1999
Central Michigan University, Midland, Michigan
GPA 3.0/4.0

Bachelor of Arts in Communications, 1996
Central Michigan University, Midland, Michigan
GPA 3.4/4.0

HONORS/AWARDS

- High School Valedictorian.
- Won citywide essay competition senior year in high school.
- Won "Best Freshman Essay" Contest out of 800 students at Armstrong State College.
- Invited to statewide Academic Recognition Ceremony at state capitol.
- Awarded distinguished *Silver A* award from Armstrong State College.

SKILLS/STRENGTHS

- Strong understanding of financial markets and market development.
- Proficient with all Microsoft Windows-based programs.
- Extensive background with performing strategic analysis of corporations.
- Developed multiple presentations outlining strategic recommendations.
- Proven tact and diplomacy in handling interpersonal relationships.

VOLUNTEER ACTIVITIES AND PREVIOUS WORK EXPERIENCE

Merrill Lynch, Lansing, Michigan
Intern (Summer 1997, 1998)
Performed financial analysis of prospective investment opportunities and worked directly with clients to support account manager

SIGMA ALPHA MU FRATERNITY, Central Michigan University, MI
Kitchen Steward (Academic Season 1996, 1997, 1998)
Established kitchen procedures, many still in use, for newly chartered chapter of this fraternity. Responsible for food budget, purchasing food and supplies, interviewing and hiring kitchen personnel, supervising kitchen and dining room operations, and preparing food. Also held positions of Scholarship Chairman and Fund-raising Chairman.

SPECIAL INTERESTS

Arts and crafts, badminton, and beginning golf.

MECHANICAL ENGINEERING COVER LETTER

ROBERT T. ROMERO
2701 Vandalia Street * St. Paul, MN 55104 * (651) 555-8848 * email@email.com

December 1, 2001

Mr. Gary Zimbale
Vice President, Engineering
Baltic Corporation
4570 Ocean Breeze Boulevard
Houston, TX 77002

Dear Mr. Zimbale:

Having researched your company and the exceptional compressors your teams produce, I have identified Baltic as an organization that is aggressive in the market. I also assume that your company values creative talent and hard work—both of which I can deliver.

Although I am certain that you receive hundreds of resumes from mechanical engineers seeking employment with your company, I urge you to consider mine. The mix of skills I possess differs from most recent graduates in the field. For example:

- As a proactive leader in my graduating class at the University of Minnesota, I gained extensive experience as a participant in the Mechanical Engineering Co-Op, completing three internships, including one with Honeywell. Additionally, I had the amazing opportunity to partner with some of today's leading firms in various University of Minnesota/industry events and projects: Ford, 3M, and Medtronic, among others.

- You'll find that I am well versed in real-world technology. I have hands-on experience working with thermodynamics, heat transfer, and gas engine technology. My grasp of the field is reflected in my graduating with highest honors.

- I have successfully joined forces with experts and enthusiasts in the mechanical engineering field to create solutions that work for a range of purposes within a cross section of scenarios. Whether it was building a solar car for world competition or coordinating the guest visit of a renowned engineer, I was actively involved.

With my unique combination of qualifications, you can welcome to your company a genuine creative talent and true professional—just as I would welcome the opportunity to meet with you. I will take the liberty of calling you shortly to see when we might get together.

Sincerely,

Robert T. Romero

Enclosure: resume

MECHANICAL ENGINEERING

ROBERT T. ROMERO
2701 Vandalia Street * St. Paul, MN 55104
(651) 555.8848 * email@email.com

"The best way to predict the future is to invent it."
—Alan Kay

HIRING ASSETS

MECHANICAL ENGINEERING PROFESSIONAL

- Well versed in the real world, and believes that hands-on reality will do quite well. Motivated to buck the trend and be hands-on ... to take something apart... to build the new.
- Well trained in experimental and computational techniques. Communicates technical information effectively.
- Successful at working on multidisciplinary design teams to meet the needs of the 21st century workplace.
- Professionally and ethically responsible; is able to adapt to emerging technologies through life-long learning.

EDUCATION

BACHELOR'S OF MECHANICAL ENGINEERING, *summa cum laude*, 2001
THE UNIVERSITY OF MINNESOTA—Minneapolis, MN
"U of M ranks third among the nation's public research facilities"—Study by The Center, University of Florida

- **Program core:** foundation in mathematics, physics, chemistry, and cross-disciplined engineering:
  – system design and control – manufacturing engineering – computer-aided design
  – thermodynamics and heat transfer – environmental engineering – power and propulsion
  – industrial engineering – materials engineering – bioengineering – mechanical-electrical engineering.

MECHANICAL ENGINEERING EXPERIENCE & LEADERSHIP

MECHANICAL ENGINEERING CO-OP   1999–2001
ENGINEERING INTERNSHIPS (3 full-time, paid industry assignments alternated with academic semesters)
    Assistant Engineering Technician   GRAY PHOTO ENGINEERING   New Hope, MN
- Developed process for creating video image onto paper, and wrote control software for recording and printing.
    Engineering Intern   HONEYWELL, INC.   Golden Valley, MN
- Collected data and documented process procedures to prepare for the "Six Sigma" initiative audit.
    Mechanical Engineer Intern   ELLISON NATIONAL LABORATORY   Minneapolis, MN
- Helped operate the Infrared Imaging Lab, part of the U.S. Department of Energy's Continuous Fiber Initiative.

AMERICAN SOCIETY OF MECHANICAL ENGINEERS   1999–2001
UNIVERSITY REPRESENTATIVE
- Acted as liaison to the Institute of Technology Student Board, and attended ITSB weekly meetings. Represented ASME at University meetings. Arranged and guided tours of local industry, and helped lead industry-related seminars, forums, and panels.

PI TAU SIGMA (Honorary Mechanical Engineering Society)   2000–2001
VICE PRESIDENT
- Selected for membership as a junior, requiring academic class ranking in the top 25%. Coordinated and evaluated Mechanical Engineering course evaluations. Arranged tours of research labs, and served as a contact between students, faculty, and administration. Networked at the National Convention in New York.

SOLAR VEHICLE PROJECT   1999
TEAM STRATEGIST
- Enhanced features of project's 1999 solar car, Aurora[4], which finished 3rd place in the cutout class in the 1999 World Solar Challenge. Made numerous appearances with Aurora[4] at schools, parades, events, and companies. Aurora[4] has a top speed of 78 mph, runs 55 mph on the power of a hairdryer, can travel over 120 miles without sun, weighs only 655 pounds, and can be driven on any U.S. road in daylight (no headlights!).

MEDICAL TECHNICIAN

LISA COUNCILMAN

265 Charlotte Street ❑ Asheville, NC 28801

email@email.com ❑ (828) 555-1212

Aggressive, empathetic top performer—who can calmly use outstanding analytical, planning, and organizing skills to set priorities and make optimum use of available resources in high-stress, rapidly changing environments—seeks full-time, permanent position as

EMERGENCY MEDICAL TECHNICIAN / PARAMEDIC
National Registry of Emergency Medical Technicians

A.A.S., Emergency Medical Science, December 2001
Asheville-Madison Technical Community College
3.85 GPA / Phi Theta Kappa National Honors Society
Who's Who in American Jr. Colleges, 2001

Completed certification requirements for:
NREMT-P, ACLS, BTLS, PALS, BCLS-I

Additional Training:

Hurst hydraulic tool operation/automobile extraction	SCBA operation/fundamentals of fire fighting
Hazardous materials awareness/recognition	Pediatric/neonatal advanced life support
Open-water scuba diving training	Helicopter scene-team training
Advanced cardiac life support	High level rescue/rappelling
Basic trauma life support	WNC CISD training

Diploma, Medical Specialists Course, Academy of Health Science, Ft. Sam Houston, TX, 1992

═══════ EXPERIENCE ═══════

Medical Specialist/SQI Parachutist, Honorable Discharge ⠀⠀⠀⠀⠀⠀⠀⠀⠀⠀1992–1996
UNITED STATES ARMY ⠀⠀⠀⠀⠀⠀⠀⠀⠀⠀⠀⠀Stationed in Saudi Arabia, Iraq, Kuwait, Turkey
4 years' training and achievement in:

❑ Field/emergency medical care—survey and sort casualties; determine and administer rescue treatment (injuries, wounds, cardiac arrest, anaphylactic shock, respiration, circulation, immobilization techniques); evacuation; supplies; and sanitation procedures. Includes psychiatric casualties. Trained to function in nuclear, biological, and chemical environments.

❑ Administration, supply, and maintenance of health records, supplies, equipment, and vehicles.

❑ Nursing care and clinic/dispensary operation.

Fox Laurel Ski Patrol, Fox Laurel, NC ⠀⠀⠀⠀⠀⠀⠀⠀⠀⠀⠀⠀⠀⠀⠀⠀⠀⠀⠀⠀1997–1998

Bartender, Barney's, Asheville, NC ⠀⠀⠀⠀⠀⠀⠀⠀⠀⠀⠀⠀⠀⠀⠀⠀⠀⠀⠀1999–Present
Part-time position while attending college.

AIMEE LAURELLE KAUKONEN

43433 Woodland Drive
Truckee, California 95737

(530) 555-0011
email@email.com

MENTAL HEALTH COUNSELOR/PROGRAM DEVELOPER

HIGHLIGHTS OF QUALIFICATIONS

- Comprehensive professional background in counseling and nursing.
- Enthusiastic and committed to career in mental health field.
- Remains calm and effective in handling crisis situations.
- Outstanding community networking and communication skills.
- Effective in balancing professionalism with sincere empathy.

PROFESSIONAL DEVELOPMENT

Master of Social Work, Counseling, University of San Diego, San Diego, California, 2001

Bachelor of Science, Nursing, California State University, Northridge, California, 1995
Marriage, Family, Child Counselor/Public Health Nurse
Certificate, Alcohol and Other Drug Studies, Delta College, Stockton, California

AREAS OF CONCENTRATION

Direct Client Services

- Adult Services
- Psychoanalysis
- Group Counseling
- Inpatient/Outpatient
- Psychological Counseling
- Youth Training Programs
- Independent Life Skills Training

- Client Advocacy
- Substance Abuse
- Dually Diagnosed
- Crisis Intervention
- Behavior Management
- Behavior Modification
- Integrated Service Delivery

Administration and Case Management

- Casework
- Social Welfare
- Client Placement
- Discharge Planning
- Program Development
- Community-Based Intervention

- Social Services
- Human Services
- Protective Services
- Treatment Planning
- Community Outreach
- Diagnostic Evaluation

AIMEE LAURELLE KAUKONEN
Page Two

___

EXPERIENCE & ACHIEVEMENTS

Social Work Intern   2001–present
Nevada County Department of Social Services, Truckee, California

- Deliver child welfare services to indigent families. Counsel chemically dependent individuals and families.
- Spearheaded and coordinated outpatient recovery treatment for substance abuse clients.
- Orchestrated child abuse prevention program for young parents with children aged 0–5.
- Compose court reports—testify at dependency hearings.
- Report and investigate up to 30 child abuse cases monthly.
- Routinely perform risk assessment of families, case management, and crisis intervention.

Mental Health Associate   1996–2001
Behavioral Health Center of Truckee, Truckee, California

- Conducted clinical assessment and humanistic and cognitive-behavioral psychotherapy for wide range of psychiatric and personal problems.
- Counseled Chemical Dependency Program inpatients.

Registered Nurse   1995–1996
Sierra Nevada Memorial Hospital, Grass Valley, California

- Managed in-home patient support service cases, trained, supervised, and evaluated 2 community outreach workers.
- Provided counseling to clients with depression, anxiety, phobias, thought, and cognitive disorders.
- Created comfortable, therapeutic home environment for terminally ill cancer and Alzheimer's patients.
- Rendered grief support to patients/family members.
- Served elderly clients in-home to prevent fiduciary abuse.

Registered Nurse Student/Intern   1993–1995
University of San Diego, San Diego, California

- Counseled boys/families. Facilitated HOPES program.
- Provided therapy for Child Sexual Assault Treatment Project, preadolescents, and Parents United group.

PROFESSIONAL AFFILIATIONS

- *American Red Cross*, Mental Health Coordinator
- *Toastmasters International*, Past President

Tammy Shanahan

9230 East 28th Street
Winston, Idaho 83400
(208) 555-1212 / email@email.com

Mental Health Case Technician—Spanish Speaking

Professional Skills

- ❖ Fluent in speaking, reading, writing, and translating Spanish.
- ❖ Familiar with admissions, initial intake assessments, and social-psycho assessments.
- ❖ Provided patients with information and assisted with applications regarding Medicare and Medicaid, family counseling for the elderly, crisis intervention, medication administration, and daily recreation for mentally disabled persons.
- ❖ Observed group counseling sessions for sexually abused women.
- ❖ BYU Internship, Utah State Hospital Children's Unit, Group and Individual Therapy for troubled children.
- ❖ CPR and First Aid certified.

Education

Brigham Young University, Provo, Utah. *Bachelor of Science Degree in Social Work*, 2001.
Ricks College, Rexburg, Idaho. *Associate Degree in Social Science*, 1988. High Honors.
Bonneville High School, Idaho Falls, Idaho. Graduated, 1986. High Honors.

Work Experience

New Beginnings for Young Women, Iona, Idaho. *Social Worker Trainee.* May 1991 to May 1994. (Family-owned business).
BYU Cannon Center. *Food Server.* Provo, Utah. June 1989 to February 1990.
New Beginnings for Young Women, Iona, Idaho. *Caretaker.* November 1987 to June 1989.
Tanya Jones Shelter Home, Rexburg, Idaho. *Weekend Caretaker.* August 1986 to February 1988.
Kathy's Hallmark, Idaho Falls, Idaho. *Sales Clerk.* July 1984 and December 1987 (Seasonal).

Volunteer Experience

Bonneville Association for Retarded Citizens, Idaho Falls, Idaho.
Idaho Falls Rape Crisis Center, Idaho Falls, Idaho.
Utah State Hospital Children's Unit, Provo, Utah.
Idaho State Child Protection Agency, Idaho Falls.

—References Available upon Request—

Tammy Shanahan
9230 East 28th Street
Winston, Idaho 83400
(208) 555-1212 / email@email.com

Page 2

Requested Supplemental Information

EDUCATION

BYU (1988–1990) Bachelor of Science Degree with emphasis in Social Work.

Related classes:
1. Spanish 201 & 202
2. Social Work 362, Social Service Practice I
3. Social Work 366, Social Welfare Policy
4. Social Work 364, Social Service Practice II
5. Social Work 389, Social Aspect of Mental Health
6. Social Work 391R, Crisis Intervention
7. Social Work 464, Interracial Minority Clients
8. Social Work 462, Social Service Practice III
9. Psychology 220, Human Development: Life Span

Ricks College (1986–1988)

Associate Degree in Social Science.

Related classes:
1. Spanish 101 & 102
2. Sociology 101, Introduction to Humanities
3. Social Work 112, Social Problems
4. Social Work 260, Introduction to Social Work
5. Sociology 200, Methods and Research
6. Sociology 205, Applied Social Statistics

RELATED WORK EXPERIENCE

Financial Adjustment Bureau.

Assisted hospital patients in completing application forms for applying for SSI benefits, Medicaid, and county benefits. Frequently spoke Spanish with patients.

Human Services.

Case Management for mentally and physically disabled. Assisted in accessing community services such as Personal Care Services, Vocational Rehabilitation Services, Counseling Services, and others that were to the benefit of the client. Followed through by visiting clients' work sites.

James Foy Sharf

email@email.com
265 Charlotte Street, Asheville, NC 28801 • (828) 555-1212

November 17, 2001

Mr. Jackson H. Jones, Jr.
Principal Nuclear Engineer
Atomic Power Co.
89 Southwest Street
Raleigh, NC 27601

RE: Entry-level nuclear engineering position

Dear Mr. Jones:

The other day my mother asked me why I chose nuclear engineering as my college major, and my answer surprised me as well as her: "Because it is the hardest."

Given that answer, it's not so surprising that my first choice for a company with whom to begin my career would be Atomic Power. In the world of power generation, it is the biggest, the most diverse, and, I'm hoping, the greatest challenge.

What are the qualities you deem most important in a candidate for a position with Atomic Power? While, as a college graduate, I have not had wide "paid" experience, I believe I can offer necessary fundamentals to be an effective contributor to the Atomic team.

- I am an Eagle Scout. I earned this honor, in part, by initiating, planning, implementing, supervising, and documenting a painting project for a local church. Teamwork and the ability to plan, implement, and complete projects was a large part of my Scouting experience.

- I am quite proficient (as you might guess) with computers and computer software.

- I am a quick and able student. I pay attention to detail, and I pay attention to instructions. The analytical and communication skills that have brought me academic success can, I believe, be successfully applied in the "world of work."

- I know how to set goals, and how to reach them through hard work, determination, and persistence. I have fine time-management and prioritizing skills.

My current goal is an entry-level nuclear engineering position with Atomic Power for early 2002. I am especially interested in nuclear fuel reclamation and waste disposal. I have enclosed my resume along with an official Atomic Power application. I hope what you see there will encourage you to consider me as a candidate. Thank you for your attention, and I very much look forward to hearing from you.

Sincerely,

James Foy Sharf

James Foy Sharf

email@email.com
265 Charlotte Street, Asheville, NC 28801 • (828) 555-1212

Profile

Successful achievement of academic and project goals in demanding curriculum with high standards, using logical, systematic problem identification and resolution skills.

Self-motivated college student with strong academic record seeks entry-level nuclear engineering position at Atomic Power Company.

- Persistent goal setter with strong analytical, research, organizational, and communication skills. Team participant.
- Computer Skills: C++, Pascal, UNIX, Windows, DOS, Word, WordPerfect, Excel, MS Works, LOGO, Internet research, some experience on Maple. Excellent keyboarding skills.
- Some fluency in German.

Education

Meritor Engineering Scholarship Finalist, Class of 2001 Competition, University Laurels

Class Rank: 8th of 200
Academic Medals for Excellence in Science & Mathematics
Perfect Attendance Award, Senior Year
North Carolina Scholar

COLLEGE OF NORTH CAROLINA—ASHEVILLE
B.S. in Nuclear Engineering   **December 2001**
- GPA: 3.7 / Dean's List
- Phi Eta Sigma National Freshmen Honor Society
- Selected Relevant Courses: Principles & Theory of Nuclear Engineering, Research & Experiment Design, Nuclear Fuel Production & Reclamation, Analytical Models of Research, Thermonuclear Analysis, Nuclear Equipment & Instrumentation, Computer Organization & Microprocessors, Nuclear/Computer Engineering Lab

JAMES B. MADISON HIGH SCHOOL, Asheville, NC
High School Diploma, with Honors   1997
- GPA: 4.21 (on 4.0 scale)
- Beta Club, Computer Club (Treasurer)
- Led team in State Computer Science and Math Competitions
- Member, Tennis Team (Best Doubles Award, 1997), 2 years

Experience

Eagle Scout, 1996

DAVY CROCKETT COUNCIL, Asheville, NC
Boy Scout Troop 46   1989–1996
- Initiated, planned, and coordinated a painting project for large, high-traffic church entrance room. Planned project, securing permission from Board via a written proposal. Recruited, organized, and led a crew of 8; calculated costs and purchased materials; assigned and scheduled crew. Maintained daily log with pictures. Upon completion, wrote and presented report in a final interview to 3-member Board of Davy Crockett Council.
- Additional volunteer work building trails, serving food to the homeless, working at St. Elmo Hospital, and performing a variety of other community services.

Red Cross Certified Lifeguard
Red Cross Certified CPR
Consistently high in service evaluations (and accompanied by raises)

BELLSON COUNTY PARKS & RECREATION, Asheville, NC
Lifeguard, Swimming & Safety Instructor   1996–2000
    Supervised an average of 150 children and adults per day during summers at Elgin Community Pool, as member of team of 8. Maintained and cleaned pool, deck, and bathrooms; watched for potential hazards and rule violators.

References

Major Advisor

Susan B. Anthony
CNCA Director of Nuclear Engineering Programs
728 Wilder Hall, Box 42, Asheville, NC 28800
(828)555-2323

Scoutmaster

Tom L. Fellers
Boy Scout Troop 46
70 Miller Street, Asheville, NC 28800
(828)555-4343

Supervisor

Clam Barton
Benson County Parks & Recreation Services
345 Rains Street, Asheville, NC 28800
(828) 555-2678

Helen Kramer, R.N., B.S.N.

1632 N. Frostwood Boulevard
Bloomington, IL 61111
Phone: 309-555-1212
email@email.com

Seeking a Position in Mental Health Nursing

Synopsis

Offering a recent Bachelor of Science in Nursing combined with training and experience in the field of mental health. Able to maintain composure and professionalism when faced with emergent patient conditions. Background includes experience in staff supervision and program development.

Education

B.S.N., Bradley University—Peoria, IL   5/02

Clinical Highlights
Mental Health Rotation, New Leaf Addictions Center: interviewed new patients, conducted assessments, and participated in group therapy. Communicated extensively with family members, answering questions and providing encouragement and support.

Additional rotations included Pediatrics, Rehabilitation, Cardiac, Cardiac Medical ICU, Neurology, Med-Surg, and Community Health.

Experience

Nurse's Aide / R.N.   9/01 to Present
New Leaf Addiction Center—Palmer, IL

Provide direct inpatient care for clients ranging in age from 18 through geriatric, including persons with disabilities, patients from multiple ethnic and socioeconomic backgrounds, persons with addictions and psychiatric conditions, and repeat offenders. Facilitate individual, group, and family therapy, and provide ongoing education. Scope of responsibility includes scheduling appointments, coordinating visits from outside agencies and family members, dispensing medications, and client transportation. Part of a multidisciplinary team of physicians, therapists, social workers, and nursing staff. Began as part-time Nurse's Aide; promoted to full-time R.N. position, 5/02.

Page 1 of 2

Helen Kramer, R.N., B.S.N.

Assistant Manager, (Part-time as needed)   5/99 to 9/01
Junction Swim & Tennis Club—Peoria, IL

Scheduled up to 20 lifeguards, opened and closed the club, maintained the pool and grounds, and provided assistance to the public. Oversaw all operations in absence of the manager. Hired as lifeguard; *promoted.*

Resident Assistant   9/99 to 1/01
Bradley University—Peoria, IL

Provided counseling for dorm living, with direct responsibility for up to 150 residents. Worked in a team with six RAs in developing activities and strategies for resolving problems. Consistently received outstanding evaluations; cited for strong communication and leadership skills.

Youth Director   Summers 1999, 2000, 2001
Sawmill Baptist Church—Sawmill, IL

Directed all youth activities and developed long-range planning. Generated and supervised creative programming, counseled youth, and taught classes and special study groups for young people ranging from primary through college level. Brought in to develop a youth program with a long-term vision; increased junior and senior high school youth involvement from one or two to 20+. Participated in the hiring of part-time, permanent replacement.

Hotline Volunteer (Part-time while in high school)   11/96 to 5/98
Lapse County—Perl, IL

Completed intensive training and staffed mental health hotline. Provided counseling and support relating to depression, addictive disorders, and family abuse. Communicated with nursing staff and therapists, and made referrals.

Certifications & Activities

- CPR, First Aid, & Lifesaving
- Bradley Nursing Student Association
- Bradley Women's Tennis Team
- National Off-Road Mountain Biking Association
- United States Tennis Association

Page 2 of 2

DAVID ZANKMAN, R.N., B.S.N.

email@email.com

54321 Dickens Street, #333 • Los Angeles, California 90024 • (323) 555-4321

REGISTERED NURSE WITH B.S.N. DEGREE
Over Four Years' Diverse Clinical Experience

Seeking Community-Based Nursing Position in a Culturally Diverse Environment

- Team-oriented nursing professional, committed to providing the highest quality of patient care.
- In-depth understanding of issues pertaining to development and delivery of community-based health care issues and services.
- Possesses excellent teaching skills with the ability to make complex information understandable at all levels.
- Reputation for establishing and maintaining exceptional relations with coworkers, administrators, physicians, and patients.
- Well organized with ability to prioritize and delegate as appropriate; detail oriented and meticulous in record keeping and program administration.

Bilingual English/Spanish

LICENSE & CERTIFICATIONS

R.N., California
CPR, PALS, NALS Certification, Hospital & Life Safety Training

EDUCATION

Bachelor of Science in Nursing, 2001
UNIVERSITY OF CALIFORNIA, Los Angeles, CA

Honors & Activities
Graduated Magna Cum Laude, Dean's List, 1999–2001
Member, Sigma Theta Tau International Honor Society of Nursing
Member, National Student Nursing Association

Clinical Preceptorship: Clinical Practicum at Veteran's Administration Hospital, Los Angeles
Rotations: 560 hours of clinical rotations in Med/Surg, Labor/Delivery/Post-Partum, Pediatrics, Psychiatry and Community Health Nursing.

R.N.—1995
LOS ANGELES VALLEY COLLEGE, Van Nuys, CA

PROFESSIONAL EXPERIENCE

Registered Nurse • 1995–1999
LOS ANGELES COMMUNITY HOSPITAL, Pediatric Unit, Los Angeles, CA
- Worked with diverse patient population, performing multiple procedures including patient isolation, ventilators, tracheotomy, NG, TPN, central IV lines, PCA pumps, dialysis, chest tubes, etc.
- Diagnoses included cystic fibrosis, sickle cell anemia, HIV/AIDS, transplants (liver, kidney, heart), diabetes, tuberculosis, RSV, multiple traumas, surgeries (plastic/reconstructive, orthopedic, otolaryngology, genito-urinary), gastro-intestinal, neurological, psycho-social, and genetic disorders.
- Conducted patient/family teaching and education.

555 Eastlawn Drive
Tyler, Texas 43099

Joan White, MS, RD
e-mail: email@email.com

Home: (512) 555-1212
Mobile: (512) 555-2121

Registered Dietitian • Nutritional Counselor

Registered Dietitian committed to providing public awareness in achieving a healthful lifestyle and extending longevity. Combines formal education with diverse work background in dietetics and previous career in physical education. Dedicated to exceptional service and performing beyond expectation, utilizing well-developed problem identification and resolution skills. Solid project management skills, with ability to balance multiple priorities in fast-paced environments. Articulate communicator, capable of working as team player with all levels of staff, management, and clients.

Areas of Knowledge and Professional Skills:

- Clinical Nutrition
- Multidisciplinary Team Work
- Enteral Feeding
- Research of Nutritional Topics
- Community Education

- Nutritional Assessments
- Customized Food Plans
- Patient Charting
- Q/A & Q/C Audits
- Curriculum Design

— Registered Dietitian; National, Licensed Dietitian, State of Texas —
— Member: The American Dietetic Association —

Educational Achievements

TEXAS WOMEN'S UNIVERSITY, Denton, Texas
Master of Science, Nutrition & Food Science, 2001

ITHACA COLLEGE, Ithaca, New York
Bachelor of Science, Health & Physical Education, 1982

Career Highlights

PHYSICAL MEDICINE & REHABILITATION, Dallas, Texas   1998 to Present
DIETETIC PRACTICE GROUP
Area Coordinator
- Manage all aspects of association contracts for members throughout a five-state area.
- Review and confirm research for articles scheduled for publication in monthly newsletter.

INDEPENDENT NUTRITION CONSULTANT, Dallas, Texas   1998 to Present
- Develop diet and exercise plans for insulin-dependent diabetics.
- Design high-fiber diets for the elderly.
- Created functional meal and exercise plans for business professionals.

DALLAS REHABILITATION INSTITUTE, Dallas, Texas   1996 to 1998
Clinical Dietitian
- Oversaw nutrition care of traumatically injured and general rehabilitation patients; caseload included patients presenting spinal cord and traumatic brain injuries, stroke, arthritis, polio, and Guillian Barre.
- Used expertise in all aspects of nutrition assessment, enteral feeding evaluation, patient care, and multidisciplinary team management of physical medicine and rehabilitation patients.

Joan White, MS, RD

Page Two

Career Highlights

DALLAS REHABILITATION INSTITUTE..._continued_
- Coordinated nutrition therapy with food service program.
- Participated in Q/A and Q/C audits, monthly financial reporting, and clinical statistics.

TRINITY MEDICAL CENTER, Carrollton, Texas   1996
Dietetic Internship
- Created personal internship program, approved by the American Dietetic Association, incorporating extensive institutional food service experience, incorporating a variety of challenging clinical opportunities in acute care, rehabilitation, extended care, and federally funded programs.

COMMUNITY RECREATION DEPARTMENT, Carrollton, Texas   1991 to 1996
Instructor
- Developed curriculum and launched publicity campaign for classes in nutrition, sports, and exercise activities for participants of all age and ability levels.

SPORTSPAGES RETAIL OUTLET STORE, Dallas, Texas   1985 to 1991
Manager
- Hired and supervised eight employees. Managed monthly financial reports; exceeded sales quota.
- Created new store layout and developed displays of upscale sports clothing and accessories.

MECHANICSVILLE HIGH SCHOOL, Mechanicsville, New York   1982 to 1985
Physical Education/Health Instructor
- Worked as classroom and sports instructor as well as a junior varsity and varsity-level coach for women's sports.
- Served as adult education instructor for aerobics and swimming.

Excellent References Furnished upon Request

OFFICE MANAGER

DAVID ROBINSON
email@email.com

5555 Ocean View Avenue, #12 • Santa Cruz, California 95062 • (831) 555-1234

Recent College Graduate—Qualified for Position as Office Manager

- Highly motivated individual with demonstrated flexibility in adapting to new and diverse situations. Proven ability to manage multiple projects in an efficient manner, meeting time and budget requirements.

- A committed team-member who works well independently as well as collaboratively. Experience in training and supervision. Track record of earning the confidence and trust of coworkers and superiors.

- Excellent oral and written communications; proficient in general office procedures and equipment.

- Computer Skills: Windows, Microsoft Office (Word, Excel, PowerPoint, Access, Outlook), Web page design, Photoshop, Painter, Illustrator, Internet, e-mail.

Strengths

Multitasking • Team Building & Leadership • Supervision & Training • Time Management • Attention to Detail
Policies & Procedures Development • Budgets • Accounts Receivable/Payable • Office Efficiency & Organization

---

EDUCATION

UNIVERSITY OF CALIFORNIA, Santa Cruz, CA • June 2002
B.A. Degree in Art History

UNIVERSITÀ DI BOLOGNA /ACCADEMIA DI BELLE ARTI, Bologna, Italy
University of California Education Abroad Program; Fall 2000–Spring 2001

Activities: Team Captain, Intramural Soccer; Cochair, Campus Art Fair

---

EXPERIENCE

Office Manager/Art Teacher   Summers 2000, 2001; Part-Time Sept. 2001 to Present
SANTA CRUZ COMMUNITY ART SCHOOL, Santa Cruz, CA
Teach painting class and assist with administrative and bookkeeping functions.
- Managed office operations during summer while owner resided abroad. Answered phones, composed correspondence, handled accounts payable/receivable and banking functions.
- Supervised part-time office assistant.
- Coordinated up to three concurrent art classes including scheduling instructors.

Receptionist / Administrative Assistant   Summers 1998, 1999
THOUSAND OAKS PEDIATRICS, Thousand Oaks, CA
Provided broad range of clerical, administrative, and bookkeeping assistance to busy pediatric office. Scheduled office visits, prepared charts for physicians, and processed patient payments.
- Demonstrated initiative in streamlining office forms, increasing office productivity.
- Organized filing system, providing easier access to vendor and patient files.

Residential Assistant (R.A.)   September 1998 to June 1999
UNIVERSITY OF CALIFORNIA, Stevenson College, Santa Cruz, CA

Sales Associate   Summers/Seasonal 1995 to 1998
BOOKS R US, Thousand Oaks, CA

ORGANIZATIONAL MANAGEMENT/COMMUNICATION

Janet Pennington

4302 Brandon Place ■ St. Paul, MN 55104 ■ 651-555-2300 ■ Email@email.com

ABLE TO MAKE IMMEDIATE CONTRIBUTIONS IN AN
ADVOCACY ASSOCIATION'S ORGANIZATIONAL DEVELOPMENT AND ADMINISTRATION

QUALIFICATIONS

- **Recent Organizational Management and Communication degree coupled with 10 years' experience as an advocate and services administrator.**
- Resource and liaison roles with law enforcement, the legislature, higher education, elected and public officials, planning groups, and professional and community-oriented organizations.
- Skilled at building teams and a sustainable presence.
- Astute at recognizing areas needing change, and leading processes to facilitate that change.

EDUCATION

CONCORDIA UNIVERSITY—St. Paul, MN
Bachelor of Arts, Organizational Management and Communication (December 2001)
- Completed accelerated learning program with a 4.0 GPA while employed full time.

EXPERIENCE

UNIVERSITY OF ST. THOMAS—St. Paul, MN   1993–present
Director's Assistant: University Women's Center
Serve as Director's "right hand," actively collaborating and participating in center's activities.
- Develop and implement educational support programs focused on equal education opportunity, women's empowerment, and women's safety.
    - Administer a $10,000 Scholarship Program for nontraditional female students.
    - Coordinate the Sexual Violence Prevention Program, a national model.
    - Colead and administer the Women's Cultural Diversity Committee.

- Manage budgets using diverse funding sources. Maintain high fiscal integrity and responsibility working with taxpayer dollars.

- Coauthor grant proposals and administer quality programs using state and local funding.

- Act as advocate for women experiencing violence, discrimination, or harassment.

- Help write, develop, and distribute promotional and educational media and materials.

- Make public presentations on women's issues, and network with campus and community.

    ✓ Cospearheaded the Women's Center organization from the ground floor. Hired to assist the Center's first Director. Literally opened the Center with an office, paper, and pen.

    ✓ The Center's programs and services have more than tripled during my tenure.

    ✓ Assisted Director in securing a 46% increase in grant funding from The Bremer Foundation and Target Corporation, used to fund sexual violence and safety programs.

    ✓ Vice-chaired the planning team that developed the University's "Women on Wednesday" weekly noon-hour lecture series. Series has become a trademark program—highly respected and successful with Twin Cities network coverage, and thousands attending.

CONSULTANT—Minneapolis/St. Paul, MN   1996
Ounce of Prevention Fund
- Conducted library research, developed bibliographies, and coordinated National Advisory Council meetings for the "Heart to Heart" project, a child sexual abuse prevention program.

Project ACCESS
- Identified and gathered information on services for single and/or displaced parents.

RETIRED & SENIOR VOLUNTEER PROGRAM (RSVP)—St. Paul, MN   1994–1996
Volunteer Recruiter
- Directed recruitments and maintained volunteer enrollments. Coordinated placements, follow-ups, and site visits. Processed and maintained contract updates with RSVP agencies.

- Developed and built rapport and relationships through publicity efforts and special events.

ST. PAUL HOSPICE—St. Paul, MN   1993–1995
Volunteer Coordinator
- Organized and cofacilitated volunteer support groups. Actively attended ongoing grief seminars, and participated in bimonthly groups addressing several issues of grief.

GRACEY WOMEN'S CENTER—St. Paul, MN   1992–1993
Program Developer/Advocate
- Provided individual and group support, legal advocacy, case management, crisis intervention, and information and referral to victims of domestic violence.

- Managed a volunteer and intern staff, and led in-service training.

- Coordinated work release program under contract with the Minnesota Department of Corrections.

UNIVERSITY OF MINNESOTA—Minneapolis, MN   1991–1992
Training Coordinator: Network for Displaced Homemakers
- Organized training for staff at 12 affiliated centers; provided technical assistance.

- Networked extensively with women's organizations at the state, regional, and national levels.

COMMUNITY & PROFESSIONAL LEADERSHIP

- American Heart Association Fund raiser, 1991–present; Board of Directors, 2000–2001
- University of St. Thomas Commission on Status of Women, 1993–present; cochair 2000
- University of St. Thomas Women's Studies Committee, 1993–present
- Take Back the Night Planning Committee, 1993–present
- Healthy Communities—Healthy Youth Initiative Collaboration Committee, 1996–present
- Minnesota Women's Funding Federation Steering Committee, 1999–2000
- Minnesota NOW/Legal Defense and Education Fund Board Member, 1999–2000
- WATCH Cofounder/Board, court-monitoring program for abuse victims, 1994–1999
- Young Parents Program Board Member, 1997–1999
- Habitat for Humanity Board of Directors, 1997–1999
- St. Paul Mayor's Task Force on Violence, 1998
- United Way of Greater St. Paul Membership Committee, 1997
- Founder, Gillette Sexual Assault Task Force, 1994
- Displaced Homemakers Network Region IX Conference Cochair, 1992
- St. Paul Aids Task Force for Community and School, 1991

PHARMACIST COVER LETTER

LEE S. WONG

33 Peachtree Boulevard
Atlanta, GA 30310
404-555-1212
email@email.com

December, 19, 2001

Ms. Mary Chase
Director of Human Resources
Lee Memorial Hospital
168 Memorial Avenue
Atlanta, GA 30301

Dear Ms. Chase:

Lee Memorial Hospital's expansion initiatives in oncology and outpatient services are of great benefit to the community. They also offer exciting opportunities for pharmaceutical professionals who want to be part of a world-class hospital. I would like to be one of them.

I earned my Doctor of Pharmacy degree this past June and have had extensive clinical training in hospital settings. I was exposed to hospital procedures and quality standards during my clinical clerkships in oncology, ambulatory care, general medicine, cardiology, and pediatrics, and as a pharmacy intern at St. Elizabeth's Hospital.

With the demand that Lee Memorial now has for chemotherapy, you may be interested to know that my high level of skills and knowledge in preparing intravenous and chemotherapy admixtures earned me the opportunity to teach other pharmacy students.

As winner of the Clinical Skills Competition of the American Society of Health-System Pharmacists, my clinical abilities are clearly sound. Equally important is my ability to communicate with other health care professionals and patients. I enjoy the educational role of the pharmacist. As an experienced tutor of college and graduate students, I know how to convey complex information clearly and simply.

Is there a time we could meet to talk about upcoming opportunities for well-trained pharmacists at Lee Memorial? I will call next week to discuss possibilities. I appreciate your attention to this letter and my enclosed resume. Thank you very much.

Sincerely,

Lee S. Wong

Enclosure: Resume

PHARMACIST

LEE S. WONG

33 Peachtree Boulevard ▪ Atlanta, GA 30310 ▪ 404-555-1212 ▪ email@email.com

PHARMACIST

COMMITTED TO PROVIDING THE HIGHEST LEVELS OF CUSTOMER SERVICE
UTILIZING AWARD-WINNING CLINICAL SKILLS COMBINED WITH NATURAL TEACHING ABILITY

— Strong critical-thinking skills —
— Accurate and highly detail oriented —
— Well-developed ability to communicate clearly and simply —
— Background in tutoring with an interest in the role of pharmacist as educator —
— Relates well with patients and health care professionals alike —
— Committed to lifelong professional development —
— Bilingual in English and Mandarin Chinese —

EDUCATION AND CREDENTIALS

Doctor of Pharmacy   2002
Georgia College of Pharmacy and Health Sciences, Atlanta, GA
  ➤ Winner, American Society of Health-System Pharmacists Clinical Skills Competition.
  ➤ Tutored fourth-year undergraduate pharmacy students in therapeutics and IV admixtures.

Bachelor of Science in Mathematics   1998
University of North Carolina, Chapel Hill, NC
  ➤ *Phi Beta Kappa*
  ➤ In senior year, tutored five freshmen in Calculus I and II throughout the academic year.

Georgia Registered Pharmacist #45190

PROFESSIONAL EXPERIENCE

Pharmacy Intern   2000–Present
Osco Drug, Atlanta, GA
  ➤ Counsel patients on use of prescription and over-the-counter drugs.
  ➤ Review drug regimens for possible drug interactions and flagged therapeutic duplications.
  ➤ Provide drug consultation to health care professionals.
  ➤ Process drug prescriptions, including reconstituting oral liquids and topical products.
  ➤ Manage drug inventory control. Maintain records on narcotic drugs dispensed.

Pharmacy Intern   1999–2000
St. Elizabeth's Hospital, Atlanta, GA
  ➤ Acted as a resource for physicians and nurses.
  ➤ Prepared intravenous and chemotherapy admixtures.

Clinical Clerkships, Rotations in General Medicine, Oncology, Cardiology, and Pediatrics   1999
St. Elizabeth's Hospital, Atlanta, GA
  ➤ Made recommendations about drug regimens, and justified them to physicians.
  ➤ Consulted with specialists on experimental drug treatments.

Clinical Clerkship in Ambulatory Care   1999
Regis Hospital Outpatient Care Clinic, Atlanta, GA
  ➤ Participated in anticoagulation clinic, cholesterol clinic, and diabetes clinic.
  ➤ Evaluated patients' medication regimens and adjusted them in consultation with physicians.

PHYSICAL EDUCATION COVER LETTER

Grace Matherly

389 Elm Street ▲ Elmwood, IL 61529
(309) 555-1212 ▲ email@email.com

June 7, 2002

Pamela Hawkins, Ph.D., Superintendent
St. James School District
St. James, IL 61234

Dear Dr. Hawkins:

It's not enough to move students through the motions of physical education as they progress from one activity to another. The dictionary definition of teaching is to cause to understand, and I would add: to cause to appreciate. As a physical education teacher, that's what I hope to do: open areas of understanding and generate a lifelong interest in physical activity.

It's a challenge to keep two dozen or more students involved and on task, but it's a challenge I gladly welcome. As indicated on the enclosed resume, I have recently completed a bachelor's degree in the teaching of physical education. During my experience as a student teacher, combined with seven years as a coach, I had the opportunity to develop any number of creative lessons and activities to capture the interest of young people and foster a positive environment for teamwork and participation.

In addition to my education, my qualifications exceed those of most new teaching graduates. For 11 years I managed a busy and growing fitness center, where I worked effectively with people of all backgrounds and ages. I learned to balance multiple concurrent responsibilities while remaining positive and upbeat in spite of unending demands on my time and resources. These qualifications will make me a more effective leader to young people.

Jane McCormick, Dean of Students at St. James High School, told me that you anticipate an opening for the coming school year and suggested I contact you. Since a resume cannot take the place of a personal interview, I would appreciate an appointment at your convenience, to exchange additional information and discuss how my experience, enthusiasm, and personal commitment to excellence could be of value to your school district.

I look forward to hearing from you.

Sincerely,

R. Grace Matherly

Encl.: Resume & Credentials File

PHYSICAL EDUCATION

Grace Matherly

389 Elm Street ▲ Elmwood, IL 61529
(309) 555-1212 ▲ email@email.com

Summary

Physical Education Teacher ▲ Coach ▲ Driver's Education Instructor
Relates exceptionally well to young people of all age levels; creates a positive environment for creativity and learning.
Incorporate each student into activities and implement diverse exercises to engage students in the learning process.
Committed to making physical education a positive experience for every student.
Coached basketball, football, and track.

Education & Credentials

WESTERN ILLINOIS UNIVERSITY—Macomb, IL   5/02
Bachelor of Science in Physical Education ▲ Minor: Safety Education

Certifications: Illinois Certifications: Physical Education, K–12; Driver's Education

Teaching & Coaching Experience

ELMWOOD SCHOOL DISTRICT—Elmwood, IL   Spring 2002

Student Teacher, Physical Education/Assistant Basketball Coach
Directed physical education activities at both the high school and the grade school, incorporating a variety of initiated tumbling, parachutes, team handball, fleetball, and flickerball. Directed class activities and assisted the basketball coach.

ELMWOOD PARK DISTRICT—Kewanee, IL (Part-Time)   1995 to 2002

High School Basketball Coach (1999 to Present)
High School Football Coach (1998 to 2000)
Assistant High School Football Coach (1996 to 1998)
Elementary Basketball Coach (1995 to 1996)

Additional Experience

JUDY'S FITNESS CENTER —Elmwood, IL   1989 to 2000
Manager/Instructor

Sample Evaluation Comments

▲ *Grace takes a personal interest in the students under her direction and tries to take them from where they are and move them forward to their maximum ability and capacity... She is very resourceful and has a keen sense of responsibility. Grace is an outstanding individual and is a person of the highest integrity. She is well respected by her peers, and her enthusiasm is a key ingredient to her successes.*

VICTOR C. FERNANDEZ

555 Woodland Terrace, Orangeburg, NY 55555
(845) 555-1212 • (914) 555-9898 Cell
email@email.com

Dear Sir or Madam:

I believe that my clinical experience coupled with my upcoming master's degree in physical therapy qualifies me for a position in your facility. I have enclosed my resume for your review and consideration.

During my experience with patients, I have become involved in a variety of situations such as performing evaluations and developing care plans on total knee, hip, and shoulder replacement patients; amputees; and stroke patients. Facing these challenges has allowed me to utilize my extensive sports background and interpersonal skills to facilitate superior levels of patient care.

I am confident that the enthusiasm and experience that I can bring to your organization will prove to be an asset. I would appreciate hearing from you regarding any existing or future openings you might have, and would welcome the opportunity to meet with you. Thank you for your time and consideration.

Sincerely,

Victor C. Fernandez
enclosure

PHYSICAL THERAPIST

VICTOR C. FERNANDEZ

555 Woodland Terrace, Orangeburg, NY 55555
(845) 555-1212 • (914) 555-9898 Cell
email@email.com

PHYSICAL THERAPIST

A dedicated, results-oriented individual who possesses excellent interpersonal and assessment skills, with the ability to put individuals at ease. Proven planning and organizational adeptness, possessing the skill to maintain superior levels of quality care under all types of circumstances. An able problem solver with the tenacity to complete assignments successfully and the flexibility to adapt to changing situations and requirements. Fluent in Spanish.

EDUCATION

Quinnipiac University—Hamden, CT
Currently Pursuing **MASTER'S DEGREE in Physical Therapy**—GPA 3.75
Expected date of graduation • December 2001
Quinnipiac University—Hamden, CT
BACHELOR of SCIENCE in Health Sciences GPA 3.89 • May 2000

PROFESSIONAL EXPERIENCE

Mercy Medical Center—Lynbrook, New York   1999
Physical Therapy Intern
- Performed initial evaluations of orthopedic and neurological patients for this medical facility.
- Arranged Cybex equipment for exercise protocols, and implemented manual therapy techniques.
- Educated patients on correct body mechanics during exercise, and performed massage.
- Managed and developed care plans for multiple patients simultaneously.
- Selected to perform an in-service for the department on Reflex Sympathetic Dystrophy.

Eddy Cohoes Rehabilitation Center—Cohoes, New York   1999
Physical Therapy Intern
- Handled initial evaluations on stroke, total knee, and hip replacement patients for this rehabilitation center.
- Performed assistive device assessments, neurodevelopmental treatments, and proprioceptive neuromuscular facilitation techniques on patients.
- Delivered an in-service on recombinant tissue plasminogen activator.
- Participated in home visits, interdisciplinary meetings, and community reentry programs.

Good Samaritan Regional Medical Center—Pottsville, Pennsylvania   1998
Physical Therapy Intern
- Performed initial evaluations on total knee, hip and shoulder replacement patients, amputees, and stroke patients at this acute care facility.
- Provided gait training for amputee patients on the use of prosthetic devices.
- Developed and trained patients on individualized exercise programs.
- Taught family members on the mechanics of transferring patients to and from wheelchairs.
- Delivered an in-service presentation on the management and care of burn scars.

PROFESSIONAL AFFILIATIONS

- American Physical Therapy Association • **Member**

Harry Perlow

626 Beacon Street
Ammon, Idaho 83000
208-555-1212 / email@email.com

OBJECTIVE

Corporate Pilot

FLIGHT RATINGS

ATP Multiengine Land CL-600/601 Type Rating
Commercial Single-Engine Land, Instrument
Private Pilot Single-Engine Sea
Flight Instructor CFI / CFII / MEI
Medical Certificate First Class
Flight Safety King Air 90 / 200 Initial Course
Flight Safety Challenger 601 3A / 600
Flight Engineer (Turbojet / Basic) Written Test
Flight Safety International Procedures Course, 2001

FLIGHT TIME

3636+ Total	3071+ Pilot in Command
1913+ Multiengine	1000+ Challenger Time
1892+ Instruction Given	580+ Total Instrument
690+ Night	1121+ Cross-Country

EDUCATION

Quinn Aero, Melbourne, Florida. 1995.
Earned Commercial, Instrument, Multiengine, CFI, MEI. 1995.
Completed all courses from PPL to CFI in six months.
Av Center, Titusville, Florida—PPL Rating. 1995.
Bachelor of Business Administration, University of Florida. 1987–1988.
Diploma in Mechanical Engineering, Switzerland. 1979–1983.

EXPERIENCE

McKinzie HBOC. Captain, Challenger 601-1A. 2001–Present.
Diamond Jet Service. Pilot, Challenger 601-3 (Part 91 and 135). 2000–2001.
AvCenter, Inc. Pilot, Challenger 600 (right and left seat). 1999–2000.
Capital Management. Flight Instructor King Air Jaguar 90. 1998–1999.
AeroMark. Part 61 Flight Training School. Co-Owner with Father. 1997–1998.
Flying Club. Part 61 Flight Training School. 1995–1997.

PROGRAM COORDINATOR

MARIE RONDEL-DELORIA
(available for relocation)

Residence
111 Mead Way
Bronxville, NY 10708

Mailing Address
PO Box 1122
Annadale, MN 55302

Phone/Fax (914) 632-6975/email@email.com

PROGRAM COORDINATOR
Utilizing Global Awareness to Promote Volunteerism Internationally

An enthusiastic and talented Program Coordinator seeking an entry-level position connecting individuals with worldwide humanitarian organizations. Dedicated rapport builder. Sensitive to cultural differences and language barriers.

CORE STRENGTHS

☑ Customer Service   ☑ Public Speaking
☑ Events Planning   ☑ Records Management
☑ Volunteer Recruitment ☑ Marketing

COMPUTER SKILLS

MS Word	Excel	Gold Mine	Quick Books	Lotus	PowerPoint

EDUCATION

Sarah Lawrence College, Bronxville, NY
Bachelor of Arts: Liberal Arts, May 2001

Junior Year Abroad: International Honors Program (Bard College Accreditation)
Studied Global Ecology, Culture, Ecology, and Justice, with extensive travel throughout England, India, the Philippines, New Zealand, and Mexico.

RELATED EXPERIENCE

CROSS-CULTURAL SOLUTIONS, New York, NY   2000–Present
Program Assistant
Recruited to provide clerical and administrative support for this nonprofit organization uniting volunteers with humanitarian projects in Ghana, Peru, India, China, and Russia. Provide timely and accurate information including travel itinerary, liability forms, and interest surveys to confirmed participants. Update and maintain volunteer records.

☑ Received high participant satisfaction ratings.

SARAH LAWRENCE COLLEGE, Bronxville, NY   1998–2000
International Program Assistant
Charged with furnishing international program information to students and their parents. Coordinated special event programs from onset through completion. Ensured the comfort of visiting dignitaries, escorting them on campus and officiating introductions.

☑ Streamlined direct mail campaign process.
☑ Redesigned recruitment material including increasing program appeal.

DONNA HANNA

1688 Clay Brooke Lane, Smyrna, GA 30082 (770)555-1212 • email@email

PROPERTY MANAGEMENT SPECIALIST

Proven track record of increasing levels of responsibility for managing complex projects for both internal and external clients. Possesses a conceptual talent for envisioning the big picture, pinpointing an organizational objective, and setting goals and priorities to achieve objectives. Able to multitask, think quickly, and make informed decisions. Computer proficiency includes Microsoft Office and an extensive knowledge of the Internet. Core competencies include:

- Project Management
- Real Estate Workouts & Recovery
- Mixed-Use Residential and Investment Properties
- Tenant Relations
- Financial Reporting
- Asset and Portfolio Management

EDUCATION & LICENSES

- **B.B.A., MANAGEMENT, New York University**, New York, NY • May 2001 • GPA 3.9 •
- **Licensed Real Estate Salesperson** • 2001

PROFESSIONAL EXPERIENCE

PROPERTY MANAGEMENT ASSISTANT   1999 to Present
National Property, LTD—New York, NY

- Provide critical support in resolving client and vendor disputes involving properties, reviewing billings, and vendor activities for this property management firm with over 25 buildings.
- Oversee the sale and rental of commercial and residential properties, maintaining documents of leases and contracts or notes and mortgages.
- Coordinate with third parties by requisitioning title searches, appraisals, and property inspections.

Selected Accomplishments:
- Identified lost revenues by preparing written and monthly income and tax expense reports and accurately updating and maintaining a property database. Create spreadsheets to track tax payments and insurance.
- Increased productivity by 47% by developing and managing external resource databases, including contractors, appraiser, title companies, and broker information.
- Developed a real estate newsletter to inform others about pertinent information.

ADMINISTRATIVE ASSISTANT   1998 to 1999
The Prudential Empire of NY, Realtors—New York, NY

- Assisted managers in all aspects of company operations with Broker/Owners, including the maintenance appointment calendars.
- Oversaw relocation department; reviewed time sheets and developed payroll reports.
- Coordinated press release development, and assisted with special event meetings, projects, and seminars.

PSYCHIATRIST

Mary Beth Rouse, M.D.
123 Eighteenth Street
Cliff Hanger, California 98666
email@email.com / (566) 555-1212

CAREER PROFILE

Practice limited to Adult and Geriatric Psychiatry

Special Expertise:

Diplomat, American Board of Psychiatry & Neurology, with added qualification in Geriatric Psychiatry.

Strengths & Work Style:

High professional standards. Strong patient-management skills. Unique in team leadership, recruitment, training, and development of well-credentialed staff. Outstanding skills in the establishment of appropriate protocols. Interdisciplinary, collaborative work style, employing excellent time management skills and tenacious multitasking habits. Highly organized manager known to create and excel in fast-paced, dynamic environments.

Communications:

An accomplished international public speaker and contributor to numerous published articles in the areas of Psychiatry. Fluent in English and Hebrew; conversant in Spanish and Romanian.

Available for Relocation.

PROFESSIONAL EXPERIENCE

UNIVERSITY OF CALIFORNIA LOS ANGELES (UCLA)—SCHOOL OF MEDICINE
Junior Faculty, Assistant Instructor—Psychiatry   1997–Present

EDUCATION & POSTGRADUATE TRAINING

Postdoctoral Associate, Yale University School of Medicine	1994–1997
Postdoctoral Fellow, Yale University School of Medicine	1993–1994
Research Assistant, Yale University School of Medicine	1991–1993
Internship, General Medicine, Ben Gurion University School of Medicine, Israel	1987–1988
M.D., General Medicine—Ben Gurion University, Beersheba, Israel	1981–1986

TEACHING EXPERIENCE

UNIVERSITY OF CALIFORNIA, LOS ANGELES (UCLA)—SCHOOL OF MEDICINE
YALE UNIVERSITY—SCHOOL OF MEDICINE
Teaching Assistant   1994–Present
Developed instruction plans and taught undergraduate and graduate level courses.

Mary Beth Rouse, M.D., page two

AWARDS

Postdoctoral Fellowship—American Psychiatric Association	1994–1997
Bayer Award—American Psychiatric Association	1996

PROFESSIONAL MEMBERSHIPS

American Association for the Advancement of Psychiatry	Since 1994
The New York Academy of Psychiatry	Since 1994
American Society of Psychiatry	Since 1994
American Society of Geriatric Psychiatry	Since 1994

PUBLICATIONS

M. Rouse, "On The Nature and Functioning of the Psyche." *Princeton University Press, 1994.*

M. Rouse, "On Pathology and Therapy." *Princeton University Press, 1994.*

M. Rouse, "On The Religious Function." *Princeton University Press, 1994.*

M. Rouse, "On Human Developments." *Princeton University Press, 1994.*

IN PREPARATION/SUBMITTED FOR PUBLICATION

M. Rouse, "The Clinton White House: A Study in Contrasts." *in preparation.*

M. Rouse, "Dogma and Natural Symbols." *in preparation.*

M. Rouse, "On the Nature of Dreams." *submitted for publication.*

M. Rouse, "Psychological Aspects of the Mother Archetype." *in preparation.*

M. Rouse, "Archetypes of the Collective Unconscious." *submitted for publication.*

M. Rouse, "The Dissociability of the Psyche." *submitted for publication.*

M. Rouse, "Instinct and Will." *submitted for publication.*

M. Rouse, "Patterns of Behaviour and Archetypes." *in preparation.*

M. Rouse, "How Your Sick Children Can Make You Sick." *in preparation.*

M. Rouse, "Motherhood: It's Not Just Having the Baby." *submitted for publication.*

PURCHASING

Ken Exum

2334 Riverside Avenue ▪ Bowling Green, OH 43403 ▪ 419-555-3623 ▪ email@email.com

PURCHASING MANAGEMENT INTERN . . . KNOWLEDGE OF:
Globalization & Supply Chain Management * *Just-In-Time Purchasing* * *Logistics*
Distribution Requirements Planning * *International and Domestic Sourcing* * *Purchasing Law*
Total Quality Movement * *Purchasing Negotiations* * *Leading-Edge Technologies in Purchasing*
Project Management Techniques & Software * *Strategic Sourcing*
Inventory Control * *Enterprise Resource Planning & Materials Management*

QUALIFICATIONS

- **Accredited Purchasing Practitioner (APP) Certified**, 2001.
- **Quick learner** who can soon master all aspects of a job, with limited training.
- **Self-starter** who can work independently and handle multiple priorities and deadlines.
- **Global thinker:** travels in Europe, South America, and Asia; Spanish fluency; active in multicultural settings.
- **Technophile:** Word, Excel, Access, PowerPoint, MSIE, ERP, AutoDesk View, and MRP software. AS400 and Windows NT/98 systems. Internet savvy.

EDUCATION

BOWLING GREEN STATE UNIVERSITY—Bowling Green, Ohio
Bachelor of Science, Business Administration (May 2002)   **3.5 GPA**
Specialization: Purchasing and Supply Chain Management   **Minor: Spanish**

Purchasing Club	Students for Cultural Understanding
Spanish Club & Studies Program Abroad	University Debating Society

RELEVANT EXPERIENCE

COLLEGE

✔ Member of E-Procurement project team that successfully implemented a global e-procurement strategy, including an electronic intranet-based spend repository, global Internet auctions across key commodities, and. a University supplier measurement system.

✔ Conducted complex research project on "Early Integration of Purchasing into Product Design."

✔ Collaborated with Purchasing Club members to implement a set of common systems and procedures for University purchasing, including a vendor rating system and a common supplier sourcing process. Resulted in a Universitywide supply-base reduction of 45%.

✔ Participated in *Individualized Studies with Spaniards Semester Program* at Universidad de Salamanca in Salamanca, Spain. *Management of Production* course offered classroom and real-world experience. Topics: location and dimension of product unity, optimal planning for the production of multiple objectives, problems of transportation, project programming at minimal cost, the "roy" method, and inventory control.

✔ Conducted data entry and spreadsheet preparation for the Debating Society.

EMPLOYMENT

✔ Participated in team-driven planning/buying for the world's largest pelletizer of RPET. Helped purchase high-volume placement parts and plan production to pelletize and crystallize recycled postconsumer PET for direct sale and reissue back into consumer plastics packaging applications.

✔ Promoted to Expeditor within one month of hire as assembler for a global designer/manufacturer of filtration tanks. Prepared requisitions, purchase orders, and bills of materials.

✔ Created and maintained a supplier database for an Internet provider.

EMPLOYMENT HISTORY

Assistant to Buyer/Planner	Plastic Technologies—Bowling Green, Ohio	2000–2001
Materials Management Expeditor	Barrett Industries—Bowling Green, Ohio	1998–2000
Office Administrator	CAROD Internet Services—Bowling Green, Ohio	1997–1998

REAL ESTATE AGENT

KELLY M. MORGAN

123 S.W. Madison Street ▪ Kewanee, IL 61443 ▪ (888) 449-2200 ▪ email@email.com

LICENSED REAL ESTATE AGENT
RESIDENTIAL & COMMERCIAL SALES

MISSION STATEMENT

To help you succeed with all of your residential or commercial property needs. To provide top quality, efficient marketing services and serve as an effective liaison between both parties in answering questions, ensuring satisfaction, preparing documentation, managing even the minutest details, and guaranteeing a win-win outcome. Offering extensive skills in:

Community Leadership/Professional Networking
Business/Marketing/Management/Communications

QUALIFICATIONS SUMMARY

- Highly qualified and enthusiastic Licensed Realtor with qualifications in both commercial and residential property sales and marketing.
- Solid academic credentials in Business, Management, Marketing, and Communications.
- Detail oriented; able to manage quickly and accurately the mundane details, and effectively interpret financial information and legal contract language into understandable terms.
- Excellent research, presentation, negotiation, and problem-solving skills.
- Computer skills include: MS Word, Excel, Access, PowerPoint, WordPerfect, Internet, e-mail, and Realty System Network.

EDUCATION & TRAINING

B.A. in Business Management/Minor in Marketing   2002
STATE OF ILLINOIS UNIVERSITY—Mercer, IL

A.A.S. in Communications   1998
ADAMS COMMUNITY COLLEGE—Keller, IL

PROFESSIONAL ASSOCIATIONS & CERTIFICATIONS

Licensed Realtor, ILLINOIS STATE REALTOR'S ASSOCIATION   2002

BUSINESS & PROFESSIONAL WOMEN'S ASSOCIATION—Mercer, IL   1996 to Present
Elected to the following positions:
Assistant Treasurer/Young Careerist State Committee Member (2001 to Present); **President of Local Chapter/District 8 Director** (2000 to 2001); **President/District 8 Associate Director** (1999 to 2000); **President Elect** (1998 to 1999); **Committee Chair** (1997 to 1998)

Member, CHAMBER OF COMMERCE—Mercer, IL (1997 to Present)

PROFESSIONAL EXPERIENCE

Administrative Assistant, TOWN & COUNTRY REALTORS—Mercer, IL   2000 to Present
Assist all Independent Realtors with administrative and research tasks. Prepare and review a wide range of financial and legal documentation for business and residential transactions.
- Developed and implemented numerous computer worksheets resulting in increased accuracy and a 99% reduction in errors.

REAL ESTATE APPRAISER COVER LETTER

Gene R. LeCompte

53 Shawmut Street
Lewiston, Maine 04240

Telephone: (207) 555-1212   Cell Phone: (207) 555-2121

November 27, 2002

Lucien Doyon, President
Property Appraisals Unlimited
33 Longbuck Drive
Sabattus, Maine 04280

Dear Mr. Doyon:

Your name was given to me recently by a mutual business associate, Arthur Hastings of Hastings Realty, as a contact for employment as a Property Appraiser with your company. I understand that you may be looking to fill this position, which is scheduled to be vacant this spring. I am very interested in speaking with you concerning this possibility and submit my resume or your consideration. Please keep in mind that I am currently undergoing all of the required training and preparation for property appraisals with the anticipation of finalizing my studies, testing, and ultimately receiving a State of Maine Property Appraisal license early this spring.

As a nontraditional student, I bring to this new career maturity and many years of experience in <u>related</u> and varied areas, which should give me an instant edge on situations when acquiring and assisting clients in performing appraisals. To date, I am at the top of my class and am very eager to begin working in a capacity, that will allow me to utilize my skills and recent training to the benefit of an employer. In summary—

- I have an extensive background In construction—having literally worked from the ground floor on up, including land excavation and landscaping. Through the years, I have made many good business contacts with the general public and business affiliates.

- I have owned, managed, and maintained multiple properties (including rental units and commercial land for development). Having been involved in property and real estate appraisals in varied forms throughout my career, the formal training I am now undergoing will give me the advanced training and insight (along with the proper credentials) to continue working in an area I truly enjoy.

The opportunity to discuss your position and my overall qualifications, would be most appreciated. I could be available to meet with you at your convenience. Please feel free to contact me at my home or on my cell phone at any time. I look forward to hearing from you.

Very truly yours,

Gene R. LeCompte

Enclosure

Gene R. LeCompte

53 Shawmut Street
Lewiston, Maine 04240

Telephone: (207) 555-1212

Cell Phone: (207) 555-2121

Career Profile:

Property Appraiser (w/current Contractor's Licensing)—Extensive and varied hands-on background in general construction. Many years of proven experience working with multiple projects of all sizes with responsibilities from the ground floor on up as a laborer, supervisor, manager, and business entrepreneur—resulting in an outstanding record of success on all jobs. Appraisal qualifications and pending credentials are further enhanced with an additional background in land excavation through landscaping at various sites. Multiple property owner and manager with full maintenance knowledge and responsibilities. Remain current on property and general real estate values, costs to maintain, legal and taxation requirements, and current business and consumer trends.

**"The expertise and assistance I offer my clients
is derived from personal experience,
specialized training, and up-to-date standards.
I handle every client as an individual and valued customer
—not just another number."**

Related Technical Knowledge:

- Complete knowledge of hand and power tools associated with general construction.
- Familiar with site-work equipment, transits, blueprints, and other systems.
- Experienced in operating heavy equipment including Bobcats, front-end loaders, backhoe-loaders, excavators, and other related equipment as needed.
- Aware of OSHA regulations for staging and other on-site safety issues.

Current Credentials:

- Real Estate & Property Appraiser—Maine/License Pending Testing, Spring 2002
- Licensed—Contractor Supervisor's License—Massachusetts
- Licensed—Home Improvement Contractor's License—Massachusetts & Maine

Related Memberships/Affiliations:

- Member—Maine Association of Home Builders & Boston Area Home Builders Association
  - Parent Organization for Both of the Above is National Association of Home Builders
- Volunteer Participant—Twenty-Four-Hour House Projects for Maine Special Olympics
  - 2 Years in a Row

Gene R. LeCompte   **Resume (Page Two of Two)**

Employment History:

Self-Employed (Varied Locations)   **1981–Present**
- **Self-employed taking on jobs** (on and off) ranging from $200 to $200,000; hire crews and subcontractors; very familiar with the "ins" and "outs" of getting jobs and completing them on time and within budget; have supervised anywhere from 1–12 individuals at a time on job sites, including working hands-on and assuming supervisory positions. Also, experienced in going from station to station at various sites and performing additional problem-solving tasks.

A.B.C. Associates (Boston, MA)   **Carpenter, 1981–1988**
- **Totally renovated existing apartments** in a high-rent district of Boston; added roof-top additions to existing buildings and supervised 2–3 personnel. (Projects ranged from $5000–$400,000.)

Quality Landscaping (Boston, MA)   **Landscape Designer/Installer, 1985–1986**
- **Mowed lawns, planted shrubs, installed flagstones**, built patios and concrete driveways, and performed all other phases of landscape work; turned a wooded backyard into a flagstone patio sod lawn. (Projects ranged from $500 to $25,000.)

Downeast Construction (Bath, ME)   **Builder, 1981–Present**
- **Framed many single-family and multifamily homes ($80,000 to a million),** on and off projects working around other jobs. Sample work included the fabrication of a 28′ × 42′ garage with 16′-high walls and installation of a 14′ × 14′ operating door. (Projects ranged from $15,000- $20,000.) Also built a Therm-O-Wall home using Styrofoam and concrete as forms (a relatively new concept in frame construction).

Bolduc Development (Boston, MA)   **Carpenters' Helper, 1977–1981**
- **Dismantled and rebuilt structures**, while gutting and renovating 5-story and 6-story brownstone buildings in the Boston area.

Education:

University of Maine   **Real Estate Courses, 2000–Present**
- Real Estate / Real Estate Law/Property Appraisals
- Course Completion Scheduled for Spring, 2002
- Eligible for Testing and Licensing upon Completion
- Currently Maintaining a 4.0 GPA

References and Credential Documentation
Available upon Request

• • •

RECREATIONAL THERAPIST

DIMITRIOS KIOUKUS
265 Charlotte Street • Asheville, NC 28801 • (828) 555-1212

College graduate with an affinity for
Challenge . . . Change . . . Diversity . . . People . . .
seeks the opportunity to learn in a multitasking environment.

B.S., Graduated with Distinction, Therapeutic Recreation
North Carolina University, Asheville, North Carolina

Additional Training in:
- Sales & SPIN Selling ◆ Crisis Prevention Intervention ◆ CPR
- Dance (Swing, Zydeco, Cajun, Contra, 2-Step, Waltz, Salsa)

ORGANIZATION, PLANNING, FOLLOW-THROUGH, TIME & PROJECT MANAGEMENT

- ❑ Proactively instrumental in improving daily workflow operations at Copeheart Adolescent Unit, e.g.: Developed checklists for tracking case-management duties, skills, and client activities; assisted rewriting of programs and group progress documentation for increased clarity and effectiveness; restructured program's leisure and functional assessment, increasing needed information and saving time and space; and changed format of groups, privilege-level system for adolescents, and program content.
- ❑ Developed and implemented assessment forms for dual-diagnosis program at Broystone Psychiatric Hospital, which more precisely mirrored client needs, and increased treatment-focused programs. Developed and restructured treatment program for the division. Planned, developed, and implemented leisure counseling and coping-skills programs; facilitated, taught, and led most of these programs.

ADMINISTRATIVE SUPPORT SKILLS

- ❑ PC proficient: Word, WordPerfect, Internet research tools.
- ❑ Supervised supply inventory at Broystone, and recorded and reported monthly statistics on department operations.
- ❑ Assisted with telephones, forms management, and filing at Copeheart.

PERSUASIVE COMMUNICATOR, DIPLOMATIC

- ❑ Sold 5 cars in first 10 days as Sales Consultant at Auto Advantage, Havenhurst, NC (2000).
- ❑ Taught group sessions on goal setting, cognitive skills, relaxation techniques, distress tolerance, problem solving, and self-awareness.
- ❑ Gregarious, genuine, inquisitive, with outstanding skills in teaching, facilitation, and leading groups.

CROSS-CULTURALLY SENSITIVE

- ❑ Willing traveler with experience in Costa Rica, Puerto Rico, and Mexico.
- ❑ Some fluency in French; exposure to Spanish.
- ❑ Active participant in language and cultural study, hiking, and backpacking.

CREATIVE & WELL BALANCED

- ❑ Instructor, coordinator, and participant in couples dancing (Swing, Cajun, Zydeco, 2-Step).

EMPLOYMENT HISTORY

Recreation Therapist: Copeheart/St. Francis Hospital, Asheville, NC (1998–2001)
- • Performed client assessments on needs and abilities; planned/developed client group programs; observed and documented client behavior and progress; wrote treatment plans and goals. Member, treatment team.

Therapeutic Recreation Specialist: Broystone Hospital, Morganton, NC (1997–1998)
- • Headed therapeutic recreation services for Admission Division. Supervised 4 full-time assistants and 1 student intern. Planned and implemented programs in coping skills, leisure counseling, and patient recreation activities.
- • Member, Admission Division Management Team.
- • Member, Treatment Team for Dual Diagnosis Program.

Kim Tynan

853 Emerald Way
Elk Grove, California 95624
(916) 555-0011 / email@email.com

RETAIL SUPERVISOR

PROFILE
Enthusiastic supervisor with proven record of achieving challenging goals of the organization. Personable and reliable team player with ability to gain trust and confidence. Improves employee morale by exhibiting cheerful, helpful attitude. Innovative and resourceful with reputation of adhering to high ethical standards.

STRENGTHS

Customer Retention	**Merchandising**	**Service Quality**
Records Management	**Inventory Control**	**Communications**
Employee Management	**Employee Training**	**Order Processing**

EDUCATION
Elk Grove High School, Elk Grove, California, 2001 (Maintained 3.79 GPA)
Certificates • One-Hour Photo Machine Technician • Cosmetician
Earned diploma while working evenings throughout high school.

ACTIVITIES
Member of 3-time championship-winning volleyball team.

EXPERIENCE
Assistant Supervisor, LONGS DRUGS, Elk Grove, California   1998–present
Work closely with service clerks to maintain smooth-running operation for self-service pharmacy and merchandise chain of 3312 stores in 43 states and Puerto Rico with over $21.2 billion in revenues.

Management
➢ Support management efforts to earn store credit for call-ins and returns.
➢ Train service clerks on Telezon, computer, new products, photo lab machine, cosmetics, and stockroom organization.
➢ Verify vendor orders and adjust stock supply discrepancies using Telezon.
➢ Manage loss protection and merchandise control with EAS tagging, keen observation, and maintaining physical presence.
➢ Stimulate sales by designing eye-catching end-cap and promotional displays.
➢ Close out registers and prepare daily cash receipts for deposit.

Customer Relations
➢ Raise profits through improved customer service and listening to needs.
➢ Secure customer loyalty by personally handling questions or complaints to assure complete satisfaction, resulting in improved corporate image.
➢ Consult with customers in selection and coordination of merchandise.

Assistant Manager DOLLAR STORE, Sacramento, California   1997–1998
Promoted from cashier to stocker to assistant manager within 6 months for nationwide bargain and closeout store. Maintained profitable operations through effective sales and merchandising techniques.
➢ Interviewed, supervised, and trained up to 20 cashiers and customer service representatives in efficient work methods.
➢ Processed employee records, recorded daily sales, and opened and closed store.

RETAIL MANAGER

LAURAL WAGNER

265 Charlotte, Asheville, NC 28801 • email@email.com • (828) 555-1212

CAREER FOCUS

". . . incredible potential and . . . ability to conquer any job that she approaches with full commitment."

RESULTS-DRIVEN TOP PERFORMER with **B.S. degree in Marketing** and 4 years' training and achievement in **RETAIL MERCHANDISING, MARKETING, AND MANAGEMENT**, with particular achievement in:

Product Management	**Merchandising**	**Report Analysis**
Competitive Market Research	**Pricing**	**Inventory Management**
Market Analysis	**Special Event Promotions**	**Loss Prevention**
Team Building & Sales Training	**Policy & Procedure Facilitation**	**Multisite Operations**

Outstanding priority- and time-management skills . . . Attentive to detail . . . Good judgment . . . Computer proficient (Windows 95, Microsoft Works, ClarisWorks, WordPerfect, Internet research) . . . Willing traveler willing to relocate . . . Speak some Spanish

Organized Leadership . . . Confident Communication . . . Passion for Retail!

HIGHLIGHTS OF EXPERIENCE

PAG INCORPORATED, Asheville, NC   1997–present
Work Study Intern   2/98–present
Recruited by store management, through an interview process for 1 of 4 management-training internships (out of 20 applicants) for national retail clothing chain with $5.5 million annual sales. Member of professional sales management team comprised of 6 full-time managers and 3 supervisors, managing 100 supporting sales associates in a dual-store environment (Pag and Pag Juniors).

- Act as Assistant Manager in intensive, 4-phase internship: Phase 1, selling and supervisory skills (3 projects); Phase 2, merchandising project (classroom and on-the-job training); Phase 3, holiday preparation (with management case-study workshop); and Phase 4, summary and assumption of assistant manager role (performance issues, merchandising, operations project, district manager store-visit project).

SALES & SUPERVISION
"Answer thousands of questions from employees and customers, and sell, sell, sell!"

Scope of responsibilities includes sales staff recruiting, interviewing, and supervision, supporting the management team through training and development of sales associates. Provide effective coaching, delegation, and feedback for maximum productivity; address unsatisfactory performance. Monitor payroll/cash flow; monitor and respond to corporate e-mail.

➤ Award of Achievement, Specialist Program. As specialist supervisor, train specialists to enhance customer experience and increase sales. Created comprehensive, flexible training program for employees to build skills and knowledge, increasing productivity and maximizing sales.
➤ Nominated by District Manager as 1 of 2 sales associates out of 500 in the district to travel to Greenville to promote Pag credit card use. Trained employees on presentation techniques, on floor and at point of sale.
➤ Promoted to Store Trainer within 1 year of hire, directing Elements of Selling program, new-employee hiring, record management. *Results*—11 out of 12 Secret Shopping reports in year 2000 rated store 85% or higher.

MERCHANDISING DOR *(1/2000–1/2001)*
"Natural eye for merchandising that makes sense . . ."

Drove results to capitalize on business trends; formulated business strategy for merchandising decisions to support key company products; developed innovative solutions to specific merchandising issues; maximized business opportunities by energizing employees; and always thought globally! Supervised 50–100 sales associates. Held sole responsibility for maps, reports, and walk-throughs; analyzed item movement and reports to react to sell-through; monitored key item placement.

➤ Took initiative to contact corporate planners to increase leather merchandise selection in our store; used store contact reports to convince them successfully of profitability.

RETAIL MANAGER (CONTINUED)

email@email.com • (828) 555-1212

OPERATIONS DOR *(1/99–1/2000)*
"We never ran out of boxes at Christmas!"

Selected and trained to assist Pag District Auditor on comprehensive summer audits of Charlotte stores (e.g., personnel, bank log deposits, register/media, operational). Identified creative options to reduce supply costs and potential causes of shortages, created plans for improvement, and rechecked for improvement in 60 days. Scope of responsibilities included inventory management, policy and procedure compliance, loss prevention, employee orientation, and staff training.

> ➤ As trainer for 3-hour, one-on-one Elements of Selling class with new hires, rewrote company manual to update product information for Asheville store.
> ➤ In response to store audit results, recommended loss prevention training for associates and was assigned liaison responsibility for management and employees, ensuring consistent procedural and policy compliance by all.

Visual Specialist • 1997–1999

EDUCATION

Bachelor of Science, Marketing, December 2001 • UNC-Asheville
- For elective Art class, created fashion portfolio, designing own spring clothing line (sketches, fabric samples); for corresponding Drama workshop, made comprehensive study of presentation styles.

UNC-Chapel Hill, 1996–1998
- Studied theatre and education systems at University of London, summer 1998.

Graduate, City High School, 1996
- National Honor Society, GPA 4.2 (4.0 scale)

Professional Retail Training (1998–present)
- Pag Management Development Program (6 sessions)
- Interviewing for Success, Pag (6 hours)
- Merchandising Training, District Field Brand Coordinator

COMMUNITY REINVESTMENT

Pag Community Action Program, Asheville, NC (1998–present)
- Initiated and organized store activities beneficial to community, e.g., American Cancer Society, Children's Hospital, Habitat for Humanity, Wellness Center.

Coordinator, Children's Hour, Foursquare Episcopal Church
- Develop crafts, reading, and activities for 20–40 children.

Volunteer, Asheville Downtown Association seasonal festivals (1997–present)

SALES COVER LETTER

Carol Pulley

89 Bonnaire Boulevard #12 • Pekin, IL 61111 • 309-555-1212 • email@email.com

August 2, 2002

Janna McQuellon, Director of Human Resources
XYZ Manufacturing Corporation
77 Seventh Avenue
Pekin, IL 63333

Dear Ms. McQuellon:

An internship in outside sales turned out to be one of the best learning experiences of my life.

When you're in the field, there are days when it seems that everywhere you go people are throwing negatives at you. I learned to turn the negatives into positives, to manage my time and stay focused on my goals, and to balance professionalism and dedication with a sense of humor. These are qualifications I would like to put to work for XYZ Manufacturing.

In addition to outside sales experience, I have had the opportunity to train and motivate sales staff, and I've even done some interviewing and hiring. I relate very well to people: I don't get tired of questions, I don't mind if I have to go over things more than once, and I'm able to sustain my enthusiasm in a way that is contagious.

I also worked in retail throughout college, and if you can make it in the pressure-cooker world of retail, you can make it anywhere! I have experience in staff training, customer relations, sales, merchandising, inventory control, and endless problem solving.

With a bachelor's degree in business management, combined with my employment experience, I believe I have a lot to offer and would welcome the opportunity to present my qualifications in person. When can we meet for an interview?

Sincerely,

Carol Pulley

Encl.: Resume

Carol Pulley

89 Bonnaire Boulevard #12 • Pekin, IL 61111 • 309-555-1212 • email@email.com

Sales/Business Development Professional
"Enhancing growth and market share in competitive markets"

Qualifications Profile

- Offering academic credentials in management and marketing accompanied by a track record of success in forging positive relationships with customers and coworkers.

- Background includes sales and account management responsibilities as well as staff training and supervision.

- Enthusiastic and highly focused motivator with the ability to draw people out and put them at ease; effective in a fast-paced and high-pressure environment.

- Computer literate; exposure to several operating systems and programming languages; proficient in Microsoft Office.

Educational Background

Bachelor of Science in Business Management; Minor in Marketing   8/02
SOUTHERN ILLINOIS UNIVERSITY—Carbondale, IL

Professional History

Sales & Marketing Intern/Sales Lead   1/02–Present
E-TECHNOLOGIES—Carbondale, IL/Peoria, IL

Called on corporate accounts, consulted with key decision makers, developed and sold targeted business solutions, and followed through to build positive client relationships. Progressed quickly from entry-level internship to leadership and staff training responsibilities.

Interviewed employees and contributed to hiring decisions. Conducted training in all aspects of the company, including intensive sales training. Supervised 20 sales representatives on a business-to-business sales campaign: made sure assignments were filled and conducted motivational and planning meetings. Also led a group on location in Minneapolis and conducted training sessions.

Sales Representative/Team Lead   1/97–12/01
TARGET—Carbondale, IL/Peoria, IL

Performed a wide range of customer service, sales, merchandising, and inventory control functions. Trained and oversaw the work of new employees. Was selected to assist in the start-up of a new location.

References Furnished upon Request

SALES COVER LETTER

Perry Geary

745 West End Ave, Apt 12J
New York, NY 10024
(212) 555-5555 • email@email.com

December 4, 2001

Mr. James O'Connor
Industrial Technologies LTD
1212 Broadway
New York, NY 10001

Dear Mr. O'Connor:

I am a dedicated, competent, and high-energy individual with a sound foundation of comprehensive training and education in sales, technical support, and customer service. I am seeking a position with your company that will present new challenges and opportunities.

My experience encompasses three years with Storm Communications and West End Products, leading distributors of networking and connectivity software. It has been during this time period that I have been involved in sales and technical support, and I have developed the skills to assist with heavy volumes of customer inquires with products and purchases. My strengths are ensuring customer satisfaction and complaint resolution.

I am a performance-oriented individual with a successful background working with diverse individuals, and I possess a demonstrated ability to adapt to widely varied environments. I perform both independently and as a team member, and I would describe myself as a well-organized, effective communicator with well-developed interpersonal skills. Additionally, I have strong ethical values and integrity, promote professionalism, diversity, and respect. I'd like to discuss your company goals and plans and my background to see if we can develop a mutual interest.

Thank you for your time and consideration. I look forward to speaking with you.

Sincerely,

Perry Geary
Enc.

Perry Geary

745 West End Ave., Apt 12J
New York, NY 10024
(212) 555-5555 • email@email.com

Sales Consultant

Dynamic sales professional with strong qualifications in identifying and capturing market opportunities to accelerate expansion, increase revenues, and improve profit contributions. Extensive background in sales support, cold canvassing, and product knowledge combined with a Bachelor's Degree in Business Administration. Strong qualifications in troubleshooting, training and development, and new business development. Excellent team building, leadership, and interpersonal relations skills. Computer experience includes Word, Excel, Microsoft Access, Windows, Lotus Notes, and J.D.Edwards.

Education

Pace University—Pleasantville, NY
B.S. • BUSINESS ADMINISTRATION • GPA 3.9, 2001
Magna Cum Laude

Areas of Expertise

- **Relationship Building**
- **Technology Management**
- **Client Relations**
- **Cisco Sales Certified**

- **Account Management**
- **Cold Calling**
- **Troubleshooting**
- **New Business Development**

Career Highlights

STORM COMMUNICATIONS—New York, NY   2000 to 2001
ACCOUNT MANAGER

- Handled sales and marketing initiatives in North and Central territories, and provided inside sales support for this multi-billion-dollar distribution firm specializing in the sale of Cisco Networking equipment and Wireless Internet-Western Multiplex.
- Coordinated troubleshooting on problem accounts and provided extensive proactive customer service to key accounts.
- Spearheaded cold canvassing programs and developed new accounts, upgraded existing accounts including the two major distributors. Provided support and assistance for 6 sales representatives.

Key Contributions:
- **Opened 75 new accounts and consistently ranked as top coordinator in Sales Support division.**
- **Exceeded sales goals by 110% for Hardware Quotas in the 2d Quarter of 2000, and surpassed service quota for the 2d quarter of 2000 by 125%.**

WEST END PRODUCTS—New York, NY   1999 to 2000
SALES SUPPORT

- Coordinated sale of software, hardware, and network Services to Fortune 1000 firms for this billion-dollar distribution firm specializing in networking and security products including Nortel Networks, Lucent Technologies, and Checkpoint Firewalls.
- Managed existing account base and developed new business through networking and prospecting of potential clients.
- Assisted less-technical account managers in positioning network solutions to increase sales potential.

Key Contributions:
- **Increased sales by 20% over previous quarter within 3 months and received a promotion supporting the top 3 account managers in division.**
- **Named Employee of the Month, August 1999.**

SALES COVER LETTER

Susan Anderson

123 NW Adams Street ◆ Kewanee, IL 61443 ◆ Phone: (888) 555-2200
E-mail Address: email@email.com

Question: **How many doors does a Marketing Representative have to knock on to get a sale?**

Answer: **As many as it takes.**

Allow me to introduce myself:

I have always believed that the three keys to successful marketing are product knowledge, product support, and perseverance, but the greatest of these is perseverance.

Let me explain. First of all, it is important to know your product inside and out, in order to sell the benefits. Second, it is extremely vital, especially within highly technical markets, to provide ongoing support. And last, but certainly not least, it is the company with the most persistent Sales Representatives (armed with these first two keys) that will ultimately clench the sale.

During my extensive tenure with Monroe Electronics, I have had the opportunity to hone my professional skills in many areas, and I have learned how to succeed in a highly competitive and ever-changing market. Starting as a Sales Representative, I have worked my way into the position of Regional Sales Manager. I am proud to say that my sales, both individually and as a region, have consistently increased every year. I truly believe that half of this success has been due to the product knowledge and support information that I have been able to convey, but the other half was definitely due to my undying persistence.

Having recently obtained my M.B.A. in Marketing, I am now ready to take my career to a new level as a Senior Level Manager, and would appreciate the opportunity to meet with you at your earliest convenience. If you require additional information, please feel free to contact me.

Thank you for your time and consideration. I look forward to hearing from you soon.

Sincerely,

Susan Anderson

Enclosure: Resume
Susan Anderson

Susan Anderson

123 NW Adams Street ◆ Kewanee, IL 61443 ◆ Phone: (888) 555-2200
E-mail Address: email@email.com

— SENIOR-LEVEL MARKETING MANAGEMENT PROFESSIONAL —

Top-Producing Marketing Professional Specializing in the Sales of
Mobile Communication Systems and Services to Fortune 500 Companies

"Susan is consistently one of the market's top producers."
Greg Foster, Senior VP
MONROE ELECTRONICS, INC./MOBILE COMMUNICATIONS DIVISION

PROFILE OF QUALIFICATIONS

Results-driven Marketing Professional spearheading the promotion of high-performance, technology-based communication system solutions designed to meet a wide range of business needs. Proven track record of sales within a very competitive and highly technical industry. Extensive experience in locating and building professional relationships with key decision makers within large corporations. Experienced team leader and project manager with a background in the full supervision and development of personnel. Possess in-depth sales training and presentation skills. Highly motivated and teamwork oriented. Professional communication, negotiation, problem solving, and conflict resolution skills; able to convey complex technical information easily in an understandable manner.

AREAS OF EXPERTISE

Marketing and Sales ◆ Strategic Planning ◆ Project Management ◆ Promotional Design
Operations Management ◆ Market Penetration ◆ Business Management ◆ Budget Management

EDUCATION & TRAINING

M.B.A. in Marketing, UNIVERSITY OF WORTHINGTON—Connersville, IL (GPA: 3.96)   2002

B.A. in Business Management, WEAVER COLLEGE—Mercer, IL   1992

Numerous corporate training programs including: Successful Marketing Strategies, Customer Relations, Technical Troubleshooting, Management Techniques, and Conflict Resolution Skills.

PROFESSIONAL EXPERIENCE

MONROE ELECTRONICS/MOBILE COMMUNICATIONS DIVISION—Chicago, IL   1996 to Present
Fast-track promotion through the following marketing and management positions:

Regional Sales Manager (2000 to Present)
Recruited to manage corporate sales accounts throughout three states in the Midwest totaling $17.5 million. Expanded current responsibilities include developing and managing an additional sales territory with projections of $2.5 million in annual revenues. Direct, train, and mentor a staff of four sales representatives. Develop and manage a $1.7 million expense budget. Instrumental in analyzing internal organizational methods, identifying goals, and developing and implementing strategic plans and training programs to achieve desired results.
◆ Successful in consistently achieving 7% in quarterly sales growth.
◆ Spearheaded a successful key account-review process focused on maintaining and expanding top-level accounts.

(Continued...)

Susan Anderson

Marketing Manager (2000)

Managed a staff of 10 in all aspects of marketing large mobile communications systems to corporations. Developed advertising materials and promotional activities targeted toward companies with high technology needs. Oversaw a wide range of support services including the development of operation manuals, specialized training materials, and targeted promotional brochures for both new and existing business accounts.

- Launched a successful market analysis program by designing an extensive customer questionnaire that resulted in valuable feedback.
- Supported sales growth from $2 million to $2.5 million within a six-month period by presenting and implementing an aggressive, bold, new-image marketing campaign. Developed new-promotional materials and redesigned existing products to reflect the new aggressive approach.
- Received a commendation from the Corporate vice president for significantly increasing sales through the development of cutting-edge promotional materials.

Sales Territory Manager (1998 to 2000)

Spearheaded a new sales/support/technical troubleshooting position for the company in a growing market segment. Oversaw product marketing and distribution throughout five counties and managed a corporate account base of 100+ clients. Collaborated with business and corporate clients in developing effective communication systems to meet their needs. Served as the main point-of-contact and liaison between clients and technical support to resolve technical issues, and made arrangements between clients and company technicians for special training as needed. Developed extensive business networking ties resulting in increased profits.

- Secured three major corporate accounts through networking, aggressive marketing, and consistent follow-up techniques.
- Played a key role in the introduction of new support services by closely collaborating with clients and technical support to make unprecedented design changes to a major client's existing mobile communication system.
- Consistently increased sales by 15% plus, annually.

Sales Team Leader (1997 to 1998)

Selected to orchestrate sales team efforts in launching new products annually and providing full technical support. Directed a team of three sales representatives and collaborated closely with technical support staff to resolve problems. Implemented numerous sales training programs to enhance marketing efforts and ensure that all team members had proper product knowledge.

- Successfully penetrated a new market territory, resulting in a promotion to management.
- Developed and implemented successful monthly and weekly training sessions in the place of random new product training, and incorporated testing to evaluate levels of product knowledge.
- Managed several key projects in the introduction of new products and services, as well as the promotion of supplementary products to existing customers.

Sales Representative (1996 to 1997)

Managed up to 30 sales accounts, including 10 key accounts, and successfully expanded sales within each through the introduction of add-on products and services. Recognized for sales achievements.

—Excellent Professional References Available on Request—

Forest Pulley

email@email.com

411 Beachtree Road
Whitehall, Ohio 43213
Home: 614.555-1212

Private Security Officer...Safety Awareness

Education Profile:

Acme Vocational School, Columbus, Ohio

Certified Security Officer
Expected Graduation (August 2002)

Comprehensive two-year secondary school training program offering 180 learning hours in:

- Ohio Peace Officer Training
- Patrol Procedures
- Criminal Investigation
- Criminalistics
- Self-Defense
- Juvenile Procedures
- Crisis Intervention
- Constitutional Law
- Community Policing
- Criminal Procedure
- Arrest & Control
- High-Rise Safety
- Hazardous Material
- Auto Theft Investigation
- Report Writing
- Crime Data Processing
- Search & Seizure
- High-Speed Pursuits
- First Aid & CPR
- Diversity Relations

Career Profile:

Guard Dog Security, Columbus, Ohio

Safety Officer/Intern (2000–Present)

Provide on-site security assistance patrolling various citywide mall parking lots and shopping venues.

- Responsible for maintaining safety and order of parking lot traffic flow during peak shopping schedules.
- Reacts to various parking obstacles and emergencies, including on-site accidents, parking lot snow removal, breakdowns, and opening locked car doors.
- Patrols vendor locations and restaurants, adhering to various time slots and routes.
- Accountable for procedure documentation including report writing relative to trespassing, ticketing vehicles for overextended parking, break-ins, and on-site assaults.
- Operates fleet vehicles comprised of Ford Explorer 4×4, Chevrolet Caprice, and patrol bicycles.

Kohl's Department Store, Columbus, Ohio

Loss-Prevention Shopper (1998–2000)

Participated in on-site security and theft-prevention efforts, patrolling sales floor, dressing rooms, and parking lots.

- Blended in with customers and minors to witness shopping and returning of stock, watching for theft and damaging of goods.
- Liaised with local police assisting in report taking relative to in-store accidents, security breaches, and detaining suspects.
- Credited with reducing shrink in selected departments.

LORI DENMAN

222 West 30th Street ◆ Danton, Idaho 83456 ◆ (208) 555-1212 ◆ email@email.com

Director, Social Services Division

PROFESSIONAL QUALIFICATIONS

- ◆ Visionary and goal oriented, inspires cooperation and teamwork.
- ◆ Strong management and leadership qualities.
- ◆ Excellent written and oral communications.
- ◆ Organized and efficient, resourceful, with a strong drive to succeed.
- ◆ Creates criteria and standard procedures for hiring new staff members.
- ◆ Manages and promotes self-directed work teams and coordination for 52 employees.

EDUCATION

Master of Science Degree in Social Work. **Walla Walla College**, Missoula, Montana. August 1999.
  Coursework included:
- ◆ Clinical Skills with Addictive Families
- ◆ Clinical Dysfunctional Behavior
- ◆ Family Violence
- ◆ Clinical Treatment of Families
- ◆ Social Work—Supervision
- ◆ Administration/Management
- ◆ Policy Issues for Clinicians
- ◆ Advanced Clinical Evaluation
- ◆ Solution-Focused Brief Therapy
- ◆ Death and Dying

Bachelor of Science Degree in Social Work. **Brigham Young University**, Provo, Utah. August 1991.
  Coursework included:
- ◆ Crisis Intervention
- ◆ Community Organization
- ◆ Group Work (Therapy)
- ◆ Individual Work (Therapy)
- ◆ Family Systems
- ◆ Abnormal Psychology
- ◆ Child Development

Associate's Degree in General Education. **Ricks College**, Rexburg, Idaho. April 1988.

LORI DENMAN
Page 2

Director, Social Services Division

EMPLOYMENT

SOCIAL WORKER. DEPARTMENT OF HEALTH & WELFARE, Anywhere, Idaho. 1992 to Present.
- Case Manager—Child Protection, Juvenile Justice.
- Investigations—Child Protection.
- Probation Officer—Fremont and Teton Counties.
- Crisis Intervention—24-hour coverage.
- Supervising—Intern and Practicum Students.
- Clinician—Children's Mental Health.

UNIT COUNSELOR. PROVO CANYON SCHOOL, Anywhere, Utah. 1989 to 1992.
- Extensive experience supervising a lock-down unit.
- Implemented new procedures for developing individual case plans.
- Taught successful life-living skills.
- Created new individual group and therapy programs to include day treatment and local children's mental health alliances.
- Organized and executed activities.

ADDITIONAL INFORMATION

- Volunteer, Utah State Hospital, 1988–1991
- Volunteer Board Member, Citizen's Advisory Board for Anthony Work Camp, 1985–1987
- Eagle Scout Award, 1981

REFERENCES

Available upon Request

SOCIAL WORKER COVER LETTER

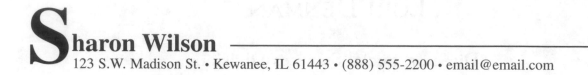

Sharon Wilson

123 S.W. Madison St. • Kewanee, IL 61443 • (888) 555-2200 • email@email.com

Allow me to introduce myself:

Serve others: that is quite simply what I wish to do with my life, and it also explains the deep passion with which I approach my work.

After working as a Care Provider for an organization that offers independent assisted-living services to the elderly and handicapped, I soon found that I wanted to do more. As a result of my hard work and passion for this service, I was eventually promoted to the position of Program Coordinator.

In the Coordinator position, I made improvements in the quality of service, implemented a successful in-house training program, served as a Crisis Intervention Representative (on call 24 hours a day), and successfully obtained additional funds from alternative sources by researching available options. It was my sincere pleasure to go well above and beyond the call of duty in order to effectively serve those who were in need.

Now that I have recently completed my B.S. in Social Work & Spanish, I am seeking to secure a position as a Social Services Counselor where my skills, dedication, and knowledge would be of benefit. With the dedication and passion for service that I have to offer, I can assure you that I will meet your highest expectations.

Thank you for your time and consideration in reviewing this material. I look forward to hearing from you soon. If you have additional questions, please feel free to contact me.

Sincerely,

Sharon Wilson

Resume Enclosed

SOCIAL WORKER

Sharon Wilson
123 S.W. Madison St. • Kewanee, IL 61443 • (888) 555-2200 • email@email.com

- SOCIAL SERVICES COUNSELOR -
Program Management/Personnel Training/Bilingual Communication

EVALUATION COMMENTS

"Sharon is a real self-starter who has demonstrated the ability to manage projects from start to finish, while maintaining exceptional quality. Her excellent organizational skills allow her to manage several different tasks concurrently. Sharon has a deep, professional commitment to her work and a personal commitment to do the best job she can do. She is passionate about her work and it shows.
Sharon lives to serve others."

REVIEW OF SKILLS

- Dedicated and caring Human Relations Professional / Program Coordinator with solid academic qualifications and an excellent professional track record.
- Experienced team leader and project manager with a background in the full supervision and development of personnel.
- Proven communication, presentation, training, negotiation, conflict resolution, and problem-solving abilities. Professional group presentation/training skills. Speaks Spanish fluently.
- Computer skills include: MS Word, Excel, Access, PowerPoint, Lotus 1-2-3, WordPerfect, Windows, Internet, e-mail, and IDHS system.

VOCATIONAL TRAINING

B.A. in Social Work & Spanish, UNIVERSITY OF SOUTHERN IOWA—Lacon, IA (2002)
A.A.S. in Human Relations, KNOX COMMUNITY COLLEGE—Knox, IA (1991)
Academic Highlights: Recipient of the Susan J. Ward Academic Scholarship • Secretary of the Student Body Association • Annual Student Body Association Fund Raiser • Member of the Spanish Club • Campus Community Club Founder & President • President's List • Dean's List

EXPERIENCE & INTERNSHIPS

Human Services Intern, ILLINOIS DEPARTMENT OF HUMAN SERVICES—Lacon, IA (2001 to 2002)
Assisted with client evaluations to determine program eligibility. Completed and submitted on-line forms, contacted clients regarding changes, and provided program information.

Program Coordinator, COMMUNITY CARE, INC.—Knox, IA (1993 to 2002)
Directed daily program support activities for 50+ participants in a community-supported independent living program for elderly and handicapped individuals. Supervised, trained, and scheduled a staff of eight in all aspects of providing full support services including transportation, prescription refills, grocery shopping, housekeeping, and basic medical care. Served as the main point-of-contact in resolving internal and external issues, providing resource information, and acting as a consumer advocate/liaison to ensure that individual needs were met.

- Drastically improved program quality, increased participants, and reduced costs by implementing in-house training, opening lines of communication, and evaluating supply needs.
- Developed policy & procedure manuals and a code of ethics for all employees.

- Excellent Professional References Available on Request -

SOCIAL WORKER

Judd Rossman
15 North Mill Street
Nyack, New York 10960
(914) 555-3160

EDUCATION

Fordham University Graduate School of Social Work—Bronx, New York
Currently pursuing Master's Degree in Social Work
Expected date of graduation, Spring 2002

Dominican College—Blauvelt, New York
Bachelor's Degree in Social Work—2002

EXPERIENCE

Stony Lodge Hospital—Briarcliff Manor, New York
Therapist—1998–Present
Provide individual, group, and family therapy to adults, children, and adolescent patients at this 40-bed resident treatment facility. Develop clinical reviews for managed-care companies and maintain extensive contacts with referral sources and families to coordinate patient care planning.
Accomplishments:
- Designed and incorporated educational groups for adolescents dealing with HIV/AIDS, sexually transmitted diseases, and alcohol/drugs.
- Prepared and presented a series of seminars on teenage suicide predictors and signs of depression for the New York Juvenile Officers Association, Rye High School, and Stony Lodge Hospital in-service training.
- Developed and presented a seminar for a local bereavement group regarding depression and psychopharmacological drugs.

Pequannock Valley Mental Health Center—Pompton Plains, New Jersey
<u>**Inquiry Worker—1997–1998**</u>
Responded to all telephone and walk-in inquires for this outpatient crisis center. Served a member of an interdisciplinary treatment team for the purpose of assessing client's strengths and needs. Implemented individual behavioral treatment plans.

REFERENCES WILL BE FURNISHED UPON REQUEST

ALLISON CHASE LANDERS

Before Dec. 16, 2001:
321 Verizon Street
Asheville, NC 28800
(888) 555-1234

email@email.com

After Dec. 16, 2001:
269 Fortrain Drive
Newport, NJ 08800
(888) 555-1212

Adaptable, motivated college graduate with strong work ethic seeks challenge and opportunity in Sports Medicine career in private, corporate, or rehabilitative environment.

- Fitness Evaluation & Assessment
- Exercise Prescription
- Cardiac Rehabilitation
- Record Management
- Patient Services
- Patient/Client Education

- Use of medical and fitness machines: telemetry heart-rate monitor, EKG, stationary bicycle, free weights, tread mills, elliptical trainers, Nautilus/Keiser/Cybex equipment.

- Evaluation and testing: % body fat, blood pressure, flexibility screening, strength and endurance testing, stress testing.

- Gregarious, with multicultural experience and good communications skills; focused listener. Goal-oriented, well-organized, excellent management of time and priorities. Multitasking rapport builder.

- Familiar with medical terminology. PC proficient—Internet, Microsoft (Word, Excel, PowerPoint).

Bachelor of Science, Exercise & Sport Science, December 2001
State University of North Carolina-Asheville

Relevant Coursework:

- Exercise Psychology & Physiology
- Exercise Prescriptions for Special Populations
- Motor Learning
- Biomechanics
- Anatomy
- Research & Evaluation
- Motor Development
- Health Management

Arnold University, Arnold, England, Spring 1999
- Overseas exposure to different cultures through International Student Association. Learned rapid adaptability to new environments, global perspectives, independence, self-reliance.
- Traveled extensively in Europe (well-traveled domestically as well).

Certifications & Continuing Professional Training:
AFAA Personal Training Certification . . . CPR Certified, Adult and Child . . . First Aid / Red Cross Certified . . . Cardiac Rehabilitation . . . NC Alliance for Health, Physical Education, Recreation & Dance Conference
(assisted set-up of seminars and aided presenters for this 3-day 2000 event)
Gymnast (8 years)

WORK HISTORY

Internship • Alliance Regional Medical Center, Asheville, NC   Spring 2001
300 hours in 238-bed full-service regional hospital

- As member of professional health team, participated in patient orientations and staff meetings. Monitored and assessed cardiac exercise program; modified exercises as needed for pain relief. As-needed office work and medical records filing.

- Ability to connect with patients ensured success in teaching motivational techniques.

ALLISON CHASE LANDERS, Page two

email@email.com • (888) 555-1234 • (888) 555-1212

WORK HISTORY
(Continued)

Occupational Therapy Volunteer • St. Francis Hospital, Asheville, NC Fall 2000
Assessed/observed OT and rehab treatments (40 hours) to better understand scope of rehabilitative choices.

Personal Training/Corporate Fitness • Constructive Stress Co., Asheville, NC January 2001–Present
Private, in-house corporate fitness facility providing one-on-one assistance, serving 300–500 employees of several tenant health care, administrative support, and financial services corporations (including Federal Express).
• Perform initial client evaluation/testing; assist in design of personal exercise programs; train clients in proper use of exercise tools. Initiated use of medicine balls in weight training program, allowing client to diversify into more precise exercise movements for specific muscle groups, lowering injury rate in certain sports. Outstanding rapport with clients.

Sales Representative • Bass Outlet, Manasquan, NJ 1996–1998
• Member of sales team responsible for this retail clothing outlet store's receiving company's 1994 Highest-Grossing Sales Award.

Manager • Summer Lake Pavillions, Summer Lake, NJ 1992–Present
Family-owned, high-volume restaurant/supply stores on New Jersey shore.
• Consistently promoted to ever-increasing responsibilities since childhood, with early exposure to all aspects of business management, including personnel supervision, customer service, menu development, and opening/closing stores. In-depth training in inventory purchasing and planning for business that is highly dependent on weather for customer traffic.

References Available upon Interview

TEACHER—ELEMENTARY COVER LETTER

SHANNON E. BENUSCAK

32 Old Schoolhouse Road • New City, New York 10956 • (845) 555-9134 • email@email.com

Dear Human Resources Professional,

I am interested in exploring teaching opportunities within your school system and have enclosed my resume for your consideration. I believe that my work with mainstream and special education elementary students coupled with my ability to develop strong rapport with students, parents, and teachers could assist your school in reaching its academic goals.

Among my many accomplishments, I participated in the successful development and implementation of thematic units to establish connections between concepts and skills learned. I am able to transfer learning from subject to subject and apply what students learn to making decisions and solving problems. I have worked with students to develop outdoor programs to enhance their learning experience and assist them in building self-esteem.

I believe that my assessment expertise, communications abilities, and teaching skills are a perfect combination for an education professional. I am confident that the enthusiasm and experience I can bring to your organization will prove to be an asset in achieving your school's goals as I have done for others.

I would appreciate hearing from you regarding any existing or future openings that you might have and would welcome the opportunity to meet with you. Thank you for your time and consideration. I look forward to hearing from you.

Sincerely,

Shannon E. Benuscak

Enc. RESUME

TEACHER—ELEMENTARY

SHANNON E. BENUSCAK
32 Old Schoolhouse Road • New City, New York 10956 • (845) 555-9134 • email@email.com

TESTIMONIALS

"Ms. Benuscak recently completed a five-week sick leave for my position as a Resource Room/Inclusion teacher. During that time she demonstrated an outstanding ability to make connections with the students...She was a great asset to Sunrise Drive Elementary School..."

Carolyn Daley
Special Education Teacher
Sunrise Drive Elementary School

"... Shannon has consistently demonstrated academic excellence. She has conducted herself with professional integrity and has demonstrated commitment to responsibilities and professional studies. She is a warm, caring, and energetic person. She has demonstrated initiative, intelligence, and preparedness. I, therefore, strongly recommend her to you..."

John P. Heaphy, Ph.D.
Dowling College
Teacher Education Program

"...Shannon worked with autistic populations of children in a highly structured environment of applied behavioral analysis. She taught with expertise, kindness, and consistency and thoroughly familiarized herself with classroom routines and with specific goals for each child. In addition, Shannon was a very pleasant addition to the adult staff that worked within the classroom. I would highly recommend Shannon as a teacher in any special education setting."

Janine Corona, CCC/Sp
Speech Teacher
Eastern Suffolk B.O.C.E.S.

EDUCATION

SUNY Stony Brook—Stony Brook, NY
Currently Pursuing Bachelor of Science in Elementary Education
Expected Date of Graduation • May 2002 • Dean's List

Suffolk Community College—Selden, NY
A.A. • **Liberal Arts** • Dean's List • 1996

CERTIFICATIONS

N.Y.S. Provisional Teaching Certification Elementary Education
N.Y.S. Provisional Teaching Certification Special Education

PROFILE

A dedicated elementary education professional with demonstrated experience in working with mainstream students to achieve goals while combining and implementing various teaching and organization strategies including direct/command, task limitation, and exploration methods. Able to establish and maintain solid relationships with coworkers, students, and parents. Recognized as a resourceful and reliable teacher with the ability to perform accurate student assessment and develop individualized education plans.

AREAS OF EXPERTISE

• **Special Ed Inclusion** • **Creative Lesson Planning** • **Thematic Units** • **Development of Instructional Materials and Learning Centers** • **Cooperative Learning** • **Multisensory Lessons** • **Multicultural Units** • **Integrated Activities** • **Individualized Education Plan Development** • **Parent-Teacher Conferences** • **Performance Assessments** • **Integration of Technology** • **Life Skills Training** • **NYS Learning Standards Compliance** •

PROFESSIONAL EXPERIENCE

2001   **STUDENT TEACHER**
            Short Hills Elementary—Middle Village, New York
- Develop and implement lesson plans for 2d, 3d, and 4th-grade students of varying abilities and intellectual levels with diverse backgrounds.
- Implement thematic approaches and integrated curriculum providing opportunity for students to build upon strengths.
- Establish connections between concepts and skills.
- Integrate language arts approaches to supplement and enrich curricula standards.
- Utilize computers for both classroom lessons and one-on-one tutoring to provide independent math and writing activities.

1999 to 2000   **STUDENT TEACHER**
            Eastern Suffolk B.O.C.E.S.—Patchogue, NY
- Provide instruction for the ABA program designed to meet the needs of elementary-aged autistic children.

Savannah McKay

123 Adams • Troy, IL 61234 • (888) 555-2200 • email@email.com

- HIGH SCHOOL TEACHER -
Motto: "I believe in leading by example."

VISION STATEMENT

To continually improve the quality of student education by providing a positive learning environment through the encouragement of classroom ownership, the integration of creative visual and audio learning methods, and the championing of direct parental involvement.

- **Classroom Ownership** stresses the importance of morals and significantly reduces disciplinary problems, providing a thriving learning environment at school.
- **Creative Learning Methods** enhance the learning process by appealing to both the audio and visual senses instilling a love of learning, which will be used throughout a lifetime.
- **Direct Parental Involvement** produces extremely successful learning results and builds a positive home/school connection.

LEADERSHIP/CREATIVITY/TEAMWORK/MOTIVATION

A dedicated and highly motivated Education Professional seeking an entry-level High School teaching position. Proven track record of successfully implementing well-planned and thoroughly integrated lessons that produce lasting results by assisting students in relating to real life. Motivated to try new, creative techniques and continually improve teaching skills.

EDUCATIONAL BACKGROUND

Bachelor of Science in Education (K-12), MISSOURI COLLEGE—Springfield, MO (2001)
• Language Arts Endorsement • Social Studies Endorsement
Major GPA: 3.9 / Cumulative GPA: 3.7

Associate of Arts in Education, WILMINGTON COLLEGE—Kewanee, IL (1997)

Academic Highlights: • Served as Secretary for the ASSOCIATION FOR STUDENT ACTIVITY PROGRAMMING • Student Body Member of the school's ETHICS BOARD • President's List • Dean's List • Recruited to assist in organizing instructional materials for the school's career center

PROFESSIONAL EXPERIENCE

Student Teacher, High School—NORTHMOORE HIGH SCHOOL—Kansas City, MO (1998–2001)
Instructed freshmen and sophomore students in English studies; was selected to provide concentrated language instruction to special needs students. Directed all aspects of two quarterly creative learning programs for up to 30 students. Integrated concurrent learning themes in English and creative learning programs to relate subject matter effectively.

- Was recruited to serve as the **Educational Facility Representative** for the Missouri State Teacher's Association (MSTA).
- Encouraged classroom ownership through various projects, including an interactive bulletin board used to present topics on current events.
- Successfully created and implemented various alternative assessment/evaluation methods to evaluate learning on all levels, as represented in *Bloom's Taxonomy of Learning*.
- Introduced, implemented, and directed several innovative programs to enhance student learning, resulting in a 30% overall improvement on test scores.
- Was selected to participate in district committee meetings for curriculum development in the reviewing, assessing, streamlining, and enhancing of current materials, unified assessment standards, and requirements for district implementation.

• Excellent Professional References Available on Request •

TEACHER—PRESCHOOL

LAURIE KAUFFMAN

318 Lindenwood Lane
Liberty, Missouri 64068
Telephone: (816) 555-5555 — Email: email@email.com

_____

OBJECTIVE:

Seeking a permanent, full-time **preschool teaching position** within the Liberty, Missouri area or within a reasonable commuting distance.

QUALIFICATIONS:

A.S. EARLY CHILDHOOD DEGREE (December, 2001)
- Currently employed at a child care facility. Many years of experience in daily teaching as the owner/operator of a home-based day care.
- Experienced volunteer preschool teacher, youth director, and puppet ministry director at church, with additional experience working with children through other varied volunteer activities.
- Homeschooled three children for several years.
- Hosted Fresh Air Child/Children (seven summers).
- Red Cross First Aid and CPR Certified.

COMMUNITY INVOLVEMENT
- **Featured Child Care Provider in Newspaper Article (*Missouri Tribune*, 1999)**
- **Recognized by Mayor Kenneth Page for Accomplishment**
  Collaborated with city officials to petition for rezoning of a residential area; gained approval to develop further a proposed Children's Nature Trail with varied accommodations for children with special needs.

EDUCATION:

Central Missouri Technical College (Liberty, MO)   **1999–2001**
Associate of Science Degree—Early Childhood Program
- Completed 3-month practicum (2001) with the Community Preschool Center, Liberty, MO; contributed to "free time" programs as well as working one-on-one with several preschool children with special needs.

Other Specialized Training & Studies:
- Child Care Provider; Training by Michael Trout at UMF, 1998
- Systematic Training for Effective Parenting, 1998
- Effective Teaching Techniques & Child Psychology, 1997
- Parenting & Homeschool Teaching, 1995

EMPLOYMENT:

Rocking Horse Day Care Center (Liberty Falls, MO)   **09/99–Present**
- Day Care Assistant—Interim Manager (35–40 Children—2–5 Years Old)

Happy Children Day Care (Home Based)   **1990–1999**
- Licensed Owner-Operator (Infants to Preschool Age—Up to 8 Children)

Child Care: Provider (Varied Locations)   **1980–1990**
- Provided care to several children at varied locations, including personal residence.

TEACHER—SPECIAL EDUCATION

MARIA LANE

11935 West 9th Street • Sun Valley, Idaho 83404 • (208) 555-1212 •
email@email.com

SPECIAL EDUCATION TEACHER

Highly dedicated, compassionate, patient, and positive professional with
numerous accomplishments working with the handicapped.

SUMMARY OF QUALIFICATIONS

- Current teaching **certificate for Elementary Education**—endorsement in Special Education.
- **Quickly develops rapport with students, employees, and staff.**
- Three years' experience (summers) working with handicapped individuals in a Developmental Disabilities Agency and writing programs for handicapped individuals.
- **Manages and promotes self-directed work teams** and coordination for three employees.
- Experienced with licensure surveys for Developmental Disabilities Agencies.
- **Strong leadership, management, and organizational skills; exceptional work ethic.**
- **Self-motivated, creative, dependable, and patient.**

EDUCATION

Current Teaching Certificate valid in Idaho and Washington. 2001.
Bachelor of Science Degree in Special Education, **Idaho State University**, Pocatello, Idaho. 1997.
Developing Capable People Seminar, **Temple Elementary**, Presented by Stacie Smith. 1997.
Managing People with Handicaps Seminar, **Temple Elementary**, Presented by Stacie Smith. 1996.

EMPLOYMENT

AIDE. DEVELOPMENT WORKSHOP, INC., Idaho Falls, Idaho.   1994 to 1996.
- Traveled to clients' homes to teach cooking, cleaning, shopping, and budgeting.
- Assisted in writing, developing, and implementing program procedures.
- Taught life skills to clients; ensured the safety of the clients.
- Monitored facility maintenance and security.
- Special project: worked with young boy, age five, who would not speak. After nine months of intense therapy, patience, and special equipment, he began speaking broken words. He is still in therapy and doing very well considering the circumstances.

LAYAWAY/SERVICE DESK CLERK. K MART, Nampa, Idaho.   1991 to 1994 (Part-Time).

CASHIER/COOK. SCOT'S DRIVE-IN, Idaho Falls, Idaho.   1988 to 1991 (Part-Time).

Have lived with and cared for a sister and brother with handicaps.

TEACHING ASSISTANT COVER LETTER

TERRY ROTHSTEIN
12345 Flatbush Avenue
Brooklyn, NY 11210 • 718-555-1212
email@email.com

Joseph Ornstein, Ph.D., Director
The Creative Years
491 9th Street
Brooklyn, NY 11215

Dear Dr. Ornstein:

Learning can be a fun and rewarding experience for both the adolescent and the facilitator, which is why I am responding to your ad in the July 23 issue of the Bay News for a part-time Teacher Assistant. I will be graduating from the Borough of Manhattan Community College in May 2001 with an Associate in Applied Science in Early Childhood Education. I have actively remained on the Dean's List for the past two years, and my cumulative GPA is 3.56.

Your opening stands out from other schools I've entertained due to the unique way that art and music are incorporated into the learning process. This position offers the opportunity I've often dreamed of, integrating my formal music training with my love of children.

Additionally, you will find that I am capable of meeting your other qualifications, including:

- **Team Player:** I understand that my role is to support the teaching staff with daily operations, including materials and meal distribution, arrivals and departures, toileting, and other related functions.

- **Creative Activities:** As mentioned above, I am formally trained in classical and folk guitar and would welcome staff collaboration on the best utilization of this talent. While at Heartshare I introduced a popular project in which children made kaleidoscopes from household objects and materials.

- **Parent–Staff Relationships:** Having worked in the educational field for the past six years, I understand the importance of fostering a family-friendly environment where together parents and staff operate in the best interest of the child. During my tenure at the Board of Education, I developed congenial relationships with parents and caregivers, alerting them to any unusual occurrence during the school day.

I welcome the opportunity to discuss program needs and will contact you early next week to schedule a convenient meeting time. Thank you for your consideration.

Sincerely,

Terry Rothstein

Enclosure

TEACHING ASSISTANT

TERRY ROTHSTEIN
12345 Flatbush Avenue
Brooklyn, NY 11210 • 718-555-1212
email@email.com

EARLY CHILDHOOD/TEACHING ASSISTANT

Talented and energetic Teaching Assistant
seeking opportunity to contribute to child development and parent satisfaction.
Patient, caring, and nurturing while establishing clear limits.
Follows directions and shares in team efforts.

CORE STRENGTHS

- Music
- Movement
- Toileting

- Storytelling
- Speech
- Arts and Crafts

EDUCATION

Borough of Manhattan Community College, CUNY, New York, NY
Associate in Applied Science: Early Childhood Education, Fall 2000 (GPA: 3.52)
(Selected Studies: Toddler Care Curriculum & Program Planning II, The Exceptional Child)
Dean's List: Fall 1998/1999, Spring 1999/2000

Brooklyn Conservatory of Music, Brooklyn, NY   1992–1998
Trained in classical and folk guitar.

CERTIFICATIONS

Red Cross, New York, NY: Infant CPR and First Aid   1999, 2000

EMPLOYMENT HISTORY

Heartshare Early Childhood Center, Brooklyn, NY   1999–2000
Teaching Assistant
Hired upon recommendation to support 3 child care providers in creating a stimulating and fun learning environment
for 12 toddlers and 4 infants. Encouraged student socialization and creative expression through art and crafts
activities, singing, and movement.

- Cited worker of the month in March 2000.

BOARD OF EDUCATION: School District 2, Brooklyn, NY   1996–1999
School Aide
Hired to manage lunchroom serving 978 students daily. Intervened in student disagreements—sustaining a
congenial, orderly, and safe environment. Promptly acquaint parents/caregivers of incidents and concerns.
Documented student information records and accident reports. Substitute for attendance clerk—calculate and enter
attendance data into AST proprietary program.

- Fostered open communication with students and their parents.
- Mastered attendance process and AST program.

References Furnished upon Request

TECH SUPPORT COVER LETTER

PAUL ROBICHEAU
1012 South Street, Apt. 2A
Cleveland, OH 44114
Tel: 216-555-1212
Cell: 216-555-2121
E-mail: email@email.com

May 23, 2002

Gerald Carboni
IT Manager
Greater Cleveland Advertising Associates, Inc.
154 Central Street
Cleveland, OH 44114

Re: Desktop Support Technician, position #105, as advertised in *The Cleveland Times*.

Dear Mr. Carboni:

I am skilled at providing PC hardware/software support both on site and over the phone. While completing my B.S. degree in Computer Science, I worked as a technical consultant to users in the university community and the Cleveland metropolitan area. I gained experience in installing, configuring, and repairing laptop and desktop PC hardware, installing and upgrading a wide range of software in multiple DOS and Windows environments, and supporting network connectivity.

Equally important to your company would be my ability to communicate effectively with business and residential clients in person and over the phone. I am able to assess problems quickly and explain in lay terms the fix required. I offer that rare combination of technical problem-solving strengths and "people skills" that has resulted in many customer requests that I do further work for them. I make customer service a top personal priority.

I have pursued extensive industry-standardized training and possess several certifications, including Microsoft Certified Professional, A+, and Network+. I am currently pursuing coursework leading to certifications as Microsoft Certified Systems Engineer and Cisco Certified Network Associate.

My skills include organizing and prioritizing jobs, multitasking, and completing jobs on schedule. I am highly motivated to get the job done well and in a timely manner, leaving behind a satisfied customer.

I would appreciate an opportunity to talk with you in person about how I might contribute to your technical support team. I will call the week of May 30th to inquire about setting up an appointment to meet. Thank you for considering this letter and the enclosed resume.

Sincerely,

Paul Robicheau

Enclosure: Resume

PAUL ROBICHEAU

1012 South Street, Apt. 2A
Cleveland, OH 44114
Tel: 216-555-1212
Cell: 216-555-2121
E-mail: email@email.com

DESKTOP SUPPORT TECHNICIAN

- Experienced PC hardware/software support specialist committed to customer satisfaction.
- Talented hands-on problem solver who gets up to speed quickly on new systems and applications.
- Able to translate technical information into lay terms for customers—a natural teacher.
- Skilled at quickly and accurately identifying problems during site visits and over the phone.
- Highly organized with a strong work ethic.

CERTIFICATIONS

- Microsoft Certified Professional (2001)
- CompTIA Network+ Certified (2001)
- Dell Certified Portable Associate (2001)
- CompTIA A+ Certified Service Technician (2000)

TECHNICAL SKILLS SUMMARY

Operating Systems: Install, configure, troubleshoot, repair PCs in DOS, Windows 95/98/2000, Windows 2000 Professional, Windows 2000 Server, and Windows XP Home Edition, and professional environments.

PC Hardware: Build and troubleshoot laptop and desktop PCs. Install power supply, motherboards, processors, memory, hard drives, floppy drives, zip drives, video cards, sound cards, network interface cards, modems, keyboards, chassis fans, ribbon cables, wiring, CD-ROM drives, CDR/RW drives, DVD drives, speakers, printers, and associated software and/or drivers.

Software and Applications: Install, upgrade, and configure Microsoft Word, Excel, PowerPoint, Access, FrontPage, McAfee Anti-Virus, Norton Anti-Virus, Norton Utilities, and multimedia plug-in applications such as Real Player, Windows Media Player, Macromedia Shock Wave, and Flash, email programs including Outlook and Outlook Express, and Palm Desktop software. Perform software synchronization. Install service packs. Proficient in the use of systems diagnostics software.

Networks and Communications: Troubleshoot network connectivity using TCP/IP tools. Install, configure, and repair hardware including cabling, hubs, routers, DSL modems, network printers, drivers, and dial-up software. Build and troubleshoot home and small office LANs.

TECHNICAL EXPERIENCE

Independent Technical Support Consultant, Cleveland, OH   1997–Present

Provide technical support services and training to small business and residential clients.

- Solve break/fix issues and perform installations, upgrades, and diagnostics for desktop and laptop systems including Windows 95/98, Windows 2000 Professional, and hardware peripherals.
- Performed troubleshooting and supported applications including MS Office and Palm Desktop software.
- Modified initialization files for optimum performance, and installed service packs.
- Installed networking hardware and software.
- Built a residential LAN and configured a small business LAN.

PAUL ROBICHEAU   216-555-1212   Page 2

EDUCATION AND TRAINING

University of Ohio, Athens, OH
Bachelor of Science in Computer Science   2000

- Paid for half of tuition by working as an independent technical support consultant.

IT Career Institute, Cleveland, OH   2000–Present
Internetworking Engineering Program

Program provides comprehensive training in the skills required to work as a PC Technician, Help Desk/Desktop Support Associate, PC/LAN Support Specialist, or LAN Administrator. Graduates possess a working familiarity with LAN hardware and software (Microsoft Windows 2000) and ability to understand, design, install, and support Microsoft LANs.

- Certifications earned: MCP, CompTIA A+, CompTIA Network Plus
- Currently pursuing coursework leading to MCSE and CCNA certifications

Coursework Completed

- Introduction to Computers and Operating Systems
- Computer Hardware Installation and Troubleshooting
- Microsoft Windows 2000 Network and Operating Systems Essentials & Supporting Microsoft Windows 2000 Professional & Server
- Supporting a Network Infrastructure Using Microsoft Windows 2000
- Implementing and Administering Microsoft Windows 2000 Directory Services
- Designing a Microsoft Windows 2000 Directory Services Infrastructure
- Designing a Microsoft Windows 2000 Networking Services Infrastructure
- Microsoft Exchange Server 5.5 Series—Design & Implementation
- Introduction to Cisco Router Configuration

TELEVISION PRODUCTION ENGINEER

SALENE HINSON

725 Sabattus Street
Lewiston, Maine 04240
Phone: (207) 555-1212 / Email: email@email.com / Cell Phone: (207) 555-2121

Career Focus:

TELEVISION PRODUCTION ENGINEER
Emphasis in Remote Production and Planning

Education:

Television Production & News Writing
Springfield Technical Community College, Springfield, MA

Training Highlights & Skills:

Video Engineer, Audio Assistant, Tech Manager, Systems Engineer, Microwave Systems, Cameras
(Mobile & Stationary Equipment Engineering Expertise)

Television Interest & Intern-Related Travel:

Follow-Up Documentary:	England & France, 16 Days	2000
Documentary:	Moscow & Leningrad USSR, 2.5 Weeks	1999
Documentary:	England & France, 5.5 Weeks	1997

Professional Experience:

Staff Engineer (Extended Internship)—
Flight 9 Satellite Services (New York City, NY)   1998–Present
  • Multicamera Productions/Equipment Maintenance/Uplink of Live Shots

Staff Assistant Engineer—
Valley Productions (Brighton, MA)   1988–1998
  • Mobile Television Services/Truck Engineering/All Production Jobs

. . .

URBAN PLANNER COVER LETTER

JAMES F. CONWAY
32 Old Schoolhouse Road, New City, NY 10956 (845) 555-1212 • email@email.com

Dear Sir or Madam:

In the interest of exploring career opportunities utilizing my education and experience in urban planning, I am enclosing my resume for your information. As you will note, I have solid experience within real estate, with additional exposure to the mortgage industry. I am a highly motivated individual with superior decision-making and problem-solving skills, and I feel that my dedication to company goals, commitment to success, and ability to implement results-oriented programs will provide the basis for increased growth and profitability for your organization.

I have consistently demonstrated my ability to develop and manage land development projects and identify problem areas, devise and implement effective management and financial controls, and ensure the attainment of goals. I have gained a solid reputation for integrity, reliability, and skill in coordinating all internal functions, resulting in strong profits and enhanced public perception. As you will note from my career overview, my particular strengths include community service, land appraisal, real estate development, and public presentations.

Realizing that a resume cannot fully convey either my desire or ability to make a significant contribution to the growth of your organization, I would appreciate the opportunity to meet with you personally to discuss my qualifications in greater detail. I am particularly interested in learning about positions that you have available at this time for an individual with my qualifications. I can be reached at the telephone number listed above to answer your questions or to set up a time for us to meet.

Thank you for your consideration. I look forward to speaking with you soon.

Sincerely,

James F. Conway

enclosure

JAMES F. CONWAY

32 Old Schoolhouse Road, New City, NY 10956 (845) 555-1212 • email@email.com

---

URBAN PLANNING SPECIALIST
Utilizing Project Management, Communication, and Interpersonal Skills

---

- Articulate and persuasive in verbal communications; adept at making public presentations; comfortable delivering briefs to senior executives and public officials.
- Highly effective in all project development phases, from initial study to project completion.
- Exceptional negotiator with a capacity for quickly developing rapport with clients, government agents, and contractors; a resourceful problem solver.
- Extremely organized and efficient; proven ability to manage multiple projects simultaneously, prioritize conflicting workloads, and meet critical, short-fused deadlines.
- Talent for responding effectively to customer-concerns issues and complaints.
- **Core competencies include:**

  - **COMMUNITY SERVICE**
  - **LAND APPRAISAL**
  - **REAL ESTATE DEVELOPMENT**
  - **PROJECT MANAGEMENT**
  - **REAL ESTATE BROKERAGE**

  - **PUBLIC PRESENTATION**
  - **PUBLIC SERVICE**
  - **LAND DEVELOPMENT**
  - **STRATEGIC NEGOTIATION**
  - **BUSINESS MANAGEMENT**

EDUCATION

- STATE UNIVERSITY OF NEW YORK AT STONY BROOK, Stony Brook, NY
  Bachelor of Arts—Urban Planning • GPA 3.8 • May 2001

PROFESSIONAL EXPERIENCE

UPSTATE LANDS REAL ESTATE, INC., NY • 1999 to Present
ASSISTANT URBAN PLANNER
- Develop comprehensive plans and programs for the utilization of land and physical facilities for this real estate brokerage firm, specializing in the purchase and development of mid- to large-sized parcels in upstate New York.
- Compile and analyze data on economic, social, and physical factors affecting land use, and prepare graphic and narrative reports on data.
- Confer with local authorities, civic leaders, social scientists, and land planning and environmental specialists to devise and recommend arrangement of land and physical faculties for residential, commercial, industrial, and community uses.
- Provide recommendations for governmental measures affecting land use, public utilities, community facilities, housing, and transportation to control and guide community development and renewal.   Review and evaluate environmental impact reports applying to specific private and public planning projects and programs.

Selected Accomplishment:
- **Coordinated all aspects of a $20-million multiuse land project, reducing costs by 27% and generating over $6 million in annual tax revenues for the town of Clarkstown.**

THE DIME—New City, NY
Mortgage Origination Assistant • 1996 to 1998
- Assisted senior loan officer in the coordination and distribution of leads and establishing loan applications for first and second mortgages and home equity lines of credit. Ran initial credit reports and developed mortgage packages for approved applicants.
- Handled concerns from clients regarding timing issues, and resolved documentation issues with underwriting departments to expedite the closing process.

Selected Accomplishments:
- **Increased loan officer productivity by 30% by developing and implementing new interoffice procedures streamlining operations.**
- **Developed targeted mail campaigns designed to attract specific clientele in the areas of home equity loans, and increased first-time buyer inquiries by 25%.**

TERESA RODRIGUES

5155 Canyon View Street, #5 • Sherman Oaks, California 91423
(818) 555-1234 • email@email.com

WAITRESS/SERVER

- ❑ Hard-working and high-energy individual with proven ability to go beyond the requirements of the job in accepting and managing multiple responsibilities.
- ❑ Works well in a fast-paced environment with high standards.
- ❑ Possesses a strong work ethic; verifiable record of punctuality and low absenteeism.
- ❑ Very personable; easily establishes rapport with customers, coworkers, and management.
- ❑ Highly motivated, as evidenced by combining academic schedule with work responsibilities.
- ❑ Natural team-building and leadership qualities; experienced in training and supervision.

WORK HISTORY

Server/Trainer   *(Part-Time Sept. 2000–Jun. 2001)* Sept. 2000–Present
ROBERTO'S ITALIAN RESTAURANT, Sherman Oaks, CA
Provide excellent service and foster guest satisfaction in fast-paced family restaurant with high guest turnover. Promoted in June 2001 to coordinate closing responsibilities and supervise other servers.
- Received top placements in various sales competitions.
- Achieved highest overall sales for all servers throughout four-store chain, September 2001.
- Train and supervise new hires and other servers.
- Maintain positive relations between kitchen and floor staffs in demanding environment with very high standards.

Hostess/Cashier   *Summer 2000*
THE PANCAKE PALACE, Van Nuys, CA
Seated guests, assisted wait staff with beverage service, relieved cashier as required.

Cashier   *(Part-Time/Seasonal)* January 1999–June 2000
SOUTHERN CALIFORNIA CINEMA, Sherman Oaks, CA
Sold tickets and provided customer information at busy multiplex theater complex. Assisted at concession stand as required.
- Accurately accounted for cash: consistently balanced registers with minimum shortages.

EDUCATION

SHERMAN OAKS SR. HIGH SCHOOL, Sherman Oaks, CA; Diploma, June 2001

Activities: Drill Team, Senior Class Secretary

ADDITIONAL INFORMATION

Computer Skills: Microsoft Word, Excel, PowerPoint, Explorer, Netscape, Internet, E-Mail

Foreign Languages: Bilingual English/Spanish

WEB DESIGNER

SAMUEL NYE

1059 Main Street ◆ Boise, ID 83704 ◆ (208) 555-1212
email@email.com ◆ www.Nyewebdesign.com

WEB DESIGNER

SOFTWARE EXPERIENCE

Web
HTML ◆ DHTML ◆ CSS ◆ XML
Dreamweaver ◆ Front Page ◆ Visual Source Safe
Netscape Navigator ◆ Internet Explorer
Cute FTP ◆ WS FTP

Graphics
3D Studio MAX ◆ PhotoShop ◆ Flash ◆ Fireworks
Illustrator ◆ PowerPoint ◆ Acrobat ◆ Distiller
PhotoTools ◆ Painter ◆ Poser
Image Robot ◆ MediaCenter

Multimedia
Sound Forge ◆ Acid PRO ◆ After Effects
QuickTime ◆ EZ CD Creator

Operating Systems
Windows 2000 ◆ Windows NT ◆ Windows 98
Windows 95 ◆ Linux ◆ DOS

Other Applications
Word ◆ Excel ◆ Windows Commander

TECHNICAL SKILLS/KNOWLEDGE

HTML/DHTML Web page development
interactive media graphic design
print-to-Web content conversion
Web user interface design
cross-browser functionality
buttons, banner ads, animation
navigation, site maps
branding/logo and icon design
tables, frames, and forms
integrating art/text/video/sound
optimized Web graphics

View Representative Work on:

www.mustangowners.com
www.eclectic.com
www.nyewebdesigner.com

SUMMARY

✓ B2B Web site design experience
✓ Multimedia graphics design skills
✓ Consistently meets deadlines
✓ Strong work ethic
✓ Team player

WORK HISTORY

Web Designer, Summers 1999, 2000, 2001
ECLECTIC.COM—www.eclectic.com, Boise, ID
A b2b trading company

◆ Made key contributions to the development and launch of a multilayered corporate Web site with 12 subsites.
◆ Created HTML site templates
◆ Optimized and edited graphics for the e-commerce Web Store
◆ Assisted in the development of Flash animations
◆ Interfaced with marketing, engineering, and other departments to create, modify, and design graphics for Web sites and intranets
◆ Advised Art Director on site look and feel
◆ Produced work across the design spectrum
Print: created 2D/3D still image and animated graphics for print ads, Web sites, and multimedia
Web: created concepts and developed Web graphics and design layouts
Multimedia/Interactive: helped create/edit Flash presentations for marketing and sales demos
Sound/Music: created/edited sound effects and music for animations and Flash presentations
Concepts: created and implemented concepts in Web, print, and interactive media formats

EDUCATION

Bachelor of Science in Computer Science, 2002
University of Colorado, Colorado Springs, CO

PC Age Learning Center, Boise, ID 1999–Present
Courses: XML. DHTML, 3 courses in HTML, 3 courses in Dreamweaver

WEBMASTER COVER LETTER

Dana Harvey
2304 Minnehaha Parkway * Minneapolis, MN 55102 * 612.555.2276 * email@email.com

WEBMASTER

November 15, 2001

Mr. Walt Trumbel
Regional Vice President
Technology Search Professionals
115 Birmingham Drive
Minneapolis, MN 55101

In today's tight job market, you undoubtedly receive hundreds of resumes every week from people seeking employment. However, you have a reputation for being able to recognize marketable talents, such as the ones I possess. A technology "geek" who thinks of technology as an addiction rather than work or a job, I thrive on sharing my broad-based expertise with others—and am continually learning from them in the process.

I am graduating this month from St. Cloud State University with a Bachelor of Science in Business Computer Information Systems. In 1998, I received an Associate of Applied Science in E-Commerce (Web Database Applications Concentration) from Brown College. I quickly mastered the academics at both schools, graduating with honors and receiving an academic scholarship at SCSU. Although technically a new graduate, my resume points out experience as a Webmaster, gained from proactively pursuing my calling for the past five years.

- Webmaster Intern (7 months) with the Greater St. Cloud Tourism Bureau, where I oversaw all aspects of their Web site from initial design through maintenance and reporting. On my last day I was honored with an "Excellence Award" as their first Webmaster—one who had set the bar high.
- Co-Creator of St. Cloud State University's Web Authors Forum, which provides the Web community with Web-related links, Web reference tools, portal projects, design assistance, and a presentations archive.
- Freelance Webmaster for businesses and nonprofits, from design through administration.

Your clients need Webmasters with as many talents as possible, who understand the Web environment from more than one perspective. My credentials and experience will enable me to make crucial contributions. Feel free to contact me at any time—I'll call you within a few days to discuss what I can do and how your clients will benefit.

Respectfully yours,

Dana Harvey

Enc: resume

Sample Resumes

Dana Harvey

2304 Minnehaha Parkway * Minneapolis, MN 55102 * 612.555.2276 * email@email.com

Webmaster

HIRING ASSETS

- Experienced in e-commerce, including Web marketing, design, construction, and administration.
- Enjoys a strong sense of architecture, navigation, and user issues.
- Fluent with hand-coding environments, including building forms and integrating language.
- Well versed in cross-browser and cross-platform issues; proficient in optimizing Web graphics.
- Able to communicate technical information in an easily understandable way. Recognized for quality performance.

EDUCATION

ST. CLOUD STATE UNIVERSITY, G.R. Herberger College of Business—St. Cloud, MN
Accredited by the Association to Advance Collegiate Schools of Business (AACSB)

Bachelor of Science, Business Computer Information Systems (BCIS), 2001   GPA 3.5

Application Software	Application Program Development	Management Information Systems
Client/Server Systems	Electronic Commerce Systems	Decision Support Systems
Competitive Technology	Entrepreneurial Technology	Data Modeling

BROWN COLLEGE—Mendota Heights, MN
Associate of Applied Science, E-Commerce
Web Database Applications Concentration, 1998   GPA 4.0

Client-Side Web Technologies	Internet Applications Architecture	Database Access on the Web
Structured Web Documents, XML	Internet Applications, VB /COM	Distributed Internet Applications

TECHNICAL SKILLS

Operating Systems: Windows XP, Windows 98, Windows 95, Windows NT, Win Beta 2000, Macintosh OS.
Software Tools: MS Office (Word, Excel, Access, PowerPoint, Outlook), FrontPage 2000, QuarkXPress.
Languages: UNIX, LINUX, CGI, PERL, XML, HTLM, DHTML, JavaScript, Java, C, C++, Visual Basic, VRML.
Applications: Net Objects Fusion, Netscape, TCP/IP, IE Microsoft, PaintShop, and majority of marketed software.
Intranets/Systems Administration & Support: Telecommunications & Phone Systems, E-mail, Workstations, Terminals, Windows NT Network, Fileservers, Search Engines, JPEG, GIF, and other Graphics Formats.

WEB MANAGEMENT EXPERIENCE & PORTFOLIO

WEBMASTER INTERNSHIP

THE GREATER ST. CLOUD TOURISM BUREAU—St. Cloud, MN   June 2000–January 2001

- Designed Bureau's Web site, and maintained hardware and software, Web page compatibility, and browser versions.
- Managed site architecture, implementation, and maintenance of technical components.
- Replied to user feedback creating cgi scripts and/or monitoring traffic through the site.
- Worked with e-commerce professionals to determine, implement, and maintain site design and content.
- Accurately managed a high volume of error-free image and text source files. Provided Web site statistics and reporting.

FREELANCE WEBMASTER PORTFOLIO (partial)   1996–present

- Converted and developed structure: hireimaging.com
- Administered changes to a public Internet site: www.tristarhuman.com
- Processed frequent site changes, and utilized JavaScript for pop-up content: www.dollarwise.com
- Helped convert an Extranet site from a conventional Web server to a dynamic, Notes Domino site: www.salem.com
- Developed and configured Java applet navigation: www.maidsrus.com

HONORS & ACTIVITIES

- **Recipient of the John Adams Scholarship**, awarded to Computer Science majors with high academic achievement.
- **Recognized by The Greater St. Cloud Tourism Bureau** with "Excellence Award" as its first Webmaster.
- **Co-Creator of the SCSU Web Authors Forum**, designed to serve members of the university Web community. Offers links on Web environment, portal projects, Web reference tools, Web page design, and a presentations archive.
- **Big Brothers/Big Sisters of Central Minnesota** volunteer.

7

Index

Note: **Boldface** numbers indicate illustrations.

About the Authors

Jay A. Block, CPRW (Certified Professional Resume Writer), internationally certified career coach and resume strategist, is the contributing cofounder of the Professional Association of Resume Writers and Career Coaches (PARW/CC). He helped develop the PARW/CC national certification process and is a widely respected national speaker, author, and career coach. Contact him at www.jayblock.com.

Michael Betrus, CPRW, has been a hiring manager in the telecommunications industry for several years, and frequently engages in academic seminars for students on campus. Michael is the author of *The Guide to Executive Recruiters* and co-author, with Jay Block, of *101 Best Resumes*, *101 More Best Resumes*, *101 Best Cover Letters* and *101 Best Tech Resumes*. Contact him at betrus@earthlink.com.